THE FRENCH SOCIALIST PARTY

THE FRENCH SOCIALIST PARTY

The Emergence of a Party of Government

D. S. Bell and Byron Criddle

Second Edition

CLARENDON PRESS · OXFORD

Oxford University Press, Walton Street, Oxford OX2 6DP
Oxford New York Toronto
Delhi Bombay Calcutta Madras Karachi
Petaling Jaya Singapore Hong Kong Tokyo
Nairobi Dar es Salaam Cape Town
Melbourne Auckland
and associated companies in
Beirut Berlin Ibadan Nicosia

Oxford is a trade mark of Oxford University Press

Published in the United States by
Oxford University Press, New York

First edition published 1984
Second edition published 1988

British Library Cataloguing in Publication Data
Bell, D. S.
The French Socialist Party: The emergence of
a party of government.—2nd ed.
1. Socialism—France
I. Title   II. Criddle, Byron
3 35'.2   HX282
ISBN 0–19–822897 X
ISBN 0–19–822870–8 (pbk)

Library of Congress Cataloging in Publication Data
Bell, David Scott.
The French Socialist Party.—2nd ed.
Bibliography: p.
Includes index.
1. Parti socialiste (France)   2. France—Politics
and government—1969–1974.   3. France—Politics and
government—1974–1981.   4. France—Politics and
government—1981–   .   I. Criddle, Byron.   II. Title.
JN3007.S6B44 1984   324.244'074   83–23707
ISBN 0–19–822897–X
ISBN 0–19–822870–8 (pbk)

Printed in Great Britain
at the University Printing House, Oxford
by David Stanford
Printer to the University

Preface

This book results from the interest we both have had in French politics and the development of the Socialist Party under the Fifth Republic. Many people have helped by reading parts of the manuscript and commenting on our earlier drafts. We have also benefited from interviews and discussion with French Socialist Party members and would like to thank them for their help, their friendliness, and their time. In particular they are: Mlle Patricia Bell, M. Maurice Benassayag, M. J.-M. Bichat, M. J.-P. Chevènement, M. J.-P. Cot, Professor J.-C. Colliard, M. J. Delors, M. Bernard Derosier, M. J.-M. Faivre, M. Roger Fajardie, Professor Bridgetta Hessel, M. Pierre Joxe, M. T. Lajoie, M. G. Le Gall, M. Bernard Manin, M. P. Maclouf, M. D. Motchane, M. M. Poupart, Mme N. Questiaux, M. A. Queval, M. J.-M. Rosenfeld, M. Thierry Leleu, and friends in the Nord and Bouches du-Rhône federations. (None of these people has any responsibility for the result, including any inaccuracies, which are our own.)

Byron Criddle would like to acknowledge the support of the British Academy, the Nuffield Foundation, the Carnegie Trust, and Aberdeen University, and David Bell would like to thank Wolfson College, Oxford, and Leeds University for their assistance in the research.

D. S. BELL
BYRON CRIDDLE

Preface to the Second Edition

For the second, revised edition of this book we have changed its subtitle from *Resurgence and Victory* to *The Emergence of a Party of Government*. This is because, four years after the completion of the first edition in 1983, we are able to reaffirm our central thesis of the Socialist Party as a pragmatic social democratic party raised by institutional and social change and by astute leadership into a dominant position in the French political system.

We remain grateful to colleagues for their advice and to the Universities of Aberdeen and Leeds for periodic financial help, but we acknowledge our own responsibility for any errors and omissions.

D. S. BELL
BYRON CRIDDLE.
May 1987

Contents

Abbreviations

CD	Centre Démocrate
CDP	Centre Démocratie et Progrès
CERES	Centre d'Études de Recherches et d'Éducation Socialistes
CFDT	Confédération Française Démocratique du Travail
CFTC	Confédération Française des Travailleurs Chrétiens
CGC	Confédération Générale des Cadres
CGT	Confédération Générale du Travail
CIR	Convention des Institutions Républicaines
CNIP	Centre National des Indépendants et Paysans
CNPF	Conseil National du Patronat Français
CRS	Compagnies Républicaines de Sécurité
DATAR	Délégation à l'Aménagement du Territoire et à l'Action Régionale
EEC	European Economic Community
EMS	European Monetary System
ENA	Ecole Nationale d'Administration
ERIS	Études, Recherches et Informations Socialistes
FEN	Fédération de l'Éducation Nationale
FGDS	Fédération de la Gauche Démocrate et Socialiste
FN	Front National
FNSEA	Fédération Nationale des Syndicats d'Exploitants Agricoles
FO	Force Ouvrière
HLM	Habitations à Loyer Modéré (Public Housing)
IFOP	Institut Français d'Opinion Publique
INSEE	Institut National de la Statistique et des Études Économiques
MRG	Mouvement des Radicaux de Gauche
MRP	Mouvement Républicain Populaire
OURS	l'Office Universitaire de Recherche Socialiste
PASOK	Panellênio Sosialistiko Kinêma
PCF	Parti Communiste Français
PCP	Partido Communista Português

PS	Parti Socialiste
PSA	Parti Socialiste Autonome
PSP	Partido Socialista Português
PSU	Parti Socialiste Unifié
RFSP	Revue Française de Science Politique
RI	Républicains Indépendants
RPF	Rassemblement du Peuple Français
RPP	Revue Politique et Parlementaire
RPR	Rassemblement pour la République
SFIO	Section Française de l'Internationale Ouvrière
SOFRES	Société Francaise d'Enquêtes par Sondages
SMIC	Salaire minimum industriel de croissance
SPD	Sozialdemokratische Partei Deutschlands
UDF	Union pour la Démocratie Française
UDSR	Union Démocratique et Socialiste de la Résistance
UGSD	Union de la Gauche Socialiste et Démocrate
UGCS	Union des Groups et Clubs Socialistes
UNCAL	Union Nationale des Comités d'Action Lycéen
UNCTAD	United Nations Conference on Trade and Development
UNEF	Union Nationale des Étudiants de France
UNR	Union pour la Nouvelle République

Paris region

departmental boundaries
regional boundaries

Introduction

Before the dramatic and unexpected victory of François
Mitterrand in the presidential election of 1981, France, it
had been observed by Maurice Duverger, had known only
three years of Left government since 1789: the Jacobins of
1793-4, the Republicans of 1848, and the Popular Front of
1936-7. In addition there had been a few years of government of a predominantly, though not wholly, left-wing
character: Combisme 1902-5, the Popular Front under
Radical leadership 1937-8, Tripartism 1944-7 and, more
debateably, the brief governments of Pierre Mendès France
and Guy Mollet in the 1950s. Mitterrand's victory in May
1981, and the Socialist Party's landslide win in the parliamentary election of June 1981, thus constituted an historic
event.

This book is in two parts. Part 1 examines first the factors
that served traditionally to frustrate the Socialists in particular and the Left in general; and second, the institutional and
social forces which in the 1950s and 1960s transformed the
environment in which the party operated and the opportunities available to it. The response made by the party to its
environment is examined. This involves a study of the process
whereby the old Socialist Party, the SFIO, was transformed
into the Parti Socialiste to become electorally the most
dynamic force in French politics—indeed, both in victory
in 1981 and in defeat in 1986, the first party of France.
Central to this process was the decision to pursue an alliance
with the Communist Party, an alliance imposed essentially
by systemic factors.

Part II comprises an examination of specific facets of the
party's situation in the 1970s and 1980s: the problems of
its relations with the Communists, its policy in government
between 1981 and 1986, its electoral strength and social
composition, and its organisational structures and factional
conflicts. The central theme of the book is that the French
Socialist Party had no alternative but to pursue the strategy

1

it did, given the presidential nature of political competition
in the Fifth Republic: that it was obliged to transform itself
into a presidential party with the prime aim of propelling its
leader into the Presidency. Such an objective in the bipolarised system of the Fifth Republic necessitated alliances with
other parties, and specifically with the Communist Party.
This alliance with the Communists was not, however, to be
taken as evidence of a significant move to the left by the
Socialist Party. It was, and is, a social democratic party in the
sense of pursuing essentially reformist objectives, though
prevented, until the 1980s, by the strategic requirement
of living with a powerful Communist Party, from embracing
overtly the reformism of north European social democracy.

By 1986 however, when the party lost an election after
five years in office during a recession and with the Communist
Party in steep decline, the Socialists were freed from
Communist-imposed constraints and able to present themselves as a pragmatic, reformist alternative to the conservative
coalition to which power was ceded after the electoral defeat.
Despite that defeat, the Socialist Party's position had been
dramatically transformed into that of the dominant party of
the Left with an electorate extensive even in defeat, a party
no longer beholden to its erstwhile Communist ally, and with
every prospect of alternating in government with its conservative competitors in a process familiar elsewhere in western
Europe. Released from a tactical alliance with a radical and
thus electorally constricting ally, the Socialist Party had,
through experience of office in the 1980s and the parallel
marginalisation of the Communist Party, finally emerged as
an electorally-credible party of government.

Part I
Environment and Strategy

1
Traditional Constraints

The year 1981 was an *annus mirabilis* for the French Socialist Party. It was the year that saw the election (10 May) of François Mitterrand as President of the Republic—only the second Socialist to occupy the office, and the first to do so since it was transformed into an executive presidency after 1958. There followed the appointment by President Mitterrand of a Socialist government under Pierre Mauroy (22 May), the dissolution of Parliament, and the election a month later (21 June) of a National Assembly containing a large majority of Socialist deputies. Thus the Socialist party took power more completely than ever before. Only once previously—in 1968 when the Gaullists won a parliamentary landslide victory—had a single party, independent of allied parties, achieved so complete a monopoly of governmental power. For the French Socialists this was a peculiarly dramatic highpoint in a history, spanning virtually the whole of the century, and yet characterized by the failure to achieve what had come comparatively easily to other European Socialist parties. In the seventy-six years of the Party's history up to 1981 it had headed governments for no more than a total of five years and participated in others for a total of only ten. In Britain over the same period the Labour Party headed governments for twenty years and participated in others for a further nine. Thus the French Socialists' record in achieving government office—an essential objective of political parties in liberal-democratic states—was markedly inferior to that of Labour in Britain, or indeed the social democrats in Scandinavia, West Germany, and Austria. The Socialist Party's record for the better part of its history after 1905 was one of failure, disappointment, and decline. Only in the 1970s was this pattern reversed as the Party moved from strength to strength in successive elections. To explain the long years of comparative failure it is necessary to examine the particular constraints within which the Socialist Party has had to operate —specifically, the nature of the party system, participation in

5

coalition politics, competition with the Communist Party, the nature of French social structure, and the political force of anti-clericalism.

The party system

From its inception in 1905 the Party had to operate within a multi-party system, and, because of the large number of parties competing for support, all governments were of necessity coalitions. The celebrated Blum government of 1936, though Socialist-led, relied for its parliamentary survival on the support of Radical and Communist, as well as Socialist, deputies. Habitually at each election during the Third and Fourth Republics there were at least five parties, each capable of attracting about 15–20 per cent of the votes, and the political outcome of all elections involved parliamentary horse-trading between parties and groups. Many, indeed most, democratic states are characterized by such a requirement, multipartism being the rule to which British bipartism is the exception. But French multipartism has been of a different order from the multi-party systems of, for example, Scandinavia. It has been more fractious and less manageable; coalition partners have coexisted less easily, and governments in the Third and Fourth Republics were in consequence of shorter duration than they usually are in multi-party states.

Giovanni Sartori has drawn a useful distinction between two different types of multi-party system: that in which the various parties are effectively poles apart and that in which they operate within two rival alliances, or in other words, around two poles, in much the same way as a two-party system operates around two parties.[1] Thus in Scandinavia the Social Democratic parties on the one hand face a coalition of Conservative, Liberal, and Agrarian parties on the other, with these latter parties forming 'bourgeois' coalition governments. The bipolar symmetry of such an association of parties is markedly different from what Sartori has called the 'polarized pluralism' of the traditional French (and Italian) type of multi-party competition where (1) the configuration

[1] G. Sartori, 'European Political Parties: The Case of Polarised Pluralism', in J. La Palombara and M. Weiner (eds.), *Political Parties and Political Development*, Princeton University Press (Princeton), 1966.

of parties is multipolar, not bipolar (i.e. does not, for operational purposes, pivot around two poles), (2) there exists a greater degree of polarity (i.e. of distance between the parties), and (3) there is a tendency to centrifugal strains (i.e. parties moving away from, rather than towards, each other, particularly at the extremes). Sartori sees such systems as characterized by a high degree of ideological rigidity; a lack of consensus at élite level; and a tendency for governments to consist of coalitions of centre-placed parties on account of the ideological distance between the parties at opposite ends of the political continuum. He cites Fourth Republic France as an example of this type, where governments of the 'Third Force' (centrist) coalition governed in opposition to the anti-system 'extreme' parties of Left (Communist) and Right.

It is clear that French parties have traditionally been divided from each other not merely by policy questions but by more fundamental matters, such as the nature of the political structure or, more serious still, the economic organization of society. In systems under which parties articulate not merely policy demands, but also structural ones, the system will be subject to strains at élite level and the conduct of inter-party relations correspondingly made more difficult. So severe was the lack of consensus over basic constitutional norms that the French polity itself was prone to a high degree of instability, with parties of significant size campaigning against the regime as well as against the Government. Governments were never trusted and regimes were always seen as partial. The Third Republic originated in an attempt to defend the interests of monarchists and their allies, and although these forces did not prevail, by the early 1920s the regime faced the hostility of the Communist Party and the right-wing *ligues*. The Fourth Republic's institutions were endorsed by a mere third of the electorate in 1946 and the regime perished after twelve years of opposition from Communists and Gaullists. Moreover, those parties that did campaign from within a 'structural' consensus—those prepared to endorse the constitutional status quo—were commonly incapable of governing easily together because of deeply ingrained ideological antagonisms. Thus the parties that accepted the constitutional provisions of the Fourth Republic—the Socialists, Radicals, MRP, and Independents—whilst accepting the need to govern together against the 'extremes' (Communists, Gaullists, and Poujadists) throughout most of the period, could not agree over essential policy matters, whether economic, colonial, or educational. For a party like that of the Socialists, committed to the liberal-democratic republic, yet aspiring to introduce socialist reforms, the dilemma was acute.

Participation

From its origins in 1905 the Party had to confront the choice of either participating in coalitions with parties to its Right in pursuit of ameliorative reforms, or to await the day when a Socialist majority would erase the need for compromise. The Socialist Party had been formed in 1905 out of a fusion of two conflicting strands, one revisionist, led by Jean Jaurès, the other Marxist and in theory revolutionary, led by Jules Guesde.[2] At the founding congress of the Party, participation in 'bourgeois' governments was specifically rejected, even though both the Jauresian and the Guesdist strands had, before 1905, practised 'republican discipline' at elections, seeking through collaboration with the Radical Party to ensure the election of a maximum number of republican deputies. They had also agreed to support the Radical Combes Ministry of 1902–5 which achieved the republican objective of separation of Church and State. Jaurès, though not Guesde, had also backed the Radical Waldeck–Rousseau government of 1899 which included the first Socialist to hold ministerial office—Alexandre Millerand. But Guesdist opposition to ministerial participation in 'bourgeois' governments played a part in dissuading ministerially inclined Socialists, such as Millerand, Viviani, and Briand from joining the new Party in 1905. The reputation of participation was thereafter damaged by the role of such ex-Socialists as Briand and Viviani in government actions seen as hostile to working-class interests, and more graphically by the subsequent career of Alexandre Millerand who effected a transition in twenty years from ministerial Socialist in 1899 to conservative President of the Republic in 1920. Given Guesde's hostility to participation it was not without a certain irony that he, after Jaurès's

---

[2] D. Ligou, *Histoire du Socialisme en France*, Presses Universitaires de France (Paris), 1962, pp. 156–75.

assassination in 1914, led the Socialist Party, in an expression of Jacobin patriotism, into the coalition government of national unity—*L'Union sacrée*—at the outbreak of the First World War.[3]

Following the split in the Socialist movement in 1920, which saw the creation of the Communist Party, the Socialists reaffirmed their resistance to ministerial participation, whilst retaining the practice of electoral collaboration with the Radicals around traditional themes of republicanism and anti-clericalism. In 1924 this took the form of the *Cartel des Gauches* followed by support for, but not participation in, Radical governments. This pattern was repeated after the election of 1932; but on both occasions half-way through the four-year parliament the Socialists withdrew their support from the Radicals, leaving them to govern with conservatives.

In 1936 the Socialists, by then the largest left-wing party (having overtaken the Radicals), took office for the first time in peacetime with the formation of Léon Blum's Popular Front government. In doing so, in coalition with Radicals and supported by Communists, the Party was opting, in Blum's words, for the 'exercise of power', that is, the 'loyal management of existing institutions and social systems in order to promote reforms'. Beyond the 'exercise' of power lay the 'conquest' of power, involving the transformation of existing institutions, but it was argued by Blum that a parliamentary party should not forgo the opportunity to achieve reforms in the context of existing structures—hence the 'exercise' of power in 1936. The record and fate of this government, the first government of the Left in French parliamentary history, has entered leftist mythology. But its survival rested on the goodwill of the Radical Party and of the Senate, which was much the same thing. Blum was effectively a hostage of the Radicals and it was they who delivered the *coup de grâce* in the Senate in 1937.[4]

Participation after the Liberation in 1944 took two forms: first, tripartism, which lasted from 1944 until 1947 and consisted of an alliance of the three large parties to emerge from the war—the Socialists, the Communists, and MRP (progressive

[3] D. Ligou, op. cit., pp. 239-55.
[4] See H. Portelli, *Le socialisme français tel qu'il est*, Presses Univeisitaires de France (Paris), 1980, pp. 53-9.

Catholics); secondly, after the ejection of the Communists from office in 1947, came the 'third-force' coalition of Socialists, Radicals, the MRP, and the Independents. With the exception of four years between 1951 and 1955 when the Socialists took a *cure d'opposition*, the Party remained in government until the start of the Fifth Republic. The Tripartist coalition, presided over for eighteen months by de Gaulle, was very much a product of wartime resistance and lasted only as long as the international climate permitted; the third-force variant—which came to characterize Socialist participation in the Fourth Republic, and which was later claimed to have had a debilitating impact on the Party's fortunes, was provoked essentially by the need to defend an unpopular regime from its authoritarian internal opponents. Guy Mollet, party leader from 1946 to 1969, showed himself more than ready to perform this defensive role—'participation', he declared at the 1949 party congress, 'has never been a question of doctrine; it is a question of circumstances.'[5] The problem, and indeed the danger, for the Party was, however, that the task of defending the Republic from its adversaries obliged the Socialists to form the exposed left flank of conservative-leaning coalitions, inside which they lacked sufficient weight to impose the social policies needed to win back working-class voters from the Communists. For much of the period of the Fourth Republic Socialist support drained away, whilst the Communists stood their ground electorally. Yet if an 'authoritarian' de Gaulle was to be kept out of power (in the late 1940s) and if the Socialists were to avoid incurring the opprobrium of the electorate for provoking a governmental crisis—indeed a crisis of the regime—the Party had little choice, even if gains in terms of ministerial portfolios had to be set against losses in the form of internal party disharmony, weakened morale, and declining membership.[6]

The Communists

For the Socialists the problem was not simply that participation in, or even merely support for, heterogeneous coalition

[5] H. Portelli, op. cit., p. 82.
[6] For accounts of the Mollet government see R. Quilliot, *La SFIO et l'exercise du pouvoir 1944–58*, Fayard (Paris), 1972, and P. Guidoni *Histoire du nouveau parti socialiste*, Tema Action (Paris), 1973.

governments involved the potential disappointment of Socialist voters and activists, but that such disappointments would be rigorously exploited by a powerful left-wing rival, the Communist Party, which had by 1936—and more especially after 1944—established a deep implantation in the working class and, from the first post-war elections in 1945, displaced the Socialists as the leading party of the Left. It is the presence of a large and effective Communist Party that has clearly constituted the most important constraint on the Socialist Party since reformist and revolutionary Socialists split at the Congress of Tours in 1920. Whereas reformists and revolutionaries, middle-class and working-class socialists, coexisted inside the same party in Britain, in France the greater force of the revolutionary-Marxist strand forced a split and thereafter a bitter struggle between rival organizations for the votes of the Socialist constituency. The breach with the Communist elements in 1920 involved the fundamental questions that have divided the French Left ever since: the belief in a revolutionary conception of Socialism and in the Leninist model of party organization. For the Socialists the Communist stance constituted—as it still does—a negation of fundamental democratic values. Thus there has been, and remains, a deep and abiding cultural divide between Socialists and Communists: a belief in democratic pluralism on the one hand, and its rejection on the other. The history of the Socialist Party since 1920 has been, in effect, the history of a party wrestling with the Communist problem. For most of that period the Party's leadership has been avowedly reformist and yet unable to acknowledge the fact by adopting a fully reformist posture (as, for example, the German Social Democrats did at Bad Godesberg in 1959) for fear of the denunciation such action would invite from the Communists. Socialist collaboration with parties to the Right has only been relatively easy when the PCF was either too weak (as in 1924) or too suspect in matters of foreign policy (as between 1947 and 1958). Collaboration with the Communists has occurred only when the PCF adopted for its own tactical reasons a collaborative stance (as in the late 1930s and for much of the period of the Fifth Republic). For most of the period since 1920 the Socialist Party in its struggle with the Communists has been at the mercy either of the international situation or of Communist tactical whims. (The problem of Socialist–Communist relations is examined more fully in Chapter 7.)

Social structure

A further major constraint imposed on the Socialist Party, and one which was highlighted in its unsuccessful competition with the Communists for the working-class electorate after 1920, was the peculiarly archaic nature of French social structure during the formative period of socialist politics at the end of the nineteenth century and during the first few decades of the twentieth century. France industrialized and urbanized slowly and remained, in André Siegfried's words in 1930, 'by its social formation, even after a century of industrial evolution, essentially a nation of peasants, artisans and bourgeois.'[7] In 1921 54 per cent of the population lived in rural communes. Even by 1946, when an urban majority at last emerged, as much as 47 per cent of the population was still village-based. At the time when the Socialist Party was being formed out of various currents in the early 1900s only three in ten of the active population were employed in industry—some 9 million people. The primary sector of economic activity was larger than either the secondary or the tertiary sectors and remained so down to the Second World War (see Table 1.1). Moreover, as Siegfried observed, even with urbanization the *'ascendance paysanne'* was never far away; a close attachment to the soil being felt even by town dwellers and a strong loyalty to locale by those in the countryside. The persistent rural and peasant bias in French society had as its most important effect the delaying of the clearcut polarization between workers and employers characteristic of urbanized society, which socialist parties classically seek to exploit.

Not only was the industrial working class smaller than in other countries, but the nature of its employment differed vastly. In 1906 half (about 4.5 million) of the French industrial labour force was working in establishments employing no more than five workers, and large-scale enterprises employing over 100 workers accounted for only 10 per cent of

[7] A. Siegfried, *Tableau des partis en France*, Grasset (Paris), 1930, p. 13.

Table 1.1

Active Population by Sector

	1901	1931	1946	1954	1962	1968	1975
Primary (Agriculture)	42.7	36.7	36.0	27.4	20.6	15.7	9.6
Secondary (Manufacturing)	30.6	33.4	29.6	36.2	38.7	39.6	38.8
Tertiary (Services)	26.7	29.9	34.4	36.4	40.7	44.7	51.6

Sources: Pierre Longone, *53 Millions de français*, Éd. du Centurion, (Paris), 1977; 'Faits et chiffres 1974', *Le Nouvel Observateur*, 1974.

the labour force. It was this fact, as much as any other, that explained the numerical, and thus the political, weakness of French trade unionism. By 1911 the CGT embraced only 700,000 members (7 per cent of the total workforce) compared with the 4 million (25 per cent) unionized in Britain and the 4.5 million (28 per cent) in Germany.[8] Numerical weakness moreover reinforced another serious deficiency: radical syndicalism. As Dupeux has noted, like all minority movements, French trade unions veered towards extremism, and the more extreme the unions' stance the more they became enclosed in attitudes of working-class sectarianism and thus less attractive to potential members. Weak in numbers and short of funds, they had to resort to ineffective one-day actions and sudden explosions of resentment.

Slow, late, and only partial industrialization produced a working-class population simultaneously weak and isolated and correspondingly lacking the strength to extract significant concessions from, or to mount an effective challenge to, the power of peasant and bourgeois politics—where the local notable ruled supreme. The political localism of peasant politics delayed the effectiveness of those parties that sought —like the Socialists—to structure the vote according to social, and not purely regional or local, criteria. The failure to impose class politics and thus to accommodate working-class

[8] G. Dupeux, *French Society 1789–1970*, Methuen (London), 1976, p. 181.

demands spawned the radical attitudes which came to characterize the French working-class movement—particularly in
the trade-union sphere where, in the Charter of Amiens of
1906, parliamentary activity in the bourgeois state was
expressly rejected. Thus, at the same time as the British trade
unions were creating their own political party to represent
them in the existing political institutions, the French unions
were declaring their hostility to all political parties *per se*.
Ultimately it was this radicalism that stimulated the formation and growth of a Communist Party whose Leninist
structures and dogmas grafted easily onto a ghetto-ized and
resentful working class.

Val Lorwin, in an examination of the link between economic development and working-class radicalism, has observed
that 'in only two countries (France and Italy), where among
all the great industrial nations capitalism has shown the least
sustained dynamism, has the wrath of the working class
permitted the Communist Party to take and hold a pre-
ponderant position among workers.'[9] Whilst economic
growth alone was unable in France to resolve the various
non-economic problems besetting the country, the very
quality of that economic growth was itself at fault: the
absence of large-scale industrialization; the quality of entre-
preneurship; the distribution of income; the nature of employer authority. 'Niggardly and tardy', as Lorwin puts it,
'in concessions to their workers, they [the employers]
flaunted inequalities by their style of living, and their class
consciousness helped shape the class consciousness of the
workers.'[10] That the bourgeoisje were able to ignore the
workers in this way, and so to provoke attitudes of utopian
radicalism in working-class ranks, was a consequence of the
social structure and the political alliance spawned to defend
established interests. The numerical preponderance of the
petty bourgeois and the self-employed in manufacturing,
retailing, and farming, down to the Second World War, and
the alliance of their political representatives with those of
the upper bourgeoisie ensured that governments reflected

[9] V. Lorwin, 'Working Class Politics and Economic Development in Western
Europe', in M. Dogan and R. Rose (eds.), *European Politics: A Reader*, Macmillan
(London), 1970, p. 28.
[10] V. Lorwin, op. cit., p. 32.

their interests and safeguarded the protection and maintenance of the status quo.

The loss of working-class support to the Communists as
the party that most markedly resisted this status quo had
major repercussions for the Socialist Party. Denied a solid
working-class base by Communist competition, the Socialists
were forced to look elsewhere—to other social classes, notably
the petty bourgeoisie. This was a process that served to cut
the Party off even further from the working-class electorate
and to expose it to a long process of 'Radicalization', that is,
the absorption of many of the characteristics of the Radical
Party. Shorn progressively of its working-class support in the
1920s and 1930s, the Party came to rely even more heavily
on a rural and small-town electorate of Radical tradition in
the unindustrialized south. The 'republican' as distinct from
'socialist' inclinations of this electorate further restricted the
Party's freedom to bid for lost working-class voters who
succumbed to the class-war militancy of the Communist
Party. By the time (1947) the Communists came to control
the CGT, the Socialist Party's failure to establish its working-
class credentials was complete. By 1956 in the working-class
suburbs of Paris two-thirds of the manual workers were
voting Communist and four-fifths of the Communist electorate
was drawn from the working class. In the seventy-one largest
towns 49 per cent of the working class were voting Communist, and a mere 17 per cent Socialist.[11]

Anti-clericalism

If the nature of French industrialization and social structure
created fundamental problems for the Socialist Party, there
was another more ancient division in French society, whose
effects constituted a further constraint on Socialist activity—
the conflict between Catholicism and anti-clericalism. Just as
the predominantly rural character of early twentieth-century
France prevented the growth of class politics, so did it also
provide fertile ground for an enduring debate between the
protagonists of faith and reason. The nineteenth century saw

[11] See M. Dogan, 'Political Change and Social Stratification in France and
Italy', in S. M. Lipset and S. Rokkan (eds.), *Party Systems and Voter Alignments*,
Collier-Macmillan (London), 1967, p. 140.

a divorce between Catholicism and Liberalism reflecting the post-1789 clash between Church and Republic, and the earlier eighteenth-century antithesis between Christianity and agnosticism. The nineteenth century established the Church's reputation as the enemy of the Republic and of all things 'progressive'. Whilst the Church's position of dominance before 1789 was irretrievably lost during the Revolution, with the State thereafter based on new secular principles, the Church, although beaten, was not routed, and in certain regimes—notably that of Napoleon III (1851–70)—it was able to reassert its influence, especially in the educational sphere where it constituted an anti-republican bulwark of the social order. The politics of the first thirty-five years of the Third Republic were, as David Thomson observed, dominated by an attempt to 'liquidate the past . . . thrashing out the old conflicts between Church and State, clerical and anti-clerical, Monarchy and Republic, militarism and parliamentarism—and by 1905 the forces of anti-clerical Republican parliamentarism had triumphed.'[12] In the remaining thirty-five years of the Third Republic, the same observer noted, new social and economic issues grew to eclipse the dynastic and ecclesiastical conflicts of the past and yet the force of the old conflicts retained a marked political salience.

In France, in place of the relatively muted English contest between Anglican Church and Nonconformist Chapel, which broadly determined electoral allegiances down to the First World War, there was a much more bitterly contested antagonism between the Catholic Church and the forces of rationalistic anti-clericalism. The religious question polarized the politics of the Third Republic before 1914: there was hardly a ministerial declaration that did not make allusion to *laïcité*. The parties of the Left echoed Gambetta's celebrated call to arms in 1877—'Le cléricalisme, voilà l'ennemi!'—and to combat the Right, of which the Church was the main bond, they combined into a coalition which in 1905 finally overwhelmed the 'menace of clericalism', achieving the separation of Church and State which had eluded the revolutionaries of 1789. The Combes ministry which effected this victory was, as has been noted, one of the earliest 'bourgeois' governments

[12] D. Thomson, *Democracy in France since 1870*, Oxford University Press (Oxford), 1964, p. 72.

to which the Socialists, as defenders of the lay Republic, lent their support.

Anti-clericalism persisted as a political force well into the century and served almost as a litmus test of Socialist bona fides, and this despite the progressive demise of the traditional struggle between the *curé* and the teacher. It was still felt to be impossible to be on the Left and go to mass, though the tangible form in which the conflict manifested itself was in the dispute over church schools. After the War, during which the Vichy regime's favoured treatment of the Church and of church schools had breathed new life into old antagonisms, merger of the Socialists with the new Christian Democratic party, the MRP, was resisted. The church-school question played an important divisive role in the Fourth Republic, the *loi Barrangé* of 1951 (which restored the state aid for Catholic schools which had been withdrawn in 1944) being the occasion for the Socialists leaving the coalition governments of which they had formed part since the Liberation. In 1959, during the debate over the *loi Debré* which reaffirmed state aid for church schools, the Socialist Minister of Education, André Boulloche, resigned rather than accept the bill, and the Socialist P.-O. Lapie was expelled from the Party for heading the commission which had examined the relationship between the state and private schools. In 1965 Guy Mollet torpedoed the idea of a Defferre candidacy in the presidential election by exploiting the difficulty of collaboration between Socialists and the MRP. More recently, in the late 1970s during a televised debate between Mitterrand and the Communist Roland Leroy, the latter, in response to Mitterrand's gibe that the Communist Party resembled a church, observed that Mitterrand ought to know a lot about churches—a reference to the Socialist leader's own upbringing in a Catholic family and his education in a Catholic school.

The electoral impact of anti-clericalism on the Socialist party was significant. Whilst it ensured the support for the Party of numberless state schoolteachers, it certainly restricted the possibility of an appeal to moderate middle- and working-class elements who were attracted, after 1944, by a rival reformist party—the Christian Democratic MRP. On the other hand, in a multi-party context, where numerous political 'brands' are in competition, it becomes inevitable for a party influenced and strongly supported by, in this case, anti-clerical schoolteachers, to seek to maintain its appeal to a restricted constituency by retaining a distinct brand image familiar to the Party's regular supporters. Nevertheless, anti-clericalism did serve to exclude the Socialists, and the Left in general, from whole tracts of the country where levels of Catholic observance remained high. As late as 1930 Siegfried had noted that 'anti-clericalism marks a frontier—one so important that it constitutes without doubt the dominant line in our politics.'[13] The political geography of France coincided in large part with its religious geography. It was confirmed in 1952 by Canon Boulard's survey that those tracts of the country such as Flanders, Artois, and Brittany, that had firmly resisted the attempt to subordinate the Church to the State in the Civil Constitution of the Clergy in 1790, were precisely those that retained in the mid-twentieth century a high level of religious observance. Moreover, church-going France was largely conservative France, even if, as Fauvet noted in 1959, 'in rural areas especially, the two [conservatism and Christianity] tend to go hand in hand only in those places where the social and religious hierarchies (presbytery and manor) tend to be confused in people's minds.'[14] Vast areas of the Catholic rural west became and remained conservative bastions. But of greater importance for a socialist party seeking to appeal to a working-class electorate was the persistence of religious observance in the industrialized departments of Alsace and Lorraine and in the Lyons and Saint-Étienne areas of the upper Rhône and Loire valleys. In 1956 in the Moselle department, which with Pas-de-Calais had the highest percentage (65 per cent) working-class population of any French department, the Left in total was capable of obtaining only 23 per cent of the vote, and in Meurthe-et-Moselle, the second most working-class department (60 per cent), only 39 per cent voted for the Left.

All the departments listed in Table 1.2 are those in which religious observance remained high. The clear implication was that the 28 per cent of industrial workers found in 1956 to be active, or regularly practising, Catholics constituted a significant barrier to the Left's capture of the working-class vote

---

[13] A. Siegfried, op. cit., p. 62.
[14] J. Fauvet, *The Cockpit of France*, Harvill (New York), 1960, p. 61.

Table 1.2
Class and Voting in Industrialized Catholic Departments (1956)

	Percentage of working-class voters	Percentage of those voting Left	Difference
Moselle	65	23	42
Meurthe et Moselle	60	39	21
Loire	53	28	25
Haut Rhin	53	28	25
Vosges	50	33	17
Rhône	49	32	17
Bas Rhin	45	17	28
Meuse	44	26	18
Loire Atlantique	43	30	13

Adapted from M. Dogan, 'Political Change and Social Stratification in France and Italy', in S. M. Lipset and S. Rokkan (eds.), *Party Systems and Voter Alignments*, Collier–Macmillan (London), 1967.

in important industrial regions of the country.[15] Whilst it is true that the force of national feeling also sustained working-class conservatism in the eastern-border departments, it is clear that the persistence of religious loyalties greatly damaged Socialist prospects. Without the clerical question it would have been possible after the War to effect the creation of a large party of the non-Communist Left by an amalgam of the Socialists and the MRP, notwithstanding the conservative character of much of the latter's electoral following. Such a party, being electorally larger than the Communists, would have been a far more effective opponent of the PCF than the weak and declining SFIO was capable of being.

For the Socialist Party, then, the problem has been not simply the conventional one identified by Gay in *The Dilemma of Democratic Socialism*[16] of how to reconcile principles and power, though that was indeed an early preoccupation and one which led Blum to define a distinction between the 'exercise' and 'conquest' of power. Additional and important problems for the Party were created by the peculiar

[15] See M. Dogan, op. cit., p. 135; also M. Dogan, 'Le vote ouvrier en France: analyse écologique des élections de 1962', *Revue française de sociologie*, 1965, pp. 435–71.
[16] P. Gay, *The Dilemma of Democratic Socialism*, Columbia University Press (New York), 1952.

nature of its environment, not least the constraints placed upon it by the division of an already constricted working-class electorate into Communist, Catholic, and Socialist loyalties, and by the related problem of an archaic social structure unconducive to socialist reformism. The French Socialists found themselves the prisoners of their past. Indeed French *politics* was overburdened by the weight of *its* past and the complexities of the party system owed much to the necessity of its handling simultaneously the unresolved conflicts of nationalism and Catholicism, democracy and authority, and worker and employer.

In Britain the first two of these conflicts had been resolved in earlier centuries, long before the introduction of universal suffrage afforded an opportunity for them to become institutionalized in partisan rivalries. In France, however, the conflicts retained a powerful force well into the present century and did become important bases for party alignments. Thus, parties of a distinctly anti-clerical identity confronted those that had clerical roots—a conflict that had the effect of cutting Socialists off from moderate reformists who happened also to be Catholic; whilst parties committed to liberal-democratic norms confronted the proponents of both left- and right-wing authoritarianism—a clash which counterposed Socialists and Communists, and thereby precluded the creation of a single working-class party.

The political and constitutional nature of the French crisis in 1958 highlighted the perennial problem of a Socialist Party seeking ideally to do no more than represent the economic interests of a particular social stratum. The new regime, with its popular leader, appeared to threaten the Socialist Party with further electoral decline, and it is to the effects of the new environment following upon the establishment of the Fifth Republic that the next chapter is devoted.

2
The New Environment of the Fifth Republic

The political crisis of 1958 brought de Gaulle to power and saw the installation of a constitution which entailed a redistribution of powers away from parliament towards the Government and an enhanced Presidency. Despite the traditional commitment of the Socialist Party, and of the French Left in general, to a parliamentary form of government, characterized by strong legislative control over the executive and a deep suspicion of personalized rule in any form, Mollet led the Socialists into the Fifth Republic as part of its *avant garde*—serving as a minister for six months—and believing de Gaulle now to be a republican bulwark against something worse, either Communism or Fascism. The Fifth Republic, born of the Algerian impasse, was a crisis-solving regime whose establishment all significant parties—except the Communists—supported.

The predominant characteristic of Fifth Republic politics has been bipolarity: the division of electoral opinion into two camps—Right and Left—and of parliamentary forces into permanent supporters of the Government on the one hand, and permanent opponents on the other. This was not the case in the Fourth Republic before 1958, nor in the Third Republic before 1940. In the Fourth Republic a constantly reshuffling pack of 'Centre' parties governed against the opposition of both Left and Right. In the 1920s and 1930s, governments at the start of parliaments usually consisted of, or were supported by, the electorally dominant parties of the Left, but slid gradually to the Right, shedding Left support by the end of the parliament, thus transforming initial government supporters into eventual government opponents. In both regimes the political complexion of governments bore no necessary resemblance to the recording of voter opinion taken at the time of the general election.

Institutional change
Fifth Republic bipolarity rests on two institutional innovations—the electoral system and presidentialism—and on the

21

impact of a unique phenomenon—de Gaulle. The electoral system introduced in 1958, *scrutin d'arrondissement à deux tours*, restored that used before 1940 during most of the Third Republic and, although it was to be replaced in 1986 by a proportional system, the government formed in that year effected its reintroduction. The system involves the election of deputies in single-member constituencies, with a candidate elected if he obtains an absolute majority (more than 50 per cent) of the votes cast. If no candidate obtains an absolute majority a second ballot is held a week later, and in that ballot a *relative* majority suffices for victory. Since few French parties have traditionally had support sufficiently wide or sufficiently concentrated to allow them to poll over 50 per cent of the vote in many constituencies at the first ballot, most of the seats (usually about three-quarters) are filled only after a second ballot. Not all candidates who contest the first ballot are permitted to contest the second; since 1976, candidates who obtain less than 12.5 per cent of the votes of registered electors at the first ballot are barred from proceeding to the second ballot. This barrier of 12.5 per cent replaced an earlier one (imposed in 1966) of 10 per cent of the registered electorate, which in turn had replaced the original barrier, installed in 1958 and comprising merely 5 per cent of those *voting*, not of the registered electorate. Thus, since 1958 the electoral system has contained a trip-wire for small parties, to reduce the field at the second ballot. Table 2.1 reveals that whilst in 1958 80 per cent of all the second-ballot contests involved three or more candidates, by 1967 most contests (79 per cent) had become straight fights, and that this proportion gradually increased in succeeding elections to cover virtually all second-ballot contests.

The traditional view associated with this particular electoral system—that the voter chooses at the first ballot and eliminates at the second—has produced the practice of tactical voting at the second ballot, and, specifically, a tendency to gang up against the least-favoured party still in the field. Thus extremist parties have tended to do badly in second-ballot contests, and can gain representation in such a system only by means of pacts with more moderate parties. By 1967 nearly all second-ballot contests were confrontations of

Table 2.1

Nature of Contest at Second Ballots in General Elections 1958-1981
(metropolitan seats only)

	1958 (%)	1962 (%)	1967 (%)	1968 (%)	1973 (%)	1978 (%)	1981 (%)
Straight fights	20.0	61.5	79.0	84.0	84.0	98.6	96.6
Triangular contests	29.0	35.0	15.0	13.0	15.0	0.2	0.3
Other	51.0	3.5	6.0	3.0	1.0	1.2	3.1*

* All walkovers.

Gaullist and Left (either Socialist or Communist) candidates (Table 2.2). But whilst permitting such a bipolarization, the electoral system does not determine it. Nor does the electoral system alone have the capacity to produce a bipolarity that is standardized across the country so that in every constituency the same two alternative parties or alliances confront each other. In the Third Republic the partisan nature of second-ballot bipolarity had been subject to considerable regional variation. In some parts of the country Radical Party candidates would be running for the Left against a 'conservative' candidate, whilst elsewhere a Radical candidate would in fact represent conservative forces opposed by a Socialist or alternative left-wing candidate. What served to standardize nationally the bipolarity of the Fifth Republic was (a) de Gaulle and (b) presidentialism.

Table 2.2

Incidence of Left–Right Bipolarization at Second Ballots 1958-1981
(metropolitan seats only)

	1958 (%)	1962 (%)	1967 (%)	1968 (%)	1973 (%)	1978 (%)	1981 (%)
Left–Right contests	0	79	94	94	95	99	100
Intra–Right contests	30	16	6	6	5	1	0
Intra–Left contests	70	5	0	0	0	0	0

Source: O. Duhamel, *La Gauche et la Ve République*, PUF (Paris), 1981, p. 327, with calculations for 1981 added.

De Gaulle's impact on the party system was dramatic. His charismatic appeal—coupled admittedly with a pre-existing low degree of partisan identification amongst right-centre voters and a sense of disillusion with the Fourth Republic—prompted the creation of a raft of electoral support extending from the right of the spectrum (though excluding elements of the ultra-Right who bitterly opposed the Algerian settlement and had in some cases opposed de Gaulle since 1940) through the Centre and into parts of the working-class electorate of the Left. This wide electoral coalition was also, in large part, assembled by the Gaullist *Party*, the UNR (Union pour la Nouvelle République) in general elections after 1962, as Gaullism came to occupy the electoral ground previously held by the weakly rooted right-of-centre parties that had emerged after the War (notably the MRP and CNIP). In 1962 this wide electoral alliance, dominated by the UNR, but including the conservative party—the RI (Républicains Indépendants) of Giscard d'Estaing—obtained an unprecedented parliamentary majority, which was maintained thereafter in a string of elections (1967, 1968, 1973, and 1978). With a degree of parliamentary discipline unknown in previous regimes, this block of pro-Gaullist deputies cohered as a disciplined majority throughout the lifetime of each parliament and came to comprise what observers have called *le fait majoritaire*, a phenomenon deriving initially from the acceptance of de Gaulle's indispensability. As de Gaulle's own appeal waned after the mid-1960s, *le fait majoritaire* took on a life of its own, habits of parliamentary discipline having been either learned voluntarily or imposed by the institutional constraints contained in the 1958 constitution, which had, by reducing parliamentary powers, made it less profitable and less easy for deputies effectively to rebel.

The specifically bipolarizing impact of de Gaulle lay in the response his coalition invited from those political forces outside it—the parties of the Left (Communist, Socialist, and Radical) and one or two small formations of the Centre.[1] To defeat the force of the Gaullist Party at the second ballot opposition parties had to employ an alliance strategy. Thus Gaullism stimulated the bipolarization of political forces

[1] See J.-L. Parodi, *La Ve République et le système majoritaire*, PUF (Paris), 1973, p. 44.

permitted, but not ordained, by the mechanics of the electoral system.

The prime institutional determinant of bipolarity however was the presidentialization of the regime after 1958. The constitution of 1958 was already a regime in which the Presidency had been enhanced with certain enlarged powers (notably the power to dissolve Parliament, invoke emergency powers, and sanction referendums), though *de facto* presidential dominance came only through precedents set by de Gaulle in the early years. The constitution was open to various 'readings'—presidential, parliamentary, or balanced,[2] and de Gaulle, in so far as he read the constitution at all, opted, as is well known, for a 'presidential' reading. In 1962 he initiated the constitutional reform—direct popular election of the President—whereby the transition to presidential dominance was completed. Moreover, the electoral law concerning presidential elections contained a more deliberately bipolarizing mechanism than the general election law in the stipulation that if no candidate obtained an absolute majority of votes at the first ballot, only the two leading candidates would be permitted to enter the second ballot. The main impact of direct election of the President was to legitimate the *de facto* presidential dominance introduced by de Gaulle and continued by his successors, Pompidou and Giscard d'Estaing. It served to lower the Presidency from the formal and lofty 'arbiter' role of the 1958 text, into a position as head of government. It largely reduced the Prime Minister to the role of a subordinate executor of presidential commands and made the Presidency the fount of all authority, patronage, and major policy-making.[3]

Presidential dominance however, was an essentially extra-constitutional concept, and rested on the solidity of the parliamentary majority, without which it could not exist. Consequently legislative elections perforce became semi-presidential elections, with presidents warning of the consequences if the incumbent parliamentary majority was not

[2] See O. Duhumel, 'La constitution de la Ve République et l'alternance', in *Pouvoirs*, PUF (Paris), 1981, p. 48.

[3] See M. Duverger, *Échec au roi*, Albin Michel (Paris), 1978, pp. 139–246; F. de Gaeque, *Qui gouverne la France?*, PUF (Paris), 1976; J.-L. Quermonne, *Le Gouvernement de la France sous la cinquième République*, Dalloz (Paris), 1980; and J. Chappel, *La Vie politique sous la Ve République*, PUF (Paris), 1981.

sustained. Thus Pompidou in 1973 declared that if the Left won a parliamentary majority he would not appoint a left-wing Prime Minister. Similarly in 1978, when faced by the prospect of a Left victory, Giscard d'Estaing stressed his intention to remain in the Élysée until the end of his term in 1981, and thus not to follow Gambetta's call to President MacMahon in 1877 'to submit or resign', if the Left won the parliamentary elections.[4] Just as presidentialism came to involve the subordination of Prime Minister to President, so it came also to mean the subordination of parliamentary to presidential elections. The Gaullists concocted the most elongated and revealing label for the 1973 legislative elections: 'Union des Républicains de Progrès pour le soutien du Président de la République', starkly abbreviated to the more explicit message, 'Une majorité pour le Président'. There could be no doubt as to what was involved in such parliamentary elections: presidential power and constitutional stability.

For the parties of the Left this new system carried severe implications, used as they were to the old parliamentary system under which each party bidded at elections more or less for its regular electoral clientele, and then negotiated with its block of deputies for representation in successive coalition governments. For the Communists, already the most isolated of the parties, the institutional innovations threatened consignment to the outer darkness. The two-ballot electoral system in general elections threatened the Party with elimination at the second ballot if it ran without the votes of allied parties to support its candidates. This was precisely what happened in 1958, when the PCF with 19 per cent of the votes at the first ballot secured only 2 per cent of the seats after the second, being reduced from 150 to ten deputies. For a party anxious to maintain a presence in the representative institutions of the country the new electoral system was a disaster, and it was hardly surprising that by 1962 the PCF had agreed a limited number of second-ballot 'withdrawals with the Socialist Party in order to boost its parliamentary representation.

Presidentialism constituted a second and more serious blow to the PCF, for no party as ideological as the Communists,

[4] See G. Bacot, 'Ni se soumettre, ni se démettre', *RPP*, 1978, Jan.–Feb., pp. 27–33.

and with as controversial a reputation, could hope to compete successfully for such an office. In an opinion survey of
public attitudes to Communist Party participation in government undertaken early in 1968, only 14 per cent declared
themselves favourable to the idea of a Communist President
(54 per cent were opposed, and 32 per cent did not respond).
On the question of a Communist Prime Minister 20 per cent
were favourable, 44 per cent opposed, and 35 per cent gave
no response. The prospect of Communist ministers in a
government was less alarming: 48 per cent being favourable,
20 per cent opposed, and 32 per cent having no opinion.[5]
The 1968 survey also revealed that 44 per cent of those
questioned believed that the PCF took too much account of
the interests of the Soviet Union. These findings confirmed
what was well known about the image of the Communist
Party. It was an image harmless enough for a party in the
context of the Fourth Republic's parliamentary regime with
its system of proportional representation, where the PCF
could survive as an anti-system force mobilizing protest, but
it was completely unsuited to the bipolarized politics of
second-ballot electioneering—whether in general elections,
where mobilization of more than the Party's immediate
support was required, or in presidential elections, where a
Communist candidate would be regarded as little more than
a defiant gesture. That said, two of the four presidential
elections since 1958 (those of 1969 and 1981) have seen
Communist candidates.

In 1969 the PCF ran a candidate to affirm the Party's
identity at a time when the non-Communist Left was broken-
backed and unable to field a credible standard-bearer. In
1981 the motive was again to reaffirm the distinct identity
of the Party in the face, this time, of a powerful Socialist
rival; but the ruse did not pay off and the PCF candidate,
Marchais, lost a third of his party's support. The painful
reality for the Communist Party under a presidential system
was that if it wanted power it could only achieve it as the
junior partner in an alliance supporting a Socialist presidential candidate. Whilst such a course implied subordination
and decline, any alternative independent strategy implied

[5] A. Lancelot and P. Weill, in F. Bon, *Le Communisme en France*, A. Colin
(Paris), 1969, pp. 295-7 and 302.

isolation, and probably an even more certain demise. Presidential politics served to incorporate parties into presidential alliances, and those parties that refused to play risked being deserted by their voters. Thus, the Fifth Republic's institutions served to make the Communists available for an alliance with the Socialists.

For the Socialists however, two alliance options have traditionally existed—'popular-front' style co-operation with the Communist Party and an alliance with the centrists *à la quatrième*. The latter, Fourth Republic, 'third-force' option was tried out in 1962 in the *Cartel des Non* which represented the last attempt made by the anti-Gaullist parties (SFIO, Radical, MRP, and some of the CNI) to resist de Gaulle's presidentialization of the regime through the introduction of direct election of the President. This stratagem failed with the poor performance of the *Cartel* in the 1962 constitutional referendum and the even worse showing of its constituent parties in the general election that followed. There was much evidence to suggest that 'Centrism' as an option was declining. Most of the electorate of the Centre parties that had risen to prominence in the Fourth Republic—notably the MRP—were conservative-inclined voters who by 1962 were voting for de Gaulle and the UNR. The attractive force of Gaullism was simply too strong for the Centre and Right parties to withstand. In the presidential elections of 1965 and 1969 the combined Centre and non-Gaullist Right vote was smaller, on both occasions, than the combined vote for candidates of the Left. (In 1965 first-ballot votes were cast as follows: de Gaulle 44 per cent; Left 32 per cent; non-Gaullist Right and Centre 23 per cent. In 1969 the distribution was: Pompidou 44 per cent; Left 31 per cent; Centre 23 per cent.[6])

Furthermore, as Duverger observed in 1967, the issues that had divided the political leaders of the Right and of the Centre were declining in force, thus making more likely the amalgamation of their electorates.[7] The divisive issues of immediate significance for politicians in the Fifth Republic included decolonization, European integration, the Atlantic Alliance, and the Fifth Republic itself. By the late 1960s even the seriously divisive impact of de Gaulle's 1962 Algerian

---

[6] See O. Duhamel, *La Gauche et la Ve République*, PUF (Paris), 1981, p. 290.
[7] M. Duverger, *La Démocratie sans le peuple*, Seuil (Paris), 1967, pp. 203–35.

settlement had waned, and the opportunity to pursue a pug-naciously independent foreign policy (as in de Gaulle's early years) was much reduced. At both presidential and legislative elections after 1968, and notably with Pompidou's election to the Presidency in 1969, came the incorporation of the 'Centre' into the Gaullist *majorité*.

If the issues that had divided the Right were declining in force it was equally arguable that the serious divisions on the Left—also largely in the field of foreign affairs—were becoming less important as international *détente* and 'peaceful coexistence' replaced the tensions of the Cold War. Whilst some Socialists—notably Gaston Defferre, mayor of Marseilles —flirted with a centrist strategy in the early 'sixties, the indicators pointed to a return to Socialist-Communist collaboration. Even Defferre, despite his staunchly anti-Communist reputation, was eventually to come to admit 'after long reflection that a Left–Right polarization permits the Left to win only in alliance.'[8] Guy Mollet also came to this conclusion—if more readily—and agreed upon mutual withdrawals with the PCF leader, Thorez, for the 1962 general election. Mollet's instinct, however, was primarily to use an alliance with the PCF merely to save Socialist parliamentary seats and as a time-buying exercise prior to an anticipated return to a traditional parliamentary system.

It was François Mitterrand who became the first politician of the Left to recognize the implications of presidential politics and the need to break out of the old multi-party system of which Mollet's SFIO was so much a part. Mitterrand was one of the first to realize that the presidential system, though apparently so disadvantageous to a disunited collection of left-wing parties in the early 1960s, offered a better prospect of achieving power than did parliamentary elections, where the nature of the *découpage* (the distribution of seats) created difficulties for the Left. Given the need to deal with the Communists, it was also necessary to restructure the non-Communist Left and to adapt it to presidential politics. It was, not least, of paramount importance for the non-Communist Left to run a candidate who had 'presidential' appeal and a capacity to aggregate votes way beyond the confines of his own party. The complete inappropriateness of

[8] J.-F. Bizot, *Au parti des Socialistes*, Grasset (Paris), 1975, p. 177.

Guy Mollet for this task was demonstrable. Mollet had never enjoyed any popularity outside his own party; even the Republican Front government of which he was Prime Minister in 1956 had been elected on the popularity of another leader —Pierre Mendès France. He lacked oratorical skills, was identified too completely with the discredited Fourth Republic, and was within his own party the source of enough discontent to provoke a split in 1958 and a long-standing conflict with the Party's leading regional notable Gaston Defferre. He was moreover unambitious for presidential power, being content to cling to the albeit declining power base afforded by his possession of the leadership of the SFIO.

As for François Mitterrand, there was not a little irony in his embracing of presidentialism. He had in 1958 been one of the more prominent figures of the Fourth Republic to have opposed de Gaulle, the new constitution and the '*pouvoir personnel*' with which it was associated. Moreover, Mitterrand, in the early years of the Fifth Republic was a man without political battalions. Never (until 1971) a member of the Socialist Party, he had risen to prominence in the Fourth Republic as a minister in many governments and as a leader of a small party, the UDSR (Union Démocratique et Socialiste de la Résistance), which shared many of the characteristics of the Radical Party, except anti-clericalism. Like the Socialist Party, which was divided over the return of de Gaulle in 1958, the UDSR split, with the leader of its right wing, René Pleven, backing de Gaulle and ending up between 1969 and 1973 as a minister in Pompidou's administration. After 1958 the UDSR, such as it was, became Mitterrand's property until, in 1965, it merged with the CIR (Convention des Institutions Républicains) a federation of left-of-centre political clubs presided over by Mitterrand and using as its official paper the former organ of the UDSR, *Combat républicain*. This new party, the CIR, became in part a vehicle for the promotion of Mitterrand's political, and specifically presidential, ambitions.

The CIR was one of a series of new political groups and parties to emerge in the early years of the new Republic, the *raison d'être* of which was primarily (though in the CIR's case not entirely) the promotion of presidential candidates. The UNR was the most obvious of these; a party created specifically as a parliamentary back-up force for President de Gaulle (1958–69) and serving the same function for his successor Georges Pompidou (1969–74). Giscard d'Estaing's party, Républicains Indépendants, formed in 1962 was equally intended to further his presidential ambitions. Even the smaller parties noted for a republican hostility to 'personalized' power succumbed to the presidential embrace. In 1969 Michel Rocard, the leader of the PSU (Parti Socialiste Unifié, a party that had emerged from left-wing defection from the SFIO in 1958), used his party to project himself onto the national stage in a presidential election, and for a few years after 1969 the Radical Party's leader Jean-Jacques Servan-Schreiber was a star in the firmament.

Such a process—the conversion of the parties to presidential politics—was assisted by the coming to prominence of a new generation of leaders. By the end of the Fifth Republic's first decade all its major political figures were men who had either enjoyed no prominent place in public life before 1958 (Pompidou, Giscard, Chirac, Servan-Schreiber, Rocard) or who, as in Mitterrand's case, had undergone a political reconstruction. Even the Communist Party, whilst not producing a type of leader who had done anything other than rise slowly through the apparatus, did, after Thorez's death in 1964, have as leader Waldeck Rochet, a man noted for his political ecumenism in the period between 1964 and 1968. Thus, by the end of the 'sixties a new generation of leaders with no particular nostalgia for the Fourth Republic was in place, prepared, and in most cases anxious, to exploit fully the opportunities offered by the new regime. Mitterrand's own particular contribution at this time was to 'presidentialize' the non-Communist Left, first by his presidential candidacy in 1965, by the alliance of the non-Communist Left parties (the FGDS, 1965–8), and by the electoral alliance made between the FGDS and the PCF; second by the capture of the leadership of the Socialist Party in 1971 and the incorporation into that party of virtually all elements of the non-Communist Left; and finally by his successful negotiation in 1972 of a programatic agreement with the PCF.

Progress along this path was not to be uneventful, nor was unity to be easily maintained, for whilst institutional rules may promote bipolarity and constrain intra-alliance conflicts, they cannot alone eradicate those conflicts. Indeed the nature

of the electoral alliance established between the Socialists
and the Communists for all elections after 1967 (withdrawal
in favour of the best-placed candidate after the first ballot)
meant that competition between the allied parties for votes at
the *first* ballot became intense and, at times on the Communists' part, extremely aggressive. Nevertheless it is clear that
the Union of the Left was a consequence of the systemic
constraints of the Fifth Republic and that Socialist dominance within the Union of the Left derived from the nature
of presidential politics, with the need for wide vote aggregation at the second ballot requiring the leadership of each
rival alliance to be in the hands of its more moderate component. The Union of the Left, in the context of presidential
politics, thus served to promote the political career of
Mitterrand and, by association, his (post-1971) party. As
bipolarization gathered apace in the 1970s with the demise
of the small Centre parties, erstwhile supporters of the
governing *majorité* had *faute de mieux* to vote for the Left
and, inevitably, for its most moderate component, the
Socialist Party. Because Left unity and Socialist dominance
within the alliance derive in large part from the institutional
changes of 1958–62, it follows that, were any one of those
institutional devices to be removed, the edifice of Left unity
would be at risk.[9] A switch, for example, to proportional
representation—to which the PS and PCF were formally
committed in the 1972 Common Programme—would remove
the need for electoral alliances, and the end of presidential
power and presidential elections would destroy all remaining
arguments for co-operation.

Social change

The Fifth Republic has also seen social changes which have
implied certain advantages for the Left and disadvantages
for the Right. The antiquated social structure outlined in
Chapter 1 was radically transformed in the post-war decades,
most notably with the decline of the peasant and the rise of
the managerial and white-collar classes. Rural depopulation
after the War served to reduce the population engaged in

[9] See O. Duhamel, op. cit., p. 553.

farming from 28 per cent in 1954 to 9 per cent in 1975, thus registering a loss of two-thirds in twenty years. Meanwhile professional/managerial and white-collar workers came to account for twice the number (37 per cent) they did in 1954 (19 per cent) (see Table 2.3). These movements reflect the essential changes in economic activity of the post-war period: the contraction of the primary sector and the expansion of tertiary-sector activity. With the latter went the expansion of white-collar and managerial employment, and the growth of urbanization—or more accurately, suburbanization. In the manufacturing sector change was of a qualitative, rather than quantitative, kind: overall numbers did not much increase, but technological changes saw the decline of traditional industries (coal, steel, textiles) and the rise of new ones (chemicals, electronics). Qualitative changes, too, came in the nature of working-class demands, with a tendency, especially in the wake of the 1968 events, towards a 'post-bourgeois' interest in participation in decision-making (*autogestion*) rather than in purely economic demands. The drift from the land was politically threatening to the Right which traditionally carried about two-thirds of the rural vote. Throughout the 'sixties the dependence on this electorate grew, at the time when it was in steep numerical decline. The political threat was masked somewhat in legislative elections by the over-representation of rural areas, but in presidential elections, with the votes counted in one single national constituency, the impact of a declining rural vote fully registered.

The expansion of the *cadres*—lower executives, supervisers, technicians—did for a while serve partially to compensate the Right for its losses in rural France. But the new white-collar class was not middle class in the traditional bourgeois sense, as Giscard d'Estaing was to observe in his reflective essay *La Démocratie française*,[10] where he described it as a 'large, expanding, amorphous, central group bordering on the one side, through its technicians, foremen, skilled workers, and certain independent workers, the industrial proletariat, and on the other side, through its managers and other independent workers, the bourgeoisie.' It was neither

[10] V. Giscard d'Estaing, *La Démocratie française*, Fayard (Paris), 1976, pp. 56–7.

Table 2.3
Occupational Categories 1954–1975

	1954 (%)	1962 (%)	1968 (%)	1975 (%)
Farmers	20.7	15.8	12.1	7.6
Farm Workers	6.0	4.3	2.8	1.7
Employers and self-employed	12.0	10.6	9.6	7.8
Professional and managerial	8.7	11.8	14.7	19.4
Non-manual workers	10.8	12.5	14.7	17.7
Manual workers	33.8	36.7	37.8	37.7
Others				
1. domestic workers	5.3	5.4	5.7	5.7
2. clergy, armed forces, etc.	2.7	2.9	2.6	2.4

Source: *Économie et statistique*, July 1977.

proletarian nor bourgeois, because it was not socially and culturally isolated, nor clearly defined by the exclusive possession of an economic and cultural heritage. It was a new group possessing a mix of values drawn from both poles. Giscard's analysis was apposite: the new white-collar class was individualistic though suburbanized; interested in consumption rather than wealth; benefiting from public rather than private provision; politically pragmatic, but interested in social justice, and concerned with qualitative as well as quantitative demands. It was, in the words of another observer: 'A population . . . [whose] values are those of a society in growth—modernity, efficiency, economic dynamism, the primacy of the expert—and yet also those of protest against promises that modern society has not yet met and the frustrations that it inflicts: [it favours] humanization of development, protection of the quality of life, protection of the environment.'[11] The same observer noted that the Socialist Party's growth appears to have been linked to the capacity of its candidates to articulate these two demands—belief in modernization on the one hand, and protest against its failings on the other. If in the 1960s this new, urbanized middle class tended to favour the Right, it was doing so during the years of Gaullist economic and political prosperity. Evidence of a

[11] P. Braud, 'Les élections législatives de mars 1978 dans la région Bretagne', *RSFP*, Dec. 1979, p. 1034.

more overt 'social democratic' alignment of the *cadres* came with the Socialist Party's penetration of the conurbations in the election of 1973.

The Right had also benefited, during de Gaulle's time, from an unusually large degree of working-class support— 45 per cent of manual workers voting for de Gaulle in the 1965 presidential election. But so 'cross-sectional' an electoral base was essentially a function of de Gaulle's charismatic appeal and of the concentration, during the early years of the regime, on issues of a non-economic kind: Algeria, foreign policy, and the Fifth Republic's institutions. That phase passed, and under Pompidou after 1969, the Right's electoral base slid perceptibly towards the countryside and the bourgeois and self-employed classes, so that by 1974 Giscard could take only 27 per cent of the working-class vote. As the social structure of the electorate changed, so did its age structure. By the 1970s the post-war baby boom was reaching the polling stations, the more so after Giscard's enfranchisement of the eighteen- to twenty-one-year-old group as one of his first reformist gestures in 1974. Thus 2.5 million young people joined the electoral rolls and showed their gratitude by favouring the Left in elections thereafter. The rejuvenation of the electorate has had a significant impact on the electoral fortunes of the Left. In 1973 the under-thirty-five-year-olds constituted 29 per cent of the electorate (Table 2.4). From this large increase of

Table 2.4
Age and Left Voting 1973–1981

| | Proportion of electorate voting for PCF and PS | | | | Age distribution of the electorate | |
	1973 (%)	1978 (%)	1981 (%)	Increase 1973–81 (%)	1973 (%)	1981 (%)
18–24 yrs }	45	53	62	+17	29	35
25–34 }		50	63			
35–49	49	44	54	+5	29	25
50–64	39	44	60	+21	22	20
65+	36	40	37	+1	20	20

Source: SOFRES opinion surveys cited in G. Le Gall 'Le nouvel ordre électoral', *Revue politique et parlementaire*, July-Aug. 1981, p. 18.

young voters it is clear that the 17 per cent increase (between 1973 and 1981) in the level of support for the Left among the under-thirty-fives (see Table 2.4) involved a large number of votes—in fact about 3.5 million (whereas the proportionately larger increase in Left support in the fifty-to-sixty-four age-group between the same years involved the transfer of only approximately 1.5 million votes). During the 1970s, as the Right became increasingly dependent on the votes of the old, so a growing proportion of the Left's strength was drawn from the younger voters; in 1967 three in ten Socialist voters were under thirty-five; by 1978, over four in ten.[12]

Secularization

Probably the most damaging change in electoral behaviour that came to affect the Right was the result of changes within the Catholic community. These were of two kinds: first the decline in the traditional identification of Catholicism with political conservatism, and second, the waning of religious practice and belief itself—in short, secularization. The historical identity of the Church as a bulwark of conservatism was undermined in France, as elsewhere, by the reforming messages emanating from the Papacy during and after the pontificate of John XXIII. In 1967 Paul VI issued *Populorum Progressio* which articulated ideas on decentralization and *autogestion* which were becoming fashionable concerns on the Left in the late 1960s. Radical themes were promoted, especially by young Catholics in the union confederation, the CFTC, which was deconfessionalized into the CFDT in 1964 and became an important organizational link between Catholicism and the working class. Meanwhile the hierarchy came to accept the possibility of a vote for any party except the Communists. The new Socialist Party after 1971 was careful not to retain the traditional laicist trade-mark and attracted many Catholic radicals. The proportion of practising Catholics prepared to support the Left also grew. In 1965 Mitterrand gained only 8 per cent of this category; by 1973 13 per cent were voting for the Left (10 per cent for the PS).

[12] R. Cayrol, *L'Express*, 13–19 Mar. 1978; and *Le Point*, 13 Feb. 1978.

Polls in 1977 suggested that 24 per cent of practising Catholics would support the Left (18 per cent of them PS), but in the elections of 1978 the figure achieved was 16 per cent (of which 13 per cent were PS)—still double the amount of devout Catholic support for the Left recorded in the mid-'sixties, but a significantly large drop from the high level of 1977, and implying that the second thoughts of Catholic voters in 1978 could have been a prime cause of the Left's defeat in that year.[13] Even more remarkable still than the move towards the Left among the laity was the shift among the clergy. In 1973 a survey showed 34 per cent of *curés* favouring the Left (25 per cent PS); and amongst young priests (under forty) as many as 64 per cent (42 per cent PS).[14] More important however, and more damaging to the Right, has been the decline of religious observance altogether. Whereas nearly nine out of ten French people identified themselves as Catholics in 1966, only eight out of ten did so by 1977. And the most devout (the regularly practising), and thus traditionally the most politically conservative, fell from being 24 per cent of the total Catholic population, to 17 per cent—a loss of a quarter of the Church's most devoted followers over a period of ten years. The loss amongst the irregularly practising was even more severe (a drop from 40 to 14 per cent). The fall in religious observance coincided with the increase in support for the Socialist Party, and whilst the waning of the religious cleavage cost the Left some votes of traditional anti-clericals, it delivered substantial gains, first in votes (1973, 1978) and then in seats (1981), for the PS in the once impregnable Catholic citadels of Brittany and Lorraine.[15] Secularization was the inevitable consequence of a society undergoing modernization, transforming itself from the rural and small-town world of the Third Republic to the urbanized cosmopolitanism of a country undergoing an economic transformation. The decline of religion—a traditional prop of the conservative order—was part of such a process.

[13] See R. Rémond, 'Echec de la gauche—est-ce la faute de catholiques?', *Projet*, June 1978, p. 735.
[14] *Le Point* survey cited in J.-F. Bizot, op. cit., p. 342; see also J. Charlot, *Quand la gauche peut gagner*, pp. 67-9. Alain Moreau (Paris), 1973.
[15] See P. Braud, op. cit., p. 1028.

New ideologies

Many of the social changes examined here have helped to spawn new ideologies: deconfessionalization and secularization have accompanied movements for women's rights; rapid urban growth and the problem of energy demands in an expanding economy have aroused the 'ecological' conscience; and the growing cosmopolitanism of remote areas undergoing rapid change has provoked a rise of regional identities, particularly in Brittany. Feminism, ecology, and regionalism are themes not readily addressed by traditional bourgeois parties. Regionalism, moreover, is resisted by those parties that stand squarely in the Jacobin statist tradition—the Gaullists and the Communists. By the latter, moreover, many of these modern causes are dismissed as mere bourgeois diversions. Of the major parties only the Socialists seriously sought to articulate the new concerns, and for two reasons: first, because the issues appealed to the new middle class which came to form the core of the Party's membership, and secondly, because there was electoral capital to be gained. The important objective of securing a 'catch-all' electorate at the second ballot has required playing to specific minority audiences. Thus in 1981 the Party promised the regional interests decentralization; specific action to secure women's rights (symbolized by the Party's support for the leading feminist lawyer, Gisèle Halimi, who was duly elected to Parliament); and a go-slow on the nuclear-power programme to entice the ecologists. After the election the traditional Interior Ministry was also given responsibility for decentralization, and a special statute to placate Corsican regionalists was introduced; at least one of the new Socialist ministers had an established reputation as a spokesman for Breton regionalist opinion. Six women were appointed to the forty-three-strong government, two of them in important ministries (Agriculture and National Solidarity) and a third, a leading feminist, was appointed Minister for Women's Rights. In the presidential election two-thirds of the ecologist voters who participated in the second ballot transferred to Mitterrand and were rewarded by the appointment of two ministers for ecological matters, one of them the leader of the MRG (Left Radicals), the Socialist Party's small *force d'appoint*, which had made a deliberate bid to speak for middle-class ecological concern. The depth of the Socialist leadership's commitment to such causes once they had come to power could, of course, be doubted. The ecologically oriented policy on nuclear power was, for example, soon dropped along with the junior Ecology Minister after the elections.[16] Nevertheless, during the 'seventies the Socialists were virtually alone among the parties in working with the grain on these issues, and electoral advantage clearly was gained.

A party whose time had come

It has been suggested elsewhere that the French Communist Party owed its emergence from the shadows after 1958 to two men, Khruschev and de Gaulle: to the former for dethroning Stalin and initiating an era of 'peaceful coexistence'; and to the latter for pursuing an independent foreign policy which entailed a *détente* with the Eastern Block, and for installing a presidential system which drew the PCF into an alliance with the Socialists.[17] If de Gaulle had, probably unintentionally, such an impact on the Communists, how much more dramatic was the effect, not only of his new institutions, but also of his eventual departure, on the Socialist Party. It has been argued here that the Socialist Party profited greatly, and almost fortuitously, from a system of bipolarized, presidential competition. Thus, although the advent of de Gaulle appeared to threaten the Party's prospects by transferring the role of government formation from Parliament to President and by attracting voters away from 'discredited' parties such as the SFIO, the post-1962, overtly presidential, nature of the regime presented the Socialists with great opportunities. Equally the withdrawal of de Gaulle in 1969 offered significant advantages by finally releasing the working-class voters who had supported Gaullism so strongly during the 'Algerian' phase of the new Republic (1958–62) and in the middle 'sixties when de Gaulle personified the twin achievements of strong institutions and national independence.

[16] See Alain Bombard (the dropped minister) in *Paris Match*, 28 May 1982, for his view of Mitterrand as a man who sees ecology as an issue people outgrow during their thirties.

[17] J. Touchard, in F. Bon *et al.*, *Le Communisme en France*, A. Colin, 1969, pp. 99–101.

Analyses of change in party systems of the sort that has characterized the Fifth Republic—the streamlining of Right and Left into a system of bipolarized competition—have tended to rely either on social and economic or on political and institutional explanations. The former view is associated with Otto Kirchheimer's analysis which traces the origins of large 'catch-all' parties to economic affluence, the demise of ideology, and the weakening of class–party alignments.[18] The picture is one of a party system 'catching up' with fundamental social and economic changes which have weakened parties tied to declining social groups or waning ideologies, and strengthened those that appeal to the voters' growing pragmatism, whether as effective parties of government (the Gaullists and Giscardians before 1981) or as moderate parties of change (the Socialists from the middle 1970s onwards). The alternative 'institutional' view sees party-system change as more directly a function of mechanical manipulation (electoral systems, presidentialism, etc.) or of political trauma (the discontinuity caused by the collapse of one regime and its replacement by another). There is, in fact, some evidence to suggest that it is only in countries that have experienced severe shocks to their political and institutional systems, such as defeat in war or the collapse of a regime, that there has been a marked propensity for the party system's configuration to change radically and for the creation of large, 'catch-all' parties.[19] It is certainly the intention to argue here that the collapse of the Fourth Republic and the nature of the institutional changes that followed were of enormous importance in reshaping the party system and in offering opportunities to the Socialist Party. Institutional changes clearly made it more probable that the Party would, given a leadership appropriate to the demands of the new political system, be well placed to harness the votes both of new social categories and of protest as the incumbency of the Right wore on into its third decade.

There is thus much force to the argument that the Socialist Party in the 1970s was a party in the right place at the

[18] See O. Kirchheimer, 'The Transformation of Western European Party Systems', in J. La Palombara and M. Weiner (eds.), *Political Parties and Political Development*, Princeton University Press (Princeton), 1966, pp. 177–200.

[19] S. Wolinetz, 'The Transformation of Western European Party Systems Revisited', *West European Politics*, 1979, pp. 5–28.

right time, a party 'whose time had come', largely through changes of which it had been more spectator than initiator. Mitterrand in 1981 observed that the 'political majority' in France had now come to coincide with its 'social majority'. That the coincidence did not occur before 1981, that the Left did not come into its electoral inheritance sooner, was due specifically to the appeal of Giscardian 'reformism' in 1974 and to concern about aggressive Communist tactics in 1978.[20] Thus, the environmental changes were not of themselves enough. Oppositions, it should be remembered, by and large do not win elections; governments lose them; and whilst the French Left spent the 1970s—particularly the election of 1978—proving the reverse, by 1981 political wear and tear in the conservative *majorité*, governing through an economic recession, was so severe as to provoke the move to a reformist alternative long prefigured in institutional and social change.

[20] See J. Capdevielle *et al., France de gauche, vote à droite*, PUF (Paris), 1981.

3
From SFIO to Parti Socialiste

The process of adaptation on the part of the Socialist Party to the Fifth Republic began effectively with the preparations for the first presidential election to be held under the new procedure of direct election in December 1965. It was in the preparations for this first electoral challenge to de Gaulle's incumbency at the end of his first seven-year term that the Party was obliged to confront, and to resolve, its choice of electoral strategies. The essential prerequisite in contemplating an alliance that would inevitably have to involve dealings of some sort with the largest opposition party, the PCF, was the creation of a Socialist Party capable of negotiating with the Communists from a position of strength. As the 1965 elections loomed two approaches were tried, the first by Gaston Defferre, the second by François Mitterrand.

Defferre's initiative opened with the launching by the magazine *L'Express* in September 1963 of a presidential bid on behalf of an anonymous 'Monsieur X', said to be capable of beating de Gaulle in 1965. By December 1963 *L'Express* had revealed the identity of 'Monsieur X' as Gaston Defferre, the right-wing Socialist mayor of the country's largest provincial city, Marseilles, and a man who had survived the Fourth Republic with a reputation largely intact. The political base for his presidential bid was envisaged as comprising the electorates of the parties lying between the Communists and the Gaullists, in other words an essentially centrist alignment which harked back, somewhat less attractively than Defferre himself, to the Fourth Republic and which had, in any case, been tried and found wanting in the autumn referendum and general election of 1962. Defferre's aspiration was not dissimilar to that of Pierre Mendès France, who had tried in the mid-1950s to stimulate the creation of a large non-Communist Left force —initially as a loose electoral coalition not unlike the American Democratic Party, a model then much in vogue. An SFIO–Radical–MRP link-up would certainly cover sufficient electoral ground to pose an effective counterweight to the PCF and one of which the Communists would be obliged to take serious account.

Defferre, who as leader of the SFIO's largest single regional power base, the Bouches-du-Rhône, was able in February 1964 to obtain his party's endorsement, nevertheless ultimately failed in his endeavour and was obliged in mid-1965 to announce his withdrawal from the presidential race. He had failed for three reasons. First, as already implied, the centrist character of his enterprise gave it a somewhat 'used' air, with the most recent elections suggesting that centrism was both politically and electorally exhausted and unable to resist the Gaullist tide. Secondly, by seeking to involve the Catholic supporters of the MRP he was flying in the face of some very firmly held left-wing anti-clerical prejudices, as well as affronting the inclinations of most MRP voters who were strongly attracted by Gaullism in the early 1960s (as they had also shown themselves to be in the early 1950s). Significantly also, in negotiations with Defferre it was the MRP leaders who specifically sought to keep the word 'socialist' out of the title of Defferre's 'federation', and who were opposed to any electoral deal with the PCF at the second ballot.[1] Thirdly, and most provocatively, Defferre had sought to assemble a collection of electorates independently of established party organizations, at first through a series of 'Horizon 80' committees and then, by the spring of 1965 through the launch of a Democratic Socialist Federation, which was intended to form the basis of a new party. From the point of view of existing party élites, Defferre's federation simply had too much of a 'free enterprise' look to it and could easily be seen —even by hostile fellow socialists—as a personal power bid for a presidential office to which many socialists, moreover, still remained unreconciled. For the SFIO leader Mollet, with whom Defferre had enjoyed poor relations for ten years, the initiative posed the greatest possible personal threat—with the incorporation of the SFIO into Defferre's new formation and the consequent loss of Mollet's own power base. It was thus, in a spirit of brotherly enmity, cloaked in a certain concern for

---

[1] F.-O. Giesbert, *François Mitterrand ou la tentation de l'histoire*, Seuil (Paris), 1979, pp. 204-5.

socialist principles, that Mollet helped to torpedo Defferre's candidacy in June 1965.[2]

Defferre failed too because of his provocative disregard for the Communist Party with whom he had, locally, very bad relations. In Marseilles, and as recently as March 1965, he had retained power as mayor through an alliance against both the PCF and the Gaullists, based not merely on the MRP but on conservatives too—in Communist eyes a deeply reactionary coalition. If Defferre's presidential bid was to be a national extension of the bitter relations prevailing in Marseilles it was indeed doomed, for there was no certainty whatever that the PCF would deliver, as Defferre assumed, its large and indispensable electorate to him at the decisive second ballot in the presidential election.

Yet, despite the collapse of Defferre's attempt, an important stage in the process of the non-Communist Left's adaptation to new political and institutional realities had been reached. Alliance-building had been attempted, undergrowth cleared, and a way made for the launching of a second presidential bid which was to establish the basis of the Fifth Republic career of François Mitterrand. Writing in 1969, Mitterrand was to declare that 'since 1962, when it was decided that the election of the President would be by universal suffrage, I had known that I would be a candidate',[3] but until Defferre, whose candidacy he had backed, was out of the way, this ambition could not be realized. Once he was, Mitterrand lost no time in launching his own bid in September 1965. He succeeded where Defferre had failed by confining himself to gaining the support of the parties of the Left—the SFIO, Radicals, *and* PCF. Both the Socialist and the Communist Parties were reassured by his avoidance of involvement with the 'anti-socialist' MRP. Guy Mollet, moreover, could accept Mitterrand as posing no threat to his own power in the SFIO: neither Mitterrand nor any of his closest acolytes had ever belonged to the SFIO and had thus never given Mollet any direct cause for offence. He was a man furthermore with only a nebulous political base of his own, comprising the small CIR and other modish, but numerically slight, political clubs of the period. Meanwhile Communist

[2] F. L. Wilson, *The French Democratic Left 1963–1969*, Stanford University Press (Stanford), 1971, pp. 129–34.   [3] F.-O. Giesbert, op. cit., p. 203.

goodwill—or at least the agreement not to run a candidate against Mitterrand—was assured by his reputation since 1958 as a resolute opponent of Gaullist *'pouvoir personnel'* and by his good relations with the PCF leader Waldeck Rochet (whom he had met in Algeria during the war). Mitterrand both saw the need and had the ability to carry the Communists with him.

Yet if one of Defferre's failings was that by seeking an essentially centrist alliance he alienated the Communists, Mitterrand was also running the risk that by dealing with the Communists he would provoke centrist voters' displeasure and also be stuck with the longer-term problem of an unreconstructed ally—the Communists having less need to liberalize if they were offered an alliance more or less on a plate. In the event, and thanks to the relatively mild leadership of Waldeck Rochet, the PCF did not seek a high price for its support of Mitterrand in 1965, even forgoing its demand for a jointly agreed programme which could have held Mitterrand to radical policy commitments. The PCF was calculating that against de Gaulle in 1965 no Communist candidate stood a chance anyway, and that a repeat of 1958 was possible—when a substantial part of the PCF electorate defected. Nevertheless, notwithstanding Communist support, Mitterrand's campaign was significantly marked by instinctive appeals to the Defferrist Centre; Communists were held at arm's length and kept off his platforms. He announced himself before the first ballot as the candidate of 'Left and Left Centre', and before the second as the candidate of 'all republicans'. He polled 32 per cent on the first ballot and in a straight fight with de Gaulle 45 per cent on the second.[4]

This outcome was doubly significant. First, it served to destroy de Gaulle's stature as the incarnation of national unity.[5] The central figure of the new Republic had been humbled into a second-ballot fight, when a first-ballot walkover had been taken for granted. This was a significant psychological blow from which the standing of de Gaulle—despite the parliamentary landslide of 1968—never recovered.

[4] *Association française de sciences politiques*, 'L'élection présidentielle du 5 et 12 décembre 1965', FNSP (Paris), 1970.
[5] P. Williams, *French Politics and Elections 1951–1969*, Cambridge University Press (Cambridge), 1970, p. 186.

Secondly, Mitterrand's strong showing established his position as *de facto* 'Leader of the Opposition' in a country used to a variety of weak and mutually suspicious 'oppositions'. Suspicions certainly remained, but a candidacy backed by the traditional parties of the Left—PCF, SFIO, and Radical—had shown itself to constitute a serious potential threat to Gaullist dominance, at the same time as the counter-threat posed by the Centre (MRP plus non-Gaullist conservatives) in the shape of Jean Lecanuet showed itself able to poll only 16 per cent of the vote. The Centre was thus shown to be of slight consequence as the voters were offered for the first time since the Third Republic a straight choice between Left and Right (for all the Gaullists' resistance to the label).

The FGDS

In September 1965 the longer-term basis for Mitterrand's political career and for the resuscitation of the non-Communist Left was secured by the formation of the *Fédération de la Gauche Démocrate et Socialiste* (FGDS), an association of the SFIO, the Radical Party, the CIR, and assorted political clubs. Mitterrand had become President of the FGDS in between the ballots of the presidential election and the implicit hope was that this loose federation of parties would progressively be tightened and its central authority increased so as to unify in one organization the non-Communist Left which could then turn in confidence to negotiate with the PCF. Both Mitterrand's performance in the presidential election and the proximity of the next (parliamentary) elections, due by spring 1967, assisted him in increasing FGDS cohesion and in dealing with the wary leaders of the component parties. After successful negotiations between the leaders of the constituent parties of the FGDS for the allocation of seats in the 1967 elections, Mitterrand appealed in March 1966 for a speedy fusion of the Federation into a single body and for the formation of a *'contre gouvernement'* (shadow cabinet). The latter was duly constituted, with leading Socialists figuring prominently: Mollet, unexcludable, was allocated the defence and foreign affairs portfolio; Mauroy, youth; Defferre, social affairs; and the Radical leader Billères education—a responsibility traditionally attractive to Radicals.

Some of Mitterrand's CIR members were also given portfolios: for example, Tron (economics) and Mme Eyquem (women's affairs). For all the need to square people whose party power bases required them to be squared, this exercise served the purpose of maintaining the momentum of unity.[6]

In December 1966 the FGDS (and later the PSU) arrived at a common national strategy for the 1967 elections with the Communist Party, based on the mutual standing down in favour of the Left candidate leading the field on the first ballot. This was an arrangement which, although prefigured in the popular-frontist amity of December 1965 was also a logical inference from the fact that half the Socialist (and Radical) deputies sitting in the 1962–7 Parliament owed their election to Communist support at the second ballot. This electoral alliance worked well in the elections of March 1967. The FGDS first-ballot vote of 19 per cent compared well with an aggregate 1962 SFIO and Radical vote of 23 per cent (which included a lot of 'Radicals' of a right-wing persuasion) and the 116 FGDS seats to a SFIO plus Radical total of 112 in 1962.[7] Of the 116 FGDS seats, sixteen were occupied by members of Mitterrand's CIR, most of them very close collaborators such as Dayan, Dumas, Rousselet, Fillioud, Mermaz, and Estier, and although all, except Mitterrand, were to lose their seats in the 1968 election, the manner of their election in 1967 was interesting. Most owed their seats to Communist generosity in constituencies where the PCF, though leading after the first ballot, voluntarily sacrificed its right under the agreement to represent the Left at the second ballot in favour of a CIR candidate considered to stand greater chance of victory. Thus in 1967 the Left (FGDS plus PCF) with 193 seats, and the Centre with forty-four, had come within a hair's breadth of denying the Gaullists a parliamentary majority; the PCF had been eased out of its isolation; Mitterrand had got fifteen of his closest supporters into Parliament and in an evenly divided Assembly was able more than ever to adopt the mantle of 'Leader of the Opposition'; and the FGDS deputies sat in the Assembly as

[6] See *La Nouvelle Revue socialiste*, 'Le renouveau socialiste et l'unité de la gauche (1958–1976)' (special number), esp. P. Joxe, 'Partis et clubs sur les chemins de l'unité', pp. 29–35 and 36 ff. (undated).

[7] Alain Lancelot, 'Les élections des 5 et 12 mars 1967', *Projet*, May 1967, pp. 549–62, and P. M. Williams, op. cit., pp. 204–25.

one group (even if this was an unavoidable necessity for the Radicals who, with only twenty-six deputies, fell short of the thirty required to constitute a separate parliamentary group).

These positive gains aside, however, it was clear that the constituent elements of the FGDS had come together essentially out of electoral necessity in the 1965-7 period and that, with these important elections passed and no more in prospect until 1972, there was still plenty of time in which mutually suspicious parties could jockey for position. In June 1967 the small PSU (2.3 per cent of the vote in 1967) reversed the collaborative posture by which it had secured four seats in 1967 (one being occupied by Pierre Mendès France), when its leadership was captured by Michel Rocard who favoured taking a route to Left unity outside the confines of the FGDS. This move precipitated a split in the PSU, with Pierre Bérégovoy defecting to the UCRG (*Union des clubs pour le renouveau de la gauche*), an organization set up by Alain Savary and other ex-members of the SFIO and the PSU in 1965, and Jean Poperen establishing his UGCS (*Union des groupes et clubs socialistes*). Both these organizations sought to retain links with the FGDS, and their leaders were to play important roles in the revival of the non-Communist Left in the 1970s.[8]

At the same time Mollet's SFIO was continuing to reject the prospect of its own dissolution within a wider organization. In theory the FGDS had decided in August 1967 to set up departmental organizations, but before this could get any further the SFIO decided to assert its independence. Within the Party 'Europe' had always been good ground on which to rally the faithful and in December 1967 the Party's *Comité Directeur* suggested a motion of censure on the Government for its hostile attitude toward British EEC entry. As it had not been put to the FGDS, this suggestion posed an affront to the Left's shaky organization and had the further consequence of poisoning relations with the PCF. Mollet manufactured more incidents of this sort with the general intention of distancing the SFIO from the FGDS without actually breaking up the Federation. The SFIO had moreover, begun to plan its own amalgamation with left-inclined Radical members

[8] See J. Mossuz, *Les Clubs et la politique en France*, A. Colin (Paris), 1970, and F. L. Wilson, op. cit., pp. 77-107.

of the FGDS—a proposal endorsed at an SFIO Congress in January 1968 and planned for early 1969. Here was a proposal for Left unity over which control could be exercised by the SFIO's old guard and not by outsiders like Mitterrand. Such manoeuvres were, however, concealed by more spectacular events—notably the signature in February 1968 of an FGDS-PCF common platform, which possessed a certain symbolic value, and yet which made no attempt to hide a wide range of disagreements over foreign policy, nationalization, and institutional matters and which fell far short of the hopes of both the PCF and the CIR for a common programme.

The major, and wholly unexpected, French political crisis of May-June 1968—which started with student unrest, expanded into a general strike, posed a threat to the continuance of the regime, and yet ended with a tremendous electoral victory for the Gaullists—knocked sideways all moves for Left unity, whether of the non-Communist Left or of the Left as a whole. Mitterrand's response to the apparent power vacuum at the height of the crisis in May, when he announced at a press conference (28 May) his readiness to assume 'the highest office', was taken by the Gaullists to imply a seizure of power, and was made, moreover, without consultation with the constituent elements of the FGDS and consequently aroused suspicions across the whole spectrum. After the (precipitated) 'red scare' elections of June, in which the Left parties lost half their seats —wiping out the gains of 1967—the Radical Party formally quitted the Federation of the Left. In August the Soviet invasion of Czechoslovakia deepened suspicions of the PCF, the more so when initial Communist condemnation of the action was retracted in favour of approval for the process of 'normalization'. The PCF was re-emerging as an unacceptable, pro-Moscow party. In November 1968, with Mitterrand's formal resignation of the Presidency of the FGDS, the organization collapsed. Discredited and directionless and denied Mitterrand's leadership, the first experiment in non-Communist Left unification had finally come to a dead end. The FGDS had foundered on the failure of established party leaders—notably those of the SFIO—to envisage loss of identity in a new organization. It was, however, clear that co-operation had brought electoral gains. The need for new structures was obvious, but after 1968 these structures were to be sought less by a federation of existing parties than by a reconstruction outwards of the Socialist Party.

This process, satisfying to the SFIO leadership, naturally caused problems for the other parties involved, and notably for the CIR, the stature of whose leader created difficulty. CIR and club elements furthermore wanted a statement of aims and principles so that they could know what they were joining and so as to prevent the backsliding on principle characteristic of Mollet's SFIO. The CIR and the UGCS (led by Jean Poperen) were also explicit in their demand for a resolutely Leftist alliance strategy for the new party and the abandonment of all Centre alliances—a demand opposed by the SFIO whose power at municipal level across France rested significantly upon such alliances. The CIR and the UGCS moreover sought an agreement on the transitional leadership of the new party, anxious as they were to avoid mere ingestion by an SFIO run by Guy Mollet. The CIR insisted on dissolution of existing structures prior to the convening of a constituent congress—a demand rejected by the Socialist Party, which was determined to control the process of transition from 'SFIO' to 'SFIO-plus'.

At a congress at Puteaux in December 1968 Mollet was successful by margins of more than two to one in carrying the conference on both principles and structures. The structures were to be virtually identical to those of the SFIO, with Mollet succeeding in delaying a decision about the proportional representation of factions on the Party's leading bodies (a principle he had suspended in 1946) until a further congress in the spring of 1969. In fact the Puteaux meeting saw all the demands put by the CIR—for a new transitional leadership, for party branches at work-places, and for a more collective decision-making structure—either rejected or shelved, an outcome which confirmed CIR hostility to the enterprise of refashioning French Socialism under existing SFIO leadership.

Within the SFIO itself Mollet's own position was fairly secure. His power had rested for twenty years on the voting strength of the two large-membership federations of Pas-de-Calais and Nord, and although the Nord was undergoing a change of leadership in 1969, with Pierre Mauroy replacing

Augustin Laurent, Mauroy's expectation of inheriting the Socialist leadership from Mollet kept him in line. Meanwhile Defferre, controller of the votes of the third big federation, Bouches-du-Rhône, although an opponent of Mollet's for some years, preferred to abstain rather than support either a 'provisional executive' or any of the other structural changes favoured by the CIR. Mollet, however, anxious not to hand the Party to an outsider like Mitterrand, was apparently reassured by the latter's declaration that he would not stand for office in the new party, for in December 1969 he announced his own retirement. Plans were laid for a constituent congress of the new party with representation of the SFIO, CIR, UCRG, and UGCS at Alfortville in 1969.

Alfortville Congress, May 1969

Preparation for Socialist Party reconstruction was, however, to be seriously disrupted by another intrusion of de Gaulle when he decided to initiate a referendum (in April) on regional government and reform of the Senate, the result of which—a majority against the President—caused de Gaulle to resign and precipitated the country into feverish preparation for an unexpected presidential election. The whole process of Socialist reconstruction thus became entangled with the problem of deciding on presidential candidates. The Alfortville Congress in May 1969 (postponed from April by the referendum) was in consequence a débâcle.

The meeting was dominated by Defferre's decision to launch himself as the Party's candidate for the June presidential election—having already won the backing of the Party's parliamentary group. Whilst Mollet's instinct was to sink such a proposal, as he had done in 1965, any alternative candidates, such as Savary of the UCRG or Mitterrand—both of whom would seek to stand on a Left unity platform backed by the PCF—would require the suspension of the congress to allow time for talks with the Communists. Mollet was both keen to avoid entanglement in talks with the Communists at this time and keener still to block Mitterrand's presidential ambitions and thus glad to reject CIR calls for a postponement of the congress. Sheltering behind the letter of the 1958 Constitution (in whose drafting he had taken a hand, but which had long since been surpassed by practice), Mollet argued in letters to Mitterrand's aide Estier and to the PCF leader, Waldeck Rochet, that talks to establish a common programme on which a single Left candidate could stand were quite inappropriate, given the 'arbiter' role ascribed the President under Article 5 of the Constitution; the President was not a chief executive and therefore did not need a programme.[9] By such dissembling Mollet closed the door on a joint Left candidate, and specifically on Mitterrand whose CIR promptly boycotted the Alfortville Congress along with Poperen's UGCS, which was strongly committed to Left unity.

Although Defferre was nominated by a large margin of 2,032 to 227 votes, the size of this majority could not be taken as evidence of enthusiasm (other confused votes were taken, one of which Defferre actually lost).[10] Mollet's rejection of a Socialist–Communist common programme and the Communists' visceral dislike of Defferre made it inevitable that the PCF would run its own candidate, Duclos. The left-wing PSU also put its own leader Rocard into the contest. Joined by Pierre Mendès France as an unofficial running-mate, Defferre—utterly devoid of the presidential qualities of oratory and charisma and with only tacit party backing—proceeded to a humiliating defeat in the election with 5 per cent of the vote, to Duclos's 21 per cent, and 23 per cent going to the centrist candidate Poher who was a briefly popular phenomenon in the months of May and June 1969, having as President of the Senate stood in as interim President after de Gaulle's resignation. The folly of Defferre's candidacy was demonstrable: many Socialist voters deserted to Poher, some to Duclos, and others to Rocard whose 3.7 per cent vote was as good a performance as Defferre's 5.1 per cent was disastrous. The self-destructive division of the Left carried through to the second ballot of the elections with the PCF calling for abstention from a contest in which the Gaullist Pompidou was confronted by the centrist Poher, the Socialists supporting Poher, and Mitterrand remaining silent.

With the Left balkanized as never before during the Fifth Republic, a number of lessons cried out to be learnt from the

---

[9] P. Guidoni, *Histoire du nouveau parti socialiste*, Tema (Paris), 1973, pp. 65-8, and R. Verdier, *PS–PC, une lutte pour l'entente*, Seghers (Paris), 1976, pp. 260-1.
[10] P. Guidoni, op. cit., pp. 73-4.

disasters of 1969. First, Defferre's exclusively Centre-Left version of socialism had been routed at the polls, securing indeed the lowest Socialist vote ever. Second, the Communist go-it-alone strategy was shown to be no way for that party to get a candidate through to the second ballot in presidential elections, despite a remarkably avuncular performance by Jacques Duclos. It had been amply demonstrated how not to play the presidential game, and the most certain long-term beneficiary of the Left's fragmentation of 1969 was François Mitterrand, who had shown four years earlier how far a united Left could go.

Issy-les-Moulineaux Congress, July 1969

Depending on one's theological point of view, Defferre was either the first candidate of the new *Parti Socialiste* or the last of the SFIO. Entirely dominated by the messy division over Defferre's nomination, the Alfortville Congress for one writer was less the founding congress of the PS than the congress at which the SFIO committed suicide.[11] In the mêlée at Alfortville the new party's launch had aborted. Only an innocuous declaration of principles had been voted and the central questions of strategy, structures, and leadership remained to be resolved. Moreover, important segments of the non-Communist Left (the CIR and UGCS), for reasons described above, avoided the Alfortville proceedings. Thus a further constituent congress was convened for July at Issy-les-Moulineaux where it was hoped—at least by the most *'unitaire'* of French Socialists—that those elements that had been at Alfortville (the SFIO and Savary's UCRG) would be joined by Mitterrand's CIR and Poperen's UGCS.

To aid such a process of reconciliation at a time when Mitterrand himself was announcing his intention of undertaking a *'tour de France'* in order to *'rassembler à la base'* all socialists, without reference to existing party structures, one of the CIR's leading figures, André Labarrère (briefly a deputy in the 1967–8 Parliament) convened a meeting of grass-roots socialists at Bagneux. This free-lance effort sought to build bridges between the new PS and the forces alienated

[11] H. Portelli, *Le Socialisme français tel qu'il est*, PUP (Paris), 1980, p. 102.

by what had happened at Alfortville, but in the event the bulk of the CIR boycotted this meeting too, leaving it to consist of only two federations and five sections of the CIR and twenty-eight federations and forty sections of the PS, including representatives of CERES (Centre d'Études de Recherches et d'Éducation Socialistes, the club organization formed within the SFIO and staunchly committed to Left unity) and representatives of Poperen's UGCS. The meeting proceeded to vote a *'base d'accord'* in which it was made clear that the PS must reject centrist alliances and institute more democratic structures. After reassurance from the leadership of the PS, at least about the new party's broad strategic orientation, the Bagneux group decided to attend the Issy Congress and there to present their own motion. The Bagneux meeting thus served to enable at least some of the elements still outside the PS to be absorbed into the Party.

At Issy the 800 delegates were confronted by four motions of significance, in the names of Savary, Mollet, Mauroy, and the Bagneux group (Labarrère's part of the CIR, CERES, and the UGCS).[12] Savary's motion contained no real indication of a new strategic direction; it recognized the Union of the Left as the normal strategic orientation of the Party, whilst at the same time not ruling out alliances with 'democratic forces' (i.e. centrists) who 'opposed the Right and certain aspects of the capitalist regime'; talks with the PCF 'without weakness' were also envisaged. Mollet's motion was very close to Savary's and stated the Party's objective as being to participate in a government supported by the whole of the forces of the Left on the basis of a common programme. Mauroy's contained anti-Communist references (for example on Czechoslovakia) and sought 'guarantees' from the PCF prior to detailed talks on a programme, but did accept the need for such negotiations. The 'Bagneux' motion called for unity of the Left as a top priority, unequivocally rejected all centrist alliances in the coming (March 1971) municipal elections, and wanted talks leading to an alliance with the PCF. There was little to choose between these texts; though Mauroy's, resting on the support of the Nord federation, was clearly the least keen on deals with the PCF.

[12] P. Guidoni, op. cit., pp. 79-84.

Of the three large federations that had dominated the Socialist Party since the War, the Pas-de-Calais, controlled by Mollet, and the Nord, led by Augustin Laurent, who in 1969 was in the process of handing the leadership to Pierre Mauroy, had both consistently backed Mollet.[13] At Issy-les-Moulineaux there was every reason—despite Pierre Mauroy's desire to see a truly renovated Socialist Party with attractive leadership— to expect Mauroy, who was considered to be Mollet's *dauphin*, to retain his links with Mollet in order to come into his expected inheritance. In the vote on the various motions Mauroy (supported by the Bouches-du-Rhône) obtained 1,135 votes, Mollet 1,013, Savary 436, and the Bagneux group 296.[14] The congress then, under Mollet and Savary's direction and with Mauroy's support, voted a political motion which included the following paragraph and which seemed to anchor the Socialists to a Union of the Left approach: 'The Union of the Left constitutes the normal strategic axis for socialists. The Party prohibits all alliances with forces representative of capitalism. It must, without preconditions, enter into and pursue a public debate with the Communist Party.'[15]

If the decision taken on the Party's strategic orientation seemed a radical change from the old SFIO's penchant for 'centrism', the decisions on structures were rather more reminiscent of the status quo. Some changes were agreed: first, that the Party should have work-place (i.e. factory and university) sections as well as geographical sections (and this barely a year after the student and worker unrest of 1968). Secondly the title of party leader was changed from General Secretary to First Secretary with the intention of instituting a more collective form of leadership. But, on the far more important question of proportional representation of all groups on the leading organs of the party the old guard triumphed, and only those who backed the Savary–Mollet– Mauroy motion at the end of the congress gained seats on the Bureau Exécutif. Although the left-wing elements— CERES and Poperen—were the more important losers in this manoeuvre, Mauroy also failed to obtain inside the Bureau

[13] Roland Cayrol, 'Les votes des fédérations dans les congrès et conseils nationaux du Parti Socialiste (1958-1970)', *RFSP*, Feb. 1975, pp. 51–75.
[14] *Le Populaire*, 16 June 1969.   [15] R. Verdier, op. cit., p. 262.

Exécutif what he had hoped to gain by supping with Savary and Mollet, namely the leadership, for Savary was elected First Secretary in succession to Mollet. Thus Alain Savary, a man with a very clean political past (*Compagnon de la Libération*, who had quitted Mollet's government in 1956 and the SFIO in 1958 over Algerian policy, who had opposed the Fifth Republic in 1958 and spent the 1960s earnestly engaged in a succession of organizations—PSA, PSU, UCRG— to 'renovate' the French Left) succeeded the wiliest and most controversial of Socialist foxes, Guy Mollet, who left party headquarters never to return. But the most unsatisfactory outcome of Issy for all but the closest of Mollet's supporters was that although Mollet had gone, the decent but essentially undynamic Savary was heavily beholden to Mollet's men who had voted him into the leadership and who were to retain control of leading posts in the Party (notably Ernest Cazelles in charge of organization). 'Demolletization' had not been accomplished, nor was this the only unsatisfactory outcome of the Issy Congress.

The new party's strategic orientation—Left unity—was neither unambiguous nor entirely credible, given that only four weeks before the congress many members of the new Bureau Exécutif, as well as Defferre and Mollet, had backed the centrist Poher at the second ballot of the presidential elections, and some effectively at the first. Nor was it clear in detail, the decision to talk to the PCF being open to varying interpretation. Savary (with Mollet) favoured talks on general philosophical and doctrinal questions ('socialism', 'democracy', etc.); anti-Communist right-wingers like Arthur Notebart of the Nord federation wanted no talks at all; Mauroy wanted them hedged with conditions; whilst CERES wanted a quick march toward the signing of a common programme.

Mitterrand's brooding absence moreover constituted a further significant drawback, for he, despite a slump in public esteem after May 1968, was still the only leader of the French Left of proven electoral worth at national level. Yet his isolation was complete; he had even detached himself from the Socialist parliamentary group and was seated among the curiosities of the *non-inscrits*. But his greatest strength now lay in his appeal to those disaffected forces inside the PS who sought the proper renewal of the party's leadership (i.e. the promotion of themselves) which had been denied them at Issy. Gaston Defferre was not on the new Comité Directeur (although some of his supporters were). Pierre Mauroy, whilst an Executive Bureau member, was kept off the Secretariat. Despite Defferre's absence, however, the Issy Congress had seen the consolidation behind Mauroy of a new alliance between the Nord and the Bouches-du-Rhône federations—an essentially destabilizing development for the heirs of Mollet for whom in the past the Nord had provided a reliable block vote.

CERES meanwhile was looking for a more categorical approach to negotiations with the Communists and whilst Mauroy and Defferre and CERES were at polar opposites in their attitudes to the PCF, each disliked Mollet and had an interest in bringing Mitterrand and the CIR into the Party as a weight with which to tilt the balance against Savary and his supporters and to provide dynamic leadership. For Mauroy and Defferre, men used to tough fights with the PCF in the Socialist municipalities of the Nord and Bouches-du-Rhône, a strengthened party was an essential precondition to dealing with the PCF, and Mitterrand was seen as the necessary ingredient in a process of building up the Party prior to such a confrontation. Thus the contours of a highly disparate alliance of Mauroy, Defferre, Mitterrand, and CERES became decipherable, even if certain events after Savary's election, such as the dispute over the municipal elections of 1971, appeared to deny its rationale.

Local election strategy, 1971

A serious test of the new party's open avowal of the leftist alliances came with preparation for the municipal elections of March 1971. This was a highly sensitive matter for two reasons: first, the Party's main strength lay in its town halls,[16] and secondly, many of its mayors and councillors had been elected as part of centrist alliances with Radicals, Christian Democrats, and in some cases anti-Gaullist conservatives. Of the 159 towns with over 30,000 inhabitants the SFIO was

---

[16] P. Guidoni, op. cit., pp. 119–20.

absent, after the previous (1965) municipal elections, from only nine councils. In fourteen the Socialists were in sole command, in eighty-two they formed part of Left alliances, but in fifty-four the alliances were of the centrist type. Amongst the councils in this group were the Socialist Party's municipal jewels: Lille, Marseilles, and Toulouse, some of which comprised support-bases for the Party's major power-brokers, such as Defferre. To resolve the problem a PS National Council meeting was held at Bondy in October 1970 at which three competing proposals were aired. CERES and Poperen sought to get the Party to reverse all centrist alliances including any with the Radicals (who, under Jean-Jacques Servan-Schreiber were enjoying a brief recovery at the time and thus being taken seriously). A motion from Savary of studious vagueness opposed all 'reactionary politics', but countenanced alliance with the Radicals, and a Mauroy–Defferre motion sought to leave the choice of alliance to local federations, whilst outlawing any pacts with the Gaullists. In a preliminary vote Savary obtained 1,066 votes, Mauroy and Defferre 1,407, and CERES/Poperen 493.

A subsequent deal ought to have been possible between Savary and CERES to ban centrist alliances, but a brutal reversal of municipal alliances would have been more than Savary's delicate leadership could stand and so a hastily cobbled compromise emerged between the leadership and the Nord–Bouches-du-Rhône—enjoining leftist alliances, but permitting freedom of choice at local level. It was duly cemented in a vote of 2,702 to 152.[17] Although in the subsequent March 1971 elections the number of PS–PCF alliances in the big towns rose from 48 per cent (1965) to 60 per cent, the proportion of centrist alliances involving the Party was virtually unchanged at 21 per cent (18 per cent in 1965). Such an outcome was deeply resented by CERES, the more so after its leader, Jean-Pierre Chevènement, was stripped of his party offices for six months after voicing opposition to the outcome of the Bondy meeting.

The Left (CERES and Poperen) was also dismayed at the slow progress of the talks between the PS and the PCF, which had opened in December 1969 and resulted in the publication of a *bilan* (balance sheet), or progress report in December

[17] D. Lacorne, *Les Notables rouges*, FNSP (Paris), 1980, pp. 47–53.

1970. The report recounted chapter by chapter the agreements and disagreements of the parties. Disagreements featured strongly in the field of foreign policy (EEC, Atlantic Alliance, etc.) and there was dispute too over *'alternance'*—the retreat from power of a Left government when beaten. On economic policy the PCF showed every sign of being able to push the Socialists well to the left on nationalization, largely because little Socialist economic doctrine existed with which to resist such pressure. Whilst these talks appeared to confirm the leftward stance of the PS established at Issy in 1969, progress was simultaneously too slow for CERES and too fast—given the Party's lack of weight in relation to the PCF—for Mauroy and Defferre.

If the botched launch of the Parti Socialiste at Alfortville and its incomplete and divisive reorganization at Issy-les-Moulineaux formed an inauspicious background for Alain Savary's leadership, certain signs of renewal were none the less evident. By the end of 1969, forty-seven of the Party's federal secretaries had been replaced with people who were both younger and of more diverse political leanings. Incipient factionalism was fuelled by journals and clubs of various sorts—a sign of life as much as of discordance. CERES began its rise by forging an alliance with the Socialist post office workers' union in Paris, led by Georges Sarre—who captured for CERES the federation of Paris in September 1969, ousting from the local leadership a staunch Molletist, Claude Fuzier. Like many of the Party's departmental federations, Paris had become moribund—virtually an empty husk. Other federations—for example Haute-Saône and Hautes-Pyrénées—had little membership to speak of and others (e.g. Basses Alpes) had more elected councillors than party members. Such anomalies began to be remedied as more effort was made to recruit new members, and to the extent that this was taking place under Savary's leadership, all was not lost.

It was, however, Savary's misfortune that his leadership of the new Party coincided with a period in which attractive reformist alternatives were in profusion. The Gaullist government of Jacques Chaban Delmas, appointed by President Pompidou in June 1969, was presenting a progressive 'new society' image to the country (aided by the future Socialist Finance Minister Delors who was at the time an adviser in

Chaban Delmas's *cabinet*). Meanwhile the Radical leader Jean-Jacques Servan-Schreiber was enjoying a meteoric sweep across the sky with his Radical manifesto *Ciel et Terre* and a famous by-election victory at Nancy. It was Savary's misfortune too to lack the leadership qualities and electoral appeal of François Mitterrand whose absence from the new Socialist Party made little sense. Negotiations to bring the CIR into the Party were thus inevitable and after Mitterrand had been warmly received at a meeting of the PS National Council in December 1970 the way was open to a further 'congress of unity' at Épinay in mid-1971.

4
Left Union 1971–1974

The second biennial congress of the new Socialist Party was duly held at Épinay in June 1971. With the absorption into the Party, at that congress, of the CIR and Mitterrand, and with the latter's replacement of Savary as leader, followed by the more resolute pursuit of a programmatic deal with the Communist Party, the Épinay meeting represented a significant turning-point, completing the process of renewal begun in the confused and inauspicious circumstances of 1969. Ironically, however, it was to be a most heterogeneous alliance that came together to ensure these changes, with the Party's right wing combining with its left to install Mitterrand as leader.

For the Nord–Bouches-du-Rhône, it was a matter of men as well as of measures. Defferre, who had an iron ward-heeler's control of the Bouches-du-Rhône federation, had long had his differences with Guy Mollet and whilst he had always remained in the bosom of the Party he had been in a minority for many years. By contrast, his relations with Mitterrand were good. In 1965 Mitterrand had loyally supported Defferre's abortive presidential campaign and had carefully waited until others had brought it down before declaring himself to be a candidate. And in 1969 Mitterrand had blamed Mollet's machinations, not Defferre's candidacy, for his failure to obtain the Left's nomination. Moreover, whilst Defferre's humiliation in the 1969 elections seemed to discredit the strategy of an alliance with centrists combined with a lofty stance *vis-à-vis* the Communists, Mitterrand's aspiration for a powerful Socialist Party and his conception of Socialism (*à la suédoise*) were not very different from Defferre's.[1] Thus an alliance was possible between the seemingly centrist Bouches-du-Rhône and apparently leftist Mitterrand supporters based on a rejuvenation of the leadership and a moderate programme. The Nord meanwhile was ostensibly as opposed to any deal with the CIR as was the

[1] See *Le Nouvel Observateur*, 24 Apr. 1971, report on the CIR *assises*.

Bouches-du-Rhône. However, in the Nord the preoccupations were slightly different: the Nord Socialists felt that renovation had not brought a rapid enough influx of new blood, which Mauroy in particular believed necessary to reinvigorate the Party and bring it national success. Neither Mauroy (nor the Nord) was moved by mere pique at his having been excluded by Mollet from the post of First Secretary. Mauroy in fact persuaded Mitterrand of the necessity for him (Mitterrand) to take this position, believing it necessary to look beyond the confines of the *'vieille maison'* for a change of leadership.

Thus was the ground prepared for Épinay. Outside the Savary majority was the 'Right'—composed of the Nord–Bouches-du-Rhône which consistently fell some 400 or 500 votes behind the leadership on disputed questions—and the radical CERES Left, with about 5 per cent of the votes, disenchanted by the leadership's slow and temporizing policies towards the PCF and hoping for a change of direction and pace. And outside the Party was Mitterrand's CIR which, once inside, could provide leadership and swing the balance against the Savary coalition.

The Mitterrand coup

Despite steadily shifting alliances within the Party, a change of leadership had not been widely expected, as Mitterrand's talks with Defferre, Mauroy, and CERES had been kept entirely secret. Co-ordination was close to the extent that the three motions submitted by each group were all written by Mitterrand's aide Claude Estier, but secrecy was so effective that criticisms of the Mitterrand *opération* did not focus on the conspiracy.

Ostensibly the issues at the congress did not appear to divide Socialists on any particularly definable lines; Savary expected the Épinay Congress to endorse his policy of 'dialogue' with the PCF and approve the agreement on ideology. Mitterrand, like Savary, wanted to rebuild the Socialist Party, unifying the non-Communist Left, and did not seem to have much to quarrel with in the actual conduct of the Party since 1969. Such criticism as he did have—for instance, the lack of a Common Programme—seemed to divide him from the Nord–Bouches-du-Rhône more than from

Savary, and Estier, in negotiating with Savary, encouraged this misperception.[2] In fact, the Nord–Bouches-du-Rhône motion appeared to imply a suspension of talks with the PCF by calling for guarantees from the Communists on crucial points: human rights, Europe, freedom from Moscow control, and '*alternance*'. Whether the Nord text could be called prudent or openly hostile depended on the interpretation of the reader, an ambiguity which was carefully nurtured to conceal from the Savary leadership the already solid alliance with Mitterrand.

The CERES motion called for a Common Programme and for united action with the PCF, demands which put a considerable distance between them and the Nord–Bouches-du-Rhône. Didier Motchane of CERES objected that the ideological dialogue had only served to put off to the indefinite future any real agreement on a Common Programme, whilst Mauroy and Defferre were calling for a pause in discussions so as to enable Socialists to regroup and to elaborate their own manifesto as a basis from which to negotiate. Meanwhile, Jean Poperen and his supporters called for parallel discussions on the programme of government and for basic ideological guarantees, but fell into line behind Savary. There were thus four competing versions of how to deal with the PCF, plus the Mermaz-Pontillion motion which was in fact Mitterrand's own. This last called for many of the same things as the Savary motion, but for tactical reasons omitted any explicit mention of a Common Programme. The motion called for common action with the PCF in parliament and in the country and envisaged that through the strategy of Left union the Party would come to occupy a strong and favourable position *vis-à-vis* the Communists. Thus the CIR hoped to unite a majority around the twin themes of a powerful and united Socialist movement and 'renovation', which they calculated would ensure the majority needed to bring Mitterrand to power in the Party. Many of the themes were unclear and it was not at all obvious what Mitterrand wanted, but it was clear that he could offer a new leadership and, importantly, one identified with success between 1965 and 1967. In summary the congress had to choose between

[2] A. du Roy and Robert Schneider, *Le Roman de la rose*, Seuil (Paris), 1982, p. 47.

the continued slow progress suggested by Savary, the pause called for by the Nord–Bouches-du-Rhône, the CERES governmental programme, Poperen's call for a government programme with guarantees on liberty, and the Mitterrandist motion.[3] Épinay involved, like much of post-1965 non-Communist Left politics, not so much personality politics as a personality: François Mitterrand. This is not to say that the various motions were mere camouflage, for there were real ideological points of difference, but it was the interplay of the two that was confusing: for example, Georges Marchais, the PCF leader, wrote to Alain Savary on the eve of the congress recalling the Communists' willingness to negotiate a Common Programme. Judging from the resolutions then being presented to the congress, the 'Union of the Left' was still in doubt; but the Party would soon show this to be a mistaken view even if the Communists, like various commentators, failed to perceive that the alliance with the PCF was not in question.[4]

At Épinay the first skirmish in the long battle came over an essential point of internal party structure: the method of election to the Party's governing bodies. Since 1946 a list system had been used and, although ostensibly open and democratic, this system was manipulated by the leadership so as to exclude opponents. CERES, like all minorities, wanted complete proportional representation even at federation (county) level so as to open out the Party to newcomers.[5] The old system would have placed difficult strains on the CIR–CERES–Nord–Bouches-du-Rhône coalition, for without proportional representation the various constituent components of the alliance would not have secured representation for their leaders in the Party's major bodies. Proportional representation would thus facilitate the Mitterrand bargain. Savary, having first opposed proportional representation, changed his mind and the congress voted in favour of this reform. But the form of proportional representation envisaged by Savary included a 10-per-cent threshold which each group's list of candidates would have to clear in order to gain representation; this would have been almost as detrimental to

---

[3] *Le Nouvel Observateur*, 14 June 1971. With the small Catholic group Vie Nouvelle, there were six motions in all.

[4] *L'Humanité*, 10 June 1971.   [5] *Le Monde*, 15 June 1971.

minorities as the old system, and was not the fully proportional system wanted by CERES. So the congress moved to
another vote, one which put Mollet in a minority for the first
time since 1946 and brought together the new Mitterrand
majority. Proportional representation with a 5-per-cent
threshold was adopted by 51,231 votes (CIR–CERES–Nord-
Bouches-du-Rhône) against 38,783 (Savary–Mollet–Poperen).
A winning coalition around Mitterrand was thus shown to be
arithmetically possible. The main speeches at Épinay were
brilliant examples of attempts to cajole and coax the crucial
marginal groups to complete this or that majority. Mauroy
and Defferre, for their part, resisted the accusation that they
were on the Right of the Party by rejecting national 'Third
Force' alliances, and recalling Defferre's position against the
Algerian war. Mitterrand's speech, made with an eye on
CERES and on other party activists elaborated on his new-
found socialism, on the 'revolutionary' nature of socialist
change, on unity, and on the necessity for an alliance with
the PCF developed through discussions and a programme of
government. This last point was specifically for CERES.
Guy Mollet, who spoke after Mitterrand, made the last big
speech of his political life. Centred on the crisis of capitalism,
the speech was a *tour de force*, taking in the problems of
inflation, unemployment, the class struggle, and dealing with
the theoretical problem of the transition to Socialism, but
not even Mollet's considerable effort was enough to save the
situation for Savary.

The various protagonists retired to the *Commission des
résolutions* where the compromises—if there could be any—
were to be thrashed out between representatives of the rival
motions voted by the congress. A composite resolution
could, in theory, have been achieved, but in this case the
decision had already been taken to try to bring CERES and
CIR supporters into the Savary majority, leaving the Nord–
Bouches-du-Rhône out in the cold. Mollet and Savary did
their best to patch together an ailing majority, but CERES
left the *commission* before the end of discussions. There was
no compromise and a confrontation therefore became
inevitable.

Back in the congress hall, the new alliance carried off a
narrow victory by 43,926 to the 41,757 of Savary, Mollet,

and Poperen. There were 3,925 abstentions, a large number, due in all probability to the refusal of some Nord and many CERES activists to follow the sharp about-turn. Savary, with dignity, defended his leadership and his conception of the Party's tasks. But the post-1969 leadership, and Savary in particular, had failed to appreciate that they could not purport to be radical about everything else except the SFIO faithful who remained in control of the organization. To be radical the Savary group could not afford to be beholden to the Molletists. It was for this reason, as much as any other, that CERES, Mitterrand, and the two big federations had formed the alliance against Savary.[6]

The new majority was committed to two actions: formulation of a Socialist Party programme with which to confront the PCF, and negotiations for a joint governmental programme with the Communists.[7] Thus the new leadership was rejecting the vagaries of marxist debate for a programme of government which could resolve indirectly the theoretical questions which Savary had tackled head on. A conference to decide the Socialist Party's programme was therefore envisaged before the negotiation of a Common Programme, which was thus to be delayed.[8] It remained for Mitterrand and the new coalition to establish the credentials of the new Socialist Party at a time when Michael Rocard's PSU was gaining support at an impressive rate, when Servan-Schreiber and the Radical Party held the front pages, and when the Communists were still by far the biggest party on the Left. Moreover, despite agreement on the immediate issues, there was still a tension between the CERES with its radical view of Socialism, and the old federations with their conceptions which were closer to the Labour Party, the Swedish Socialists, and the SPD than to the 'workers' control' Left.[9]

Mitterrand takes over

After the Épinay Congress the Party's *Comité Directeur* was composed as follows: 28 Savary–Mollet supporters, 23

[6] *Le Nouvel Observateur*, 19 Aug. 1971. Stanislas Levif, 'Le Parti Socialiste: Quel Renouveau?', *Études*, May 1972, pp. 719–30.

[7] *Le Monde*, 15 June 1971.

[8] Jean Poperen, *La Gauche française*, Vol. ii, Fayard (Paris), 1972, p. 331 ff.

[9] R. C. Macridis, 'Oppositions in France: an interpretation', *Government and Opposition*, Winter 1972, pp. 166–85.

Mauroy–Defferre, 13 Mermaz–Pontillon, 7 CERES, and 10 Poperen, giving the new alliance a five-vote majority. Mitterrand was elected First Secretary, and assembled beneath him an extremely heterogeneous Secretariat—with his own men (Estier, Fillioud, Joxe) outnumbered by those with an SFIO background; Mauroy, Jaquet, Loo, Pontillon, Chevènement, and Sarre—the first four of whom were firmly to the right of centre within the Party. The Communists were not slow to criticize this new leadership, seeing it as composed of the Party's Right, and determined to postpone a 'dialogue' with the PCF. As a symbol of PCF suspicion Savary was privileged to be interviewed by *L'Humanité*. Mitterrand wrote to Marchais reaffirming the outcome of Épinay and during the summer the new Secretariat went to work issuing press releases and statements on policy. Working committees were set up to prepare a Socialist manifesto and steps were taken to revive the moribund party press. Mitterrand, who had joined the Party only days before his election to its leadership, naturally enough had to work hard to become accepted by party workers.[10]

During the period of Socialist renovation, the Communist Party had been having its own troubles. The ailing Waldeck Rochet had let slip his hold on the Party and George Marchais had since 1970 slowly established himself as leader. In the process the PCF had published its own programme, *Changer de cap*, a document which was the fruit of much work in the Communist bureaucracy. Its publication in November 1971 was timely. Communist activists henceforth had an explanation of their party's role in society. The Socialists were now confronted with an established Communist position and given notice of the issues over which they would have to negotiate, notably European, defence, and nationalization policies.

As a counterpoint, the Socialist programme was hammered out under the guidance of the CERES leadership, and in particular of Chevènement, who co-ordinated the five study groups at work. Under such management it was no wonder that the document emerging was adventurous in its propositions and extreme in its language. However, in December 1971

---

[10] F.-G. Dreyfus, *Histoire des Gauches en France 1940–1974*, Grasset (Paris), 1975, pp. 328 ff.

the draft began a very rough passage through meetings of
party activists. The document's key concept was *'autogestion'*,
roughly translatable as 'workers' control' but which, although
vague, meant much more: the decentralization of decision-
making and administration and an appreciation of the value
of small units individually controlled. Disagreements also
concerned defence (the original document drawn up by
Chevènement was decidedly 'neutralist'), Europe, nationalization, education, and indeed, the radical stylish language of
the document itself. Mitterrand, acting as a Solomon among
ideologues, realized that the Party was deeply split by the
propositions forwarded by Chevènement's committees:
elements of the Épinay majority were bitterly opposed to
the document, as was the Savary–Mollet group.

A national conference was held at Suresnes in March 1972
in order to ratify the programme. A motion to overturn
Mitterrand could not be presented at Suresnes, but could be
disguised as a point of principle. Not for the first or the last
time, factional warfare broke out amongst the many currents,
with Poperen using the occasion to table a kind of 'preamble'
which was really designed to replace the political resolution
passed by the majority at Épinay, whilst CERES, adept
at this game, took the opportunity to hold a meeting open
to the entire Left to discuss *autogestion* and to increase its
own audience among Socialists within and outside the Party.
At Suresnes the Party had to debate the major problems of
the proposed programme and come to some combined conclusion if possible. On economic democracy, Pierre Mauroy
and Pierre Joxe had put down a motion which gathered a
54-per-cent vote, although the strongly *autogestion* CERES
motion had taken 23 per cent and Poperen 24 per cent.
The debate on *autogestion* was of labyrinthine complexity.
For Poperen and the Mollet–Savary supporters, the main
objective was 'appropriation by the collectivization of the
means of production', for without nationalization there
could be no Socialism; hence collectivism first. CERES, however, was of a directly contrary opinion: first, workers'
control, in particular over matters such as conditions of
work, hours of pay, unemployment, and social and industrial
security. The final resolution sought a compromise by
providing for the right of veto for workers and limited trial

autogestion in nationalized industries. All that remained was to batten on a concern for 'planning' which was conceded in characteristically vague terms. Finally a resolution from Marc Wolf (then of CERES) inserted a *'petite phrase'* into the programme which allowed workers to ask for their factory to be nationalized. This came later to be regretted, for it opened the door to an almost infinite series of nationalizations.

Political institutions, and in particular the 'legislative contract', were seen by Mollet's supporters to be under attack from the new leadership. The point at issue here was whether subsequent loss by a Left government of its parliamentary majority automatically entailed dissolution or whether there could be a search for another majority within the Assembly. Automatic dissolution was supposed to prevent any rightward drift and within the Savary–Mollet camp most were of the opinion that automatic dissolution should be the rule where the 'contract' was broken. The PCF had, however, exalted the principle to the status of holy writ and as it stood the proposal would have given the Communists (by breaking the contract) the final say on the timing of dissolution. It was therefore decided that in such cases the President should nominate a Prime Minister, but if the new Prime Minister could not find a majority the Assembly should then be dissolved—that is, only after a second hostile vote. This demanded a President prepared to behave in the approved manner and kept the door discreetly open to Fourth Republic experiments in finding new governments from within the Assembly.

European policy provided still further cause for disagreement. The Poperen minority were isolated in their call for an end to the construction of Europe and were at the head of those wishing to dispose of the Atlantic Alliance. A heterogeneous minority composed of the supporters of Mollet and some of those around Savary wanted to strengthen the supranational institutions of Europe, but the clear majority was behind the text presented by Robert Pontillon, the Party's International Secretary. Pontillon's text stated flatly that Europe would be acceptable only in so far as it permitted a 'Socialist experiment' in France. It also envisaged a simultaneous dissolution of the two military blocs—harking back to an old idea of Léon Blum's.[11] Despite many disagreements,

[11] Jean Lacouture, *Léon Blum*, Seuil (Paris), 1978.

a final motion on the Atlantic Alliance rejected a unilateral withdrawal by France, but strong 'Atlanticists', such as Notebart and Énock, were in a minority and were outnumbered by the advocates of neutralism (CERES–Poperen–Estier), a trend which appeared to be growing within the Party. But no sooner was the Socialist Party programme, *Changer la vie*, published than it was forgotten; it was a document setting out a negotiating position for the talks with the PCF but without committing the Party on any detailed points of policy.

With the Socialist Party's acceptance of François Mitterrand as its leader and with its decision to pursue exclusively the alliance with the Communist Party, the Left entered its period of closest harmony. The years 1972–4 constituted a time of steady progress for the Left and of rapid development for the Socialist Party, but without the squabbles and suspicions characteristic of more normal times. This exceptional quiescence was due, on the one hand, to the Communist Party's feeling that the Socialists posed no threat and their need to win them over to the cause of Left union, and on the other hand to the Socialist Party's steady growth. Left union was sealed with the signing of the Common Programme of the Left in preparation for the parliamentary elections of 1973.

The EEC referendum 1972

Before negotiations on the Common Programme could be properly started however, President Pompidou tried to capitalize on the disagreements inside the Socialist Party and the differences between the parties of the Left, by calling (16 March) a referendum in April 1972 on the accession to the EEC of Britain, Denmark, Ireland, and Norway.[12] Whatever the feelings inside the new party may have been, the old ex-SFIO members would never have supported an anti-EEC campaign. Indicators were therefore set fair for abstention, which Mitterrand ultimately recommended, but before that was decided, an agreement with the Communists had to be

[12] See Michael Leigh, 'Linkage Politics: The French Referendum and the Paris Summit of 1972', *Journal of Common Market Studies*, December 1975, pp. 157–70.

attempted. Pompidou meanwhile was counting on the PCF
to organize the opposition to EEC enlargement, and thus to
legitimize British accession for his own Gaullist Party, many
of whom were still loyal to the memory of de Gaulle's ten-
year veto on British entry. Pompidou's move was viewed
by the press as one of great tactical subtlety and did in fact
suspend the discussions between the PCF and the Socialists
for a few weeks.

A referendum on the Common Market posed no real problems for the PCF which hardly hesitated before flinging
itself into the battle as the only *'non'* force. PCF strategists
hoped to extend their influence into areas not traditionally
pro-Communist: to nationalists and Gaullists, particularly
working-class Gaullists. Moreover, the PCF could demonstrate
its patriotism, accentuate its long hostility to the EEC, condemn the Mansholt plan, and make a general assault on
'conservative and social democratic' politics. At one point,
and for a short time, the CGT had advised abstention,
but quickly changed when the PCF formally advised a
negative vote.

A series of events illustrated the impossibility of a PS–PCF
agreement. The PCF asked for a 'secret' meeting between the
leaders of the two parties: Marchais and Mitterrand met on
20 March (Mitterrand having informed the PS Comité Directeur) and they exchanged views without coming to any
conclusion. The PS then refrained from taking any definite
stand for some days until negotiators could meet, but the day
before the envisaged working-group discussions, *L'Humanité*
called for a *'non'* vote. Immediately after the PCF had thus
pre-empted negotiations, the two parties met and Marchais
revealed the 'secret' discussions (of 20 March). This was
regarded as sharp practice by the PS delegation to whom
Marchais's behaviour came as a surprise. Discussions went on
throughout the afternoon and evening, but the Communists
stuck to the idea of a *'non'* campaign.[13] Thus the two parties
went into the referendum divided: the PCF running its
campaign against enlargement and the PS abstaining.

The results of the referendum were not difficult to inter-
pret; they reflected the electorate's view of the futility of a
vote on a question already effectively decided. Participation

[13] *Le Monde*, 29 Mar. 1972.

was very low, with 13 million (47 per cent) abstaining and only 30 per cent of the electorate voting '*oui*'. Just over 5 million voted '*non*', but the PCF could not claim that these were all Communist votes. The PCF fiefdoms (Paris, Paris suburbs, and the Nord) did not vote '*non*' overwhelmingly, whereas many Gaullists, remembering the General's views on British entry to the EEC, did vote '*non*'. The Socialists drew some comfort from the fact that abstentions were 25 per cent higher than usual in French elections and were especially high in Socialist areas, but the number was more a reflection of general apathy about the referendum than of a PS break-through.

The Common Programme of June 1972

The Common Programme was negotiated, and agreed within two months—from 27 April to 27 June 1972. However, before negotiations with the Communists could be completed, there was the important matter of the Radicals and the centrists. Premier Chaban Delmas had just been autocratically sacked by President Pompidou, a dismissal implying a move to the Right and the end of Gaullist experiments with Chaban's 'new society', which had appeal for Centrists. Times therefore seemed propitious for a move to the Centre to encompass the Radicals, simultaneously with a move to make an agreement with the PCF. The Radical leader, Servan-Schreiber, was doubtful about the Union of the Left, although he appeared able to overcome the 'contradictions' between the newly published Radical Party manifesto *Ciel et Terre* and the Socialist Party programme by stating that they were in basic agreement. In negotiations the Socialists and Radicals surprisingly agreed on nationalization, factory democracy, and taxation, but the Radicals could not accept the electoral discipline of the Left which entailed voting for Communists on the second ballot.[14] The failure of negotiations with the Radicals however, encouraged *L'Humanité*, which saw in it a refusal by the PS to be tempted by the sirens of the Right and the allures of Third Force politics.

To negotiate the Common Programme, four working groups were set up: on Institutions, with Joxe and Boulloche

[14] Robert Fabre, *Quelques baies de genièvre*, Ramsay (Paris), 1976.

for the PS and Ballanger for the PCF; on Economics with
Chevènement and Piette for the PS and Jourdain for the PCF;
on Social Services, with Mauroy and Bérégovoy for the PS
and Madeleine Vincent for the PCF; and on International
Affairs with Jaquet and Énock of the PS and Kanapa for the
PCF. By June only a few disagreements remained. The
envisaged problems on workers' control, on resignation from
office following a defeat in elections, and on the Middle East
were settled with ambiguous formulas, but without doing
violence to Socialist principles. This left disagreements over
the 'legislative contract' (whether there should be an automatic dissolution as soon as the Left alliance was defeated in
the Assembly), on the number of nationalizations, and on
foreign policy.

On 26 June these issues were still unresolved.[15] The
question of the legislative contract was settled, despite PCF
misgivings, by adoption of the Socialist preference for no
automatic dissolution. On defence there was to be a simultaneous disbandment of both the Warsaw Pact and NATO,
and no reintegration of France in the military structures of
the latter, but equally no withdrawal from the Alliance
either. This formula represented a Socialist victory of sorts,
but ambiguity reigned. On the question of the EEC, the gulf
opened up by the recent referendum was bridged by an
acknowledgement of the Community and the Treaty of
Rome as a 'fact', and with calls, largely generated by the
PCF, for democratization, pursuit of workers' demands, and
retention of freedom of action for a French Left government.
On nationalization policy the gap was wide, with the Socialists
worried about the electoral consequences of the long list
('pages and pages', in Mauroy's words[16]) proposed by the
PCF. Deadlock was broken only by Mitterrand's threat to
close the meeting and agreement was made to take over nine
companies: Dassault, Roussel–UCLAF, Rhône–Poulenc,
Honeywell–Bull, ITT–France, Thomson–Brandt, Pechiney–
Ugine–Kuhlmann, Saint-Gobain-Pont à Mousson, and Compagnie Générale d'Électricité. Excluded from this list were

[15] See Pierre Uri, *Plan quinquennal pour une révolution*, Fayard (Paris), 1973,
Philippe Alexandre, *Le Roman de la Gauche*, Plon (Paris), 1978, pp. 291-2.
[16] F. O. Giesbert, *François Mitterrand ou la tentation de l'histoire*, Seuil (Paris),
1977, p. 272.

many other major concerns which had been on the PCF's shopping list, notably, the Compagnie françaises des pétroles (CFP), Hachette (the publishers), Peugeot–Citroën, and steel and merchant-shipping companies. The PCF thus 'lost', but in conceding as many as nine major companies, the PS could scarcely be said to have 'won'.

Thus, in the early hours of 27 June, the Common Programme was agreed. It was of prime symbolic importance; not only confirming the Socialist Party's Épinay strategy, but also capping the myth of Left unity, recalling 1936 and the Popular Front, and implying, to the more myopic, a reversal of the historic schism of 1920. But the Common Programme also served to rally the Right by supplying it with a common enemy. Nationalization, a neutralist-sounding foreign policy, the ambiguity, lack of economic sense, and general incoherence of the Programme were to be attacked many times over. Although a small group of left-inclined Radicals around Robert Fabre (becoming in July 1972 the *Mouvement des radicaux de gauche*) broke ranks and agreed to sign, other Radicals grouped around Servan-Schreiber were among the first to attack the barn-door target represented by the Programme. Some Socialists, including the deputy, Max Lejeune, left the Party and were to fight the next elections as *Réformateurs* (centrists).

Discordant harmony—the 'honeymoon'

Communist Party leaders may have privately feared that in signing the Common Programme the Socialists were on to a winner; if they did, they did not say so and most of them expected the PCF, as in 1936, to gain disproportionately from any Left agreement.[17] Immediately the Common Programme was signed and sealed, the Communist Party threw its enormous machine behind its publication—so much so, that by far the most common version distributed was that of the PCF, prefaced by Marchais. Communists called for joint meetings 'at the base' (i.e. between activists at grass-root level), a call echoed by CERES. Given Socialist weakness at the grass roots, this was a challenge they knew the PS

[17] This is the view of Jacques Duclos in *Cahiers du Communisme*, February 1972, pp. 941–58.

could not face. In the 'honeymoon' period of the 'Union of the Left', competition did not appear particularly pressing, but it was an inherent feature of the alliance from the beginning.

The Socialists hoped that there would be a rebalancing of forces on the Left and that the PS would grow, possibly even at the expense of the PCF. However, the Socialist Party had another and longer-term problem. It had to recapture the Centre without risking its new base. As a political programme the Socialist-Communist agreement, forged by activists, was extremely radical and would not appeal to the average Centre —or even Socialist—voter. Not for the first time were the Socialists caught trying to oversell a policy to interested parties and to undersell it to the electorate. But for the present, the success of signing the programme submerged other problems.

Meanwhile, the Socialist Party still had lines open to the PSU, whose most dominant personality was Michel Rocard, and which had important relations with the leading non-Communist union, the CFDT. But the PSU was even more faction-ridden than the Socialists and its hostility to Left union was undisguised. In 1972 Rocard was talking of 'revolution', and of the Common Programme as 'reformist'. However, the journalist, Gilles Martinet, forsook the PSU to join the PS as part of CERES, with which he worked closely for a while, and the PS began to take up the threads which led from the former PSU members to the expanding CFDT.

The 1973 elections

The parliamentary elections of March 1973 were the first to be fought by the re-formed Socialist Party and the first to test the credibility of the new Union of the Left. In an unprecedented campaigning effort, the Socialists introduced the electorate to the Party's new 'rose in the fist' symbol. Socialist-Communist relations were publicly harmonious, the Communists even offering to let the PS represent the Left at the second ballot in certain seats where the PCF led on the first ballot, but where it was reckoned a Socialist had a better chance of winning. Offers of such *'cadeaux'* (from which

Mitterrand's own CIR candidates had profited in 1967) were, however, wisely rejected by Mitterrand who could not afford to be tied so obviously to the PCF and who calculated that the PS was well placed in any case to overtake the PCF in more constituencies than previously. Joint meetings with the Communists were likewise avoided, although a liaison committee of the three Left parties (PCF, PS, and MRG) met frequently. Hopes were high, but serious expectations of a Left victory were not entertained: the extent of the 1968 parliamentary landslide meant that the Left had simply too much ground to make up. Moreover, the presence in the Élysée of Georges Pompidou, with nearly half his presidential term still to run, made it possible for the conservatives to concentrate upon the constitutional difficulties that would flow from a victory of the Left.

The election results were instructive: it was already possible to see the emerging physiognomy of the PS of the 1970s and the disappearance of the SFIO (see Chapter 9). On the first ballot (4 March) the PCF polled 5,156,619 votes (21.3 per cent), the UGSD (Socialists and Left Radicals) 4,939,603 (20.4 per cent), the PSU 470,000 (1.9 per cent), and the extreme Left, 299,000 (1.26 per cent): a total for the Left of 10.9 million votes. The Left had 45 per cent as compared to 40 per cent in June 1968 and 44 per cent in March 1967. The PCF had retained its dominant position, but the Socialist Party had stemmed a long decline by putting its own vote up to 4,579,000.[18] Many seats taken from the Party in the Gaullist avalanche of 1968 were restored to the fold and many of the Party's new leaders brought into Parliament. Among the newly elected Socialists were Jean-Pierre Chevènement, Jean Poperen, Pierre Joxe (radical son of the former Gaullist minister), Pierre Mauroy (who won the Lille seat once held by the Popular Front minister, Salengro), Alain Savary (who defeated the Gaullist Sanguinetti in Toulouse), Jean-Pierre Cot (son of another famous Popular Front minister), Charles Josselin (who ousted the ex-Premier and pompidolian minister, René Pléven), and many other total newcomers. There was also a shift expressed not simply in the arrival of new faces, but in the disappearance of a number of ex-Socialist centrists,

[18] Alain Lancelot, 'La France de M. Bourgeois-République', *Projet*, September 1974.

some of whom were beaten and others who had cut their ties with the Party for good: for example, Max Lejeune and Paul Alduy, who held their seats as centrists. The core of the parliamentary group was still composed of men of the old SFIO, but the new and younger men were a symbol of renovation.[19]

The Grenoble Congress—June 1973

The first party congress at which the Mitterrandist majority presided as incumbents was held at Grenoble in June 1973. It was a meeting of near-unanimity which reaffirmed the 'grand coalition' at the head of the Party—indeed extending it by the incorporation of Alain Savary and Jean Poperen into the majority. Although Mitterrand's grip on the Party was thus confirmed, CERES was revealed to have grown disproportionately, rising to 21 per cent of the congress votes and thus increasing from seven to seventeen its representation on the Comité Directeur. Meanwhile the number of 'Molletists' fell from fourteen to six, and Poperen's supporters from fourteen to eight.

At Grenoble the number of members had risen by 40,000 to 110,000, most of these having joined in waves since Épinay (10,000 since the 1973 elections). Just as the Party's influence was spreading nationally, its recruitment of activists was also becoming more evenly spread: the relative size of the big federations fell from 43 to 33 per cent and there were very few federations with under 200 members—most had over 700. Amongst the new activists there were many younger people and, a new feature, Catholics. The Party also began to organize industrial branches in metal working and in new technology industries, in which (unlike the Post Office and banks) it had not been represented since the War. These organizations, *sections d'entreprises*, were however somewhat limited and, compared with those of the PCF, paltry: but they were a beginning and most of the steam behind them was provided by CERES. Activists were being attracted by Mitterrand, Left unity, renovation, and the feeling of progress.

[19] Jean Edouard, 'Le groupe parlementaire à l'assemblée nationale: renouvellement et continuité', *Nouvelle Revue Socialiste*, No. 1, 1974.

A 'true shadow theatre' was how Pierre Guidoni, Paris councillor and member of CERES, described the Grenoble Congress and this, to some extent, it was.[20] Mitterrand's leadership was no longer challenged, but CERES began to make its irritating presence felt. It was now numerically strong, well organized, and united by a 'clan' spirit. Sarre and Chevènement refused to sign Mitterrand's original motion calling for a 'return to the spirit of Épinay' and although, on the face of it, there was not a great deal of difference from the rest of the majority, CERES wanted to pull the Party leftward. But neither CERES nor Mitterrand wanted a complete break; Mitterrand noted: 'Je suis partisan d'un parti unifié mais aussi d'un parti bouillonant.'[21] CERES was the fastest-growing part of the PS and indeed gave the Party much of its vivacity and life.

The Grenoble Congress seemed to indicate that there were three main currents of opinion within the Party: (1) the old Molletist current which was losing its momentum and represented, with Jean Poperen's ERIS, only 13 per cent of the votes (even in Pas-de-Calais and Haute-Vienne, where the Molletists were supposedly strong, the Mitterrand motion collected respectively 40 and 31 per cent of the votes); (2) the broad Mitterrand governing current which included Defferre, Mauroy, the ex-CIR, and now Savary, and accounted for about 60 per cent of the Party (its strong points being in the Bouches-du-Rhône (94 per cent), the Nièvre (93 per cent), Gard (84 per cent), Nord (77 per cent), Puy-de-Dôme (70 per cent), Isère (70 per cent), and Gironde (60 per cent); and (3) the left-wing *'autogestion'* group mainly represented by CERES, which was part of the majority, but which also included the Catholics of Objectif Socialiste and Vie Nouvelle which were not. CERES drew support from Poperen's group and from Savary's supporters, but their main force came from their 'white anting' activity in the small and marginal federations where new members contributed to swell CERES forces.

Nothing, however, managed to spark the Grenoble Congress into life. This may have been a consequence of the anaesthetizing effect of the previous elections. In effect the outcome of the Congress had been decided in advance and the leadership's

---

[20] *Le Nouvel Observateur*, 2 June 1977.   [21] *Le Point*, 14 May 1973.

motion was assured a majority. Mitterrand preached at CERES for its 'party within a party' attitude and for trying to make a 'false Communist Party with real petty bourgeois', but behind closed doors a composite motion was agreed. None the less CERES tried to push its major preoccupations on *autogestion*, Europeanism disengaged from Atlanticism, municipal alliances with Communists, and so on. Savary asked whether CERES should even retain its seats in the Secretariat but the old guard closed ranks and defended the 'young turks' who were, they said, 'l'aile marchant du parti'. Within CERES, some, like Didier Motchane, were prepared to sever links with the Mitterrand majority but others, such as Gilles Martinet, were not. The delicate problem of third force municipal alliances was shelved for a while; 'Europe' and *autogestion* were declared subjects on which special conferences were to be held later, and CERES's refusal to go into opposition ensured that there would be no rallying point for Mitterrand's opponents on the Left, for a while.

As Mitterrand had avoided any commitment to the congress, he was free to choose his own Secretariat and whilst this could have meant CERES's exclusion, they were given three places out of twelve, with responsibility for workplaces, the Third World, and ideology. CERES had stayed with the party leadership mainly because they saw it as guaranteeing the Épinay strategy, but bad blood had been created between them and the rest of the Party. This became increasingly evident in the months that followed as clashes occurred on a series of issues; notably on Chile, when CERES issued a joint poster with the PSU (although the Party had decided to campaign with the PCF); on the Middle East, when the CERES-dominated Paris federation published a distinctly pro-Arab communiqué;[22] and over the Young Socialists whose membership, under CERES control, had actually fallen.

In the course of preparing for a national conference on European policy at Bagnolet in December 1973, an even worse quarrel broke out—worse, because it associated the Mitterrandists Pierre Joxe and Claude Estier with CERES. In November, stung by a visit of SPD officials to the Gaullist

<hr>

[22] Robert Verdier, *PS–PC: une lutte pour l'entente*, Seghers (Paris), 1976, pp. 279–82.

Party Congress, Mitterrand proposed sending a PS delegation to EEC Socialist parties to explain French Socialist views and then subsequently to define a European policy. Joxe questioned confining the visit to EEC parties and proposed the inclusion of Scandinavia and Eastern Europe. At this, Mitterrand developed one of his diplomatic 'rages' and declared that he would resign as leader unless the Party came out clearly for the EEC orientation, and by twelve votes to eight in the Party's Bureau, it was decided to send delegates to EEC Socialist parties only. The next day Mitterrand sent a letter to Pierre Mauroy again threatening resignation if the Party did not adopt a 'sensible' European policy. No opposition was forthcoming because the Bagnolet conference agreed to a compromise containing something for everyone, for Joxe and Motchane, Left and Right. Like all Socialist policy documents, it was devised to secure the maximum agreement and the minimum content. At all events, it was consistent with the Common Programme and squashed party squabbles over European policy for a while.

Left union: the first problems

The legislative elections of 1973 had illustrated Mitterrand's determination to create a Socialist Party powerful enough to deal with the Communists on Socialist terms. Marchais's problem was a particularly difficult one. He had only recently been appointed his party's leader; he had to maintain the PCF's overall domination and to deal with an increasingly assertive Socialist Party. But there was one further element in the situation which had been added since the signature of the Common Programme: the gathering economic crisis. Since the War, no economic crises had hit France for any length of time, but in 1973 the signs were ominous: increasing inflation, falling growth rates, and then the Arab oil price rise.

In the spring of 1973 the Communists had tried to make the running in a series of demonstrations after the Socialist Party had refused to participate in a Communist demonstration, using as an excuse 'the lack of any joint preparation'. The Communists were worried about the challenge posed by extreme-Left parties to their ability to control and mobilize demonstrations; indeed they had only just regained control of UNCAL, the schoolchildren's union. To this extent, the *autogestion* debate in the PS clearly worried the PCF because it served both as a rallying point for the young and the extreme Left, thus out-flanking the Communists, and because the idea of 'decentralization' contained within *autogestion* went counter to the hierarchic way the PCF ran and controlled organizations.

The Arab oil cartel also revealed new differences. The Socialist Party was pro-Israel and Mitterrand had been accused once before, in 1972, of supporting expansionist Israeli policies. A more ominous development was the Communist Roland Leroy's denunciation of 'European solidarity' with the Dutch against the Arab oil embargo which, he alleged, could deprive the French workers of heating and transport. Marchais and others in the Party began to note the effects of inflation and to reject the notion, as they put it, that the 'workers should pay'; that working-class living standards should remain static or fall during the economic crises. A gathering polemic was only stopped short by the sudden presidential election in 1974.

The presidential elections—1974

For the Left generally, and for François Mitterrand and the Socialist Party in particular, the presidential elections came at an opportune moment.[23] Pompidou's death on 2 April found the Right for the first time seriously divided, without an agreed candidate, and menaced by a deteriorating economic climate, with inflation at 17 per cent and unemployment increasing. The Left, despite minor skirmishes, was now united for the first time in many years; the Socialist Party was internally quiescent and François Mitterrand was an unrivalled and obvious choice as presidential candidate.

However, Mitterrand's campaign was a personal one. To start with, he was 'common candidate of the Left', supported without reservation by the parties, but without being a candidate of particular parties. Thus he succeeded in freeing

---

[23] Serge Hurtig, 'Never So Near to Victory', in H. R. Penniman (ed.), *France at the Polls*, American Enterprise Institute (Washington), 1975.

himself from party and Common Programme control. He resigned, symbolically, as First Secretary of the PS (a position taken up by Mauroy for the duration of the campaign), and did not regard himself as bound by previous Socialist agreements. He chose his own advisers, including Mendès France, Rocard, and others from outside the PS, and, significantly, evaded reference to the Common Programme. Independence from the parties of the Left, especially from the PCF, yet being coupled with a united Left effort from the outset, gave Mitterrand enormous advantages.

Although not tied down by the Common Programme, Mitterrand's weak position on economic policy was none the less evident. Instead of the Common Programme he had a three-phase plan to deal with inflation, unemployment, and growth. There would be a preliminary six months of price control, government loans, price-indexed savings, increased spending (social and industrial), and cuts in VAT on certain goods. A second stage, of eighteen months, would be a phase of industrial reorganization; and a third stage (over five years) would involve the completion of the Left's programme (but exactly how and what was unclear). Mitterrand's foreign policy included a commitment to the Atlantic Alliance; his Prime Minister would be a Socialist, while the Communists agreed through Marchais that they would not impose demands for particular ministries. But Giscard d'Estaing made convincing attacks on Mitterrand's economic programme in two major debates, and the Communists insisted, if not openly, that Mitterrand was still bound by the Common Programme.[24]

On the first ballot Mitterrand drew less than the 45 per cent which, it was believed, would guarantee victory, polling only 43.2 per cent. This meant that he had to draw together at the second ballot the votes of René Dumont, the ecologist candidate (1.3 per cent), the extreme Left (2.3 per cent) and the dissident Gaullists (those disenchanted by Chaban-Delmas's first-ballot defeat), centrists, new voters, and others. In the event, it was a very narrow defeat: 49.2 per cent to Giscard's 50.8 per cent. Mitterrand had polled a clear 2 million votes more than the Left's total in 1973, but even this

[24] See M. Charlot, 'The Language of Television Campaigning' in H. Penniman, op. cit.

had been bought at the expense of an avoided Common Programme and a neglected PCF.[25] The Socialist Party, by contrast, emerged reinforced and with a leader of unparalleled popular standing. Mitterrand had shown that the Left could, united, make enormous progress and aspire to power in the near future. The problem was that Left unity could not survive the clear dominance of the Socialists and the popularity of their leader at a time when the Communist Party had hoped for considerable gains itself. Mitterrand's showing in the 1974 election thus sowed the seeds from which dissension grew and finally broke up the unity under Socialist leadership upon which the success of 1974 had depended.

[25] *Le Monde* (Dossiers), 'L'élection présidentielle de mai 1974', and J. Ozouf, 'L'élection présidentielle de mai 1974', *Esprit*, July–August 1974, pp. 14–37.

5

1974–1978: 'L'Union est un combat'

The near victory in the presidential elections of 1974 represented the high point of the Union of the Left. Communist-Socialist relations were harmonious, the Left made steady advances in the polls, and an eventual move into government appeared to be within reach. The Socialists had, however gained disproportionately from the alliance, both in activists and in voters, while the Communist Party remained more or less static. It was this imbalance in gains that prompted the PCF to launch in late 1974 a series of attacks on its Socialist partner which culminated in the eventual collapse of the Left alliance in 1977.

Mitterrand's increasing stature and the rising popularity of the Socialist Party were at the same time the cause of disaffection within the alliance and the condition of its success.[1] The Left could win only if the Socialists appeared to dominate the Communists (the greater the domination the more attractive the alliance), but this was something the Communists could not accept. Thus the strategy of Left union, with which Mitterrand had been identified since the mid-1960s, was increasingly called into question. The Union of the Left was not rejected outright by the Communist Party, but its basis was called into question in a series of escalating attacks. The Communists hoped to redress the balance inside the alliance by an emphasis on their own left-wing credentials and by presenting themselves as sole guarantors of a truly left-wing programme. It was alleged that, without a strong Communist Party, the Socialists were bound to drift to the Right, but as the polemic developed and it became clear that the Communist Party was not increasing its audience or its support, the tactic then changed to one of trying to cut the Socialist Party down to size even at the expense of a Left victory.

In the immediate aftermath of the presidential elections the Socialists wanted to capitalize on their near victory. At

[1] *Le Nouvel Observateur*, 11 June 1974.

the suggestion of Pierre Mauroy a meeting, the *assises du socialisme*, was planned for the autumn of 1974 to complete the process of unifying the Socialist Left by bringing together diverse individuals and groups, including the PSU and CFDT. Incorporation of the latter would serve to create the union link desired by both the Socialists and the CFDT leader Edmond Maire. However, neither the CFDT nor Rocard's PSU had supported the Common Programme; there were even objections inside the Socialist Party to such an incorporation, notably from CERES, which feared PSU competition over *autogestion*, and which saw itself as the guardian of the Common Programme against those who had not put their names to it.[2] When PSU leaders, ex-Gaullists, CFDT personalities, and others joined the PS after the *assises*, the party leadership was satisfied. But in the PSU, although Rocard and Chapuis joined along with 5,000 members, the majority refused to follow. Much the same hostility existed inside the CFDT, which objected to such close links with a political party. The *assises* therefore became an occasion for the incorporation of individuals rather than for a mass influx. At the *assises* the main rallying point was *autogestion*, a fact which drew the concentrated fire of the PCF for whom the idea was then anathema. Moreover the final document produced by the *assises* was vague and utopian, and by significantly failing to mention the Common Programme it offered a further provocation to the PCF. Nebulous and rambling, the document pledged to end the 'exploitation of man by man', to abolish the division of labour, to do away with the cash-nexus and to dissolve the State; all, of course, long-term objectives.[3] The anti-statist *autogestionnaire* tone was in keeping with the Socialist Party programme of 1972, but now backed by PSU and CFDT politicians, *autogestion* seemed to take on a new seriousness and to be further evidence of a PS move away from the Common Programme.

No warning was given to unsuspecting Socialists that they might be subjected to Communist attacks after a cluster of by-elections in late September, when it was evident enough that the Communist second-ballot vote did not equal the Left's combined first-ballot total; that Socialist voters were,

---

[2] *Pour le Socialisme; le livre des Assises du Socialisme*, Lutter–Stock 2 (Paris), 1974. [3] *Ibid.*, pp. 177–80.

in other words, deserting PCF candidates. The Communist attacks started by concentrating on this desertion and then moved on to assault the new Socialist recruits, Rocard and Chapuis. Marchais also complained that the Socialists were intent on growth at Communist expense. For *L'Humanité* they were in this sense the accomplices of the monopoly capitalist Right.[4] It was pointed out that Socialists were still allied with centrists in local government and this, the Communists complained, was incompatible with Left unity, a point finding echo inside the PS itself. Municipal alliances were a serious target for PCF criticism because, if there was one area in particular where the Communists might expect to gain from Left union, it was in local government where they were seriously under-represented.

All these criticisms were designed to show that at heart, and fundamentally, the Socialist Party was still a centrist electoral organization which only took up Left union to further reformist aims and was ready to drop the Common Programme at the least excuse. PCF spokesmen argued that the economic crisis did not, as Rocard and others maintained, make the Common Programme outdated, but rather, more necessary. The Communists were merely reformulating the old idea of the Marxist Left that the crisis of capitalism provides the chance for Socialist transformation and not the pretext for its postponement. Moreover, the only way to guarantee the application of the Common Programme, Communists argued, was to ensure a strong Communist Party.[5]

The polemic on the Left

During Mitterrand's election campaign the Communists had been loyal, self-effacing, and unobtrusive allies; when they did appear it was to correct the impression that they might be over-demanding partners.[6] However, in the autumn of 1974 this strategy (identified with Marchais) was sharply

[4] See also François Hincker and Leo Lorenzi, 'Le PS aujourd'hui', *France nouvelle*, 27 Jan. 1975.

[5] Paul Laurent, 'Programme Commun, Référence formelle ou base de combat politique', *Les Cahiers du Communisme*, February 1975.

[6] On 11 June 1974 Marchais stated, 'The orientation of the Socialist Party remains quite clear. We have no worries on that score.' (*L'Humanité*)

reversed. Paris Communists had tried to capitalize on the momentum of the presidential election by mounting 'operation open heart' in which they showed people around the PCF headquarters and explained Communist policy to enquirers. But this example had not been followed by other Communist federations and the initiative had not been a resounding success. Marchais may have wanted particularly to 'liberalize' the PCF and the 21st Congress in November 1974 was probably intended to achieve this. However, it turned out to be the occasion of Marchais's humiliation and a change of line. Marchais himself seems to have been unaware of the opposition to close collaboration with the Socialists which was building up within the Party; he had, for example, met Mitterrand on a private basis only days before the polemic started. But having declined to do battle with his opponents, he was left to find some other way of restoring his battered authority and this he did with the classic *fuite en avant*, by outrunning his critics. He therefore took the lead in attacks on the PS, at the same time struggling to control the Communist Party through a long and exhausting campaign in the provinces, building up support and placing his own men in positions of influence.

Other attacks from the Communists arose from their perception that the Socialists were conniving at the Government's policies. That the workers should not pay for the crisis is an old theme in PCF propaganda, but with the opening of the polemic it came well to the fore. The Socialists accepted that the budget had to be squeezed in times of crisis, thus providing confirmation for the Communists that PS economists accepted the need for the sort of austerity measures being applied by the Government. The Communists proposed joint action of party activists to obstruct these very policies, knowing that the Socialists would be reluctant to accept, given their lack of means to compete with Communist organization. Such was the dishevelled condition of the Left at the beginning of 1975 despite a near victory at the elections six months earlier. With the Communists using CERES, who sympathized with much of the PCF's case against Mitterrand, the need for a new leadership alignment within the Socialist Party seemed to become more pressing.

The Pau Congress, January 1975

The Socialist Party Congress at Pau on 31 January 1975 was enlivened by factional disputes and by Communist attacks on the Party's leading spokesmen. Like the earlier PS congresses, Pau served to confirm the personal authority of François Mitterrand. Since the Épinay Congress in 1971 the PS had been Mitterrand's party, if only on the basis of an unlikely coalition within which the left-wing CERES component was inflating alarmingly. At Épinay CERES won only 8.5 per cent of the votes, but at Grenoble in 1973 it obtained 21 per cent: the more the Party grew, it seemed, the more CERES benefited. CERES had recruited from the PSU newcomers at the *assises*, conducting a campaign around the themes of *autogestion* and 'Left union', and were in effect more of an opposition than a part of the Mitterrand majority.[7] CERES was now well implanted in those areas of party activity to which they had been given access (the youth movement, factories and businesses, and Third World policy) and there were accusations that they had used these posts to further their own recruitment rather than to aid the Party. Rocard and Chapuis, unlike others of the *assises* influx, did not join CERES, and although Rocard kept aloof from factional in-fighting, Mitterrand did use Chapuis and some former PSU activists, Acquier of the CFDT metal-workers and Martinet, who tabled an amendment at Pau which was *autogestionnaire* in tone, in an attempt to reduce the strength of CERES. CERES nevertheless managed to poll 25 per cent, the Molletist Bataille Socialiste only 3.4 per cent, Notebart 3.1 per cent, and Mitterrand's majority, built upon the Nord–Bouches-du-Rhône and CIR, a massive 68.1 per cent.[8]

CERES had continued to make progress in the Catholic and former conservative areas where the Socialists were not traditionally strong, and felt in a position to bargain strongly with Mitterrand. However the leadership could now draw for reinforcements on the ex-PSU group and use them to oust CERES from its footholds in the youth movement and workplace *sections*. Mitterrand therefore felt that CERES could be pushed into opposition by refusing a composite motion. Thus in the middle of a polemic with the Communists

[7] *Le Monde*, 4 Feb. 1975.   [8] Ibid.

Mitterrand ejected his Party's Left out into the cold, and brought people who had been cool to the Common Programme onto the Secretariat, in the process 'personalizing' his power more completely. Following the reshuffle within the Secretariat the ex-PSU members, led by Rocard, did not immediately rise to the top, but were kept in the background, though Poperen and Martinet were promoted and more Mitterrandists lifted to prominence, with a consequent increase in authority for Mitterrand's personal court. Half of the thirteen-man Secretariat now consisted of the leader's own men. Former CERES's responsibilities were given to more reliable people: Alain Rannou replaced Sarre, who had had responsibility for workplace organization, and Lionel Jospin, who had almost succeeded in breaking CERES's control in the Paris federation, began his short rise to power with responsibility for Third World policy. CERES was going to be slowly ground down.

Meanwhile the Communists, noting the ejection of CERES, saw the Pau Congress as a slide to the right.[9] Shortly after Pau, on 10 February, Marchais moved the polemic into a higher gear by attacking Mitterrand personally for being 'increasingly sure of himself and domineering'. Thus the Pau Congress served to animate rather than to defuse the quarrel between the Communists and the Socialists, with the scope of Communist attacks widening and further aggravating internal Socialist difficulties. Although relations steadily deteriorated, the Communists and Socialists arranged a Left-liaison committee meeting for 27 February (the first since the end of June 1974). At this meeting the Socialists conceded the case for mass demonstrations in the departments, calling on the Government to renounce its current economic policy. Giscard then puckishly intruded into the Left's difficulties by visiting Gaston Defferre in Marseilles (where Socialist–Communist relations had always been extremely bad), to 'take a look at the city's problems'. Faced with continuing attacks and a mounting polemic, the Socialists turned to their favourite resort in such cases: a party convention. However, since no party meeting on the split would be able to resolve anything, as the initiative lay with the PCF, nothing was decided. Marchais then compounded Socialist

[9] *L'Humanité*, René Andrieu, 3 Feb. 1975.

confusion by publishing his secret report which had been presented to the Central Committee after the signing of the Common Programme in June 1972.[10] The report warned that the Socialist Party was unreliable and open to reformist temptations.[11] Socialist responses to all such charges were low key; they tended to ignore PCF accusations and Mitterrand's replies were made with an eye on the opinion polls.

Mitterrand attempted to legitimize his own party's approach to the Communists by building up a (presumably French-led) bloc of southern-European Socialist parties. This came to nothing, although it remained a constant Socialist theme even until the 1981 elections. Meanwhile a southern-European question—that of Portugal—came to preoccupy the French Left in a markedly different way. Events in Portugal after the 1974 Revolution and until mid-1975 were confused and quasi-revolutionary; the Socialists walked out of the Government in May to oppose the *'gauchiste'* military and the Portuguese Communists (PCP). The French Socialists naturally defended the new Portugal and the Portuguese Socialist Party of Mario Soares, although CERES dissented. The PCF, on the other hand, defended the Portuguese Communist Party, and launched attacks on Mario Soares whom they typified as an 'arch social-democratic reformist'.[12] The most serious aspect was the PCF's defence of the seizure of *Republica*, the Portuguese Socialist journal, which did nothing for the French Communists' defence of liberties, of which they were making a good deal at the time. The French Communists could hardly claim to be the only 'true' defenders of liberty and at the same time support the suppression of a journal.

The 1977 municipal elections

In the context of the Union of the Left, the 1977 local elections had inevitably to be approached in a less ambiguous fashion than those of 1971. Neither the PCF, which was

---

[10] Étienne Fajon, *L'Union est un combat*, Éditions Sociales (Paris), 1975. The book consisted of a speech by Fajon and reports on Left union by the three post-war PCF leaders.

[11] *Le Monde*, 18 Apr. 1975.   [12] *Le Monde*, 31 May 1975.

anxious for more local representation, nor the enthusiastic young Socialist activists inspired by Left unity, would permit the continuation of any centrist alliances. Furthermore, the Socialist Party had grown enormously in the years since the 1971 Épinay Congress and its younger elements had to be given some means of expression and some proving ground for their leadership qualities. Municipal changes were thus inevitable and would enable the first thoroughgoing rejuvenation of the Party under Mitterrand. Such an abrupt reversal of alliances would not of course be easy, particularly at local level, where stability is a key feature and politics are often personalized. A further inevitable consequence of the reversal of alliances was that the Party would no longer have a basis of town and village positions separate from the turbulence of national politics; from 1977 onwards the Socialists would be irredeemably committed to the alliance with the PCF at all levels and there could be no retreat. The 1977 municipal elections therefore marked the point of no return away from third-force politics for the Socialist Party.

The Socialist Party strategy for the municipal elections had been decided by unanimous vote on 16 May 1976 at a special conference in Dijon.[13] The conference decided to reject all alliances other than Left alliances, but demanded a binding PCF commitment on annual council-budget votes, a commitment particularly needed, given the Communists' refusal to vote for certain Socialist budgets in November 1975. It also left open the door to 'homogeneous' Socialist (i.e. PS only) lists and reserved the right to review contentious cases at an autumn conference.[14] The Socialists refused negotiations at leadership level between the parties and instead made individual sections responsible for bargaining with the PCF on the composition of joint lists.[15] This was a decision which pushed the problem down to the base of the Party and thus created a mosaic of different compromises across the country. A meeting took place with the PCF on 28 June 1976 resulting in a communiqué which was to become a cause for divergences of interpretation, the PCF arguing that an agreement had to be sought in all communes where the signatories

---

[13] *Le Poing et la rose*, No. 50, 1976.
[14] On PS local election strategy see D. Lacorne, *Les Notables rouges*, FNSP (Paris), 1980. [15] *Le Poing et la rose*, No. 52, 1976.

were present and the Socialists that an agreement was to be sought if it was possible.[16] The PCF increased the pressure on the PS, but in a number of cases in towns with more than 30,000 inhabitants—and notably in Aix-en-Provence, Laval, Marseilles, and Villeurbanne—there were, because of PS–PCF antipathy, no joint lists.[17] In the event, however '*Union à la carte*' was to be the order of the day in 204 of the 221 largest towns.

The extension of Left–Right bipolarity down into municipal politics in these elections produced substantial gains for the new Left alliance and correspondingly large losses for the Right, which lost half of the big (30,000+) towns it had controlled since 1971. The Socialists gained thirty-five big towns to take their total to eighty-one, and the Communists twenty-two, taking theirs to seventy-two. Socialist gains were especially notable in the Catholic west where Rennes, Nantes, Le Mans, Saint-Malo, and Roche-sur-Yon all fell to PS-led Left lists, though they were rather less good in the east where towns such as Nancy, Metz, and Strasburg stayed in government hands. Nor did the Socialists recover enough ground to recapture the former south-western bastion of Toulouse. But the Left alliance, with 54 per cent, had attained a national majority.

The Communists, clearly profiting from the respectability conferred by association with the Socialists, substantially increased their local-government presence. The number of (big city) councils to which they had access rose from sixty-seven to 147 and the number of PCF councillors in those towns doubled from 1,256 to 2,306.[18] While Socialist gains were as spectacular, the PS did lose six towns which it had previously controlled, whereas the Communists lost none of their municipalities. The PCF moreover was starting from a somewhat lower base and there was some justifiable debate in Socialist ranks as to whether the Party had not in its local negotiations handed too much to the Communists on a plate. It was clear that in some areas—often those where CERES

[16] *L'Humanité*, 18 Apr. 1976. Much was made in the PCF press of the Communist interpretation—to keep up pressure on the PS.

[17] The Communists were displeased with these exceptions: 'Où se situ l'exception, où se situ la règle?' M. Gremetz, *Liberté*, 11 May 1976.

[18] See D. B. Goldey, 'The French Municipal Elections of 1977', *Parliamentary Affairs*, 1977.

was locally dominant—inter-party bargaining had not been sufficiently rigorous and that the PS could have used the potential gains on which the Communists had set their sights as a bargaining counter in the Socialist quest for a realistic updating of the Common Programme. As it was, the PCF's gains cost the Party nothing.

After the municipal elections of 1977 the updating (*'actualisation'*) of the Common Programme became the major issue between the parties, it having been conceded by the Socialist Party that such an updating was necessary— though it would have to be limited. For the Mitterrandist majority of the Socialist Party, but not for CERES, the worsening economic climate, the gradual reintegration of France into the Atlantic Alliance under Giscard, and the position of the Left at the threshold of power made the Common Programme too radical and out of date. On one wing of the Party were the Rocard supporters, who argued a moderate case with considerable vigour, and on the other wing CERES, believing, like the PCF, that the way out of the economic crisis was not to abandon the Common Programme but to apply it in totality.[19] Against such background the Socialists met for their National Congress at Nantes.

The Nantes Congress, June 1977

For the Socialist Party, the Nantes Congress meant a continuation and a consolidation of the Mitterrandist majority which emerged at Pau in 1975 augmented by the support of the ex-PSU and *assises* elements. Nantes was a congress infused with the sense of coming victory heralded in the municipal results, and the atmosphere was more one of anticipated celebration than reflection or political hard bargaining. Nevertheless, as at Pau, the internal balance of the Party had effects both on the state of the Union of the Left, and on the general electorate, to whom the PS was trying to present itself as a 'natural governing party'.

The Party's problems with the PCF continued to arise from a number of sources but notably from the refusal of Mitterrand to accept CERES back onto the Secretariat. Bitter

[19] The Communist case is given in *Le Programme commun de gouvernement actualisé*, Éditions Sociales (Paris), 1978. Figures on pp. 184–5.

recriminations against CERES were made by members of
Mitterrand's entourage; in particular they were accused of
having delivered several town halls to the Communist Party
(Reims was a case in point) at the municipal elections by not
having bargained hard enough with the local PCF. CERES's
desire to appear as *the* unitary and pure Left current of the
Socialist Party had, it was argued, made them weak and
pliable when facing Communist negotiating demands. Other
accusations of a similar nature turned on CERES's action in a
few small communes where, although in a majority, the PS
had conceded the position of mayor to a Communist. However, the real problem underlying diverse grievances against
CERES was the need to update the Common Programme and
hence for a united front in negotiations with the PCF.
Socialist strategy demanded an opening to the French middle
classes and the Centre supporters to whom the rhetoric of the
Common Programme, as expressed by radicals, was deeply
abhorrent. Discipline was therefore the order of the day as
the Party edged towards a prospective victory in 1978.[20]

Mitterrand brutally, and rather unnecessarily, slapped
CERES down at the Nantes Congress, demanding the dis-
mantling of the Left group's quasi-party organization within
the PS. Furthermore many of the themes which CERES was
articulating were similar to Communist negotiating demands,
notably extended nationalization, an increased SMIC (minimum wage), and above all a transformation of the capitalist
economy. It was this latter theme and the Mitterrandist
reaction to it that captured the attention of the Communist
press in what was otherwise an intra-party dispute of marginal interest. Rocard, for example, giving almost a definition
of the market economy, declared that the PS was a free-
market party. In this—if not in the manner of expressing it—
he was no more than echoing the thoughts of Mitterrand's
economic advisers. Nantes definitively squashed the notion
that for Mitterrand, as for the Party itself, there would be an
alternative or third-way transition to Socialism: for the Left,
led by CERES, there could thereafter be no excuse for believing otherwise. At certain points in the congress the despised
notions of incomes policy, wage restraint, and social contract
were floated. For CERES and for the PCF these were the

[20] *Le Monde*, 19 June 1977.

familiar formulas of the Barre government merely disguised by a veneer of Socialist rhetoric.

Neither Mitterrand nor his economic policy-makers were under any illusions that the margin of manoeuvre was very slight; the Socialist Party in power would not be able to conduct a policy much different from that of the Giscard–Barre administration. Time after time, first with the Giscard–Mitterrand television debates, and with the Barre–Mitterrand debate in May 1977, Socialist economic policy had been its weakest point. Mitterrand and the Socialist Party had to be convincing: they could make no concessions to CERES rhetoric if they were to retain any credibility with the 'target' group of Centre voters who had given the PS a resounding victory in the municipal elections and who would be needed to win the elections in 1978. With the negotiations to update the Common Programme in the offing, Mitterrand thus used the Nantes Congress to demonstrate his control over his party and to issue a series of ultimata to the Communists.[21]

Nantes was also the occasion for the 'discovery' by the press of Michel Rocard who, in a brilliant speech, was largely responsible for crushing CERES. Rocard, whose intellectual brilliance outruns his tactical subtlety, managed to annoy Mitterrand by appearing rather too keen on his status as 'the man most likely to succeed'. But it was more for CERES, and for Marchais, that there was a disconcerting quality of menace about the Nantes Congress; making the Left alliance more precarious, even if facilitating the Socialist line of development towards the Centre. Mitterrand, no novice at Fourth Republic style in-fighting, knew how to play the long-term future of the Party, but Nantes left unresolved the basic question of how to deal with an unco-operative Communist Party.

Updating the Common Programme

Between maximalist (PCF) and minimalist (PS) interpretations of the Common Programme the distance was immense. Communists believed that the Socialists had begun to retreat in the face of a possible victory; that it was now necessary to

---

[21] *Le Point*, 27 June 1977.

anchor the treacherous 'social democrats' to a very precise series of measures. Negotiations started in May 1977, when the Communists revealed a series of policy changes on social, economic, and defence matters, which served to show that their preparations for the preliminary meetings had been deep and thorough. Mitterrand, who wished in no way to be tied to such measures—certainly not on the eve of a presumed victory—remained studiously vague.

The beginning of the Communist campaign for 'updating' came with the publication of their costing of the programme on 11 May 1977 and caused maximum embarrassment to Mitterrand who was due to debate the economy with Prime Minister Barre on TV the next day. The PCF, in its costing, calculated the revenues from the application of 'their' Common Programme. These assumed a growth rate of 6.8 per cent in the first year and 6 per cent thereafter, inflation at 6 per cent, and enormous public expenditure amounting to 489 billion francs. Figures such as these were clearly unacceptable to the Socialists, especially as they were based on the rejection of the free-market economy. French electors were therefore astonished to learn that there apparently never had been any Common Programme in the sense of an agreed set of propositions about its economic foundations.

By July there was a range of disagreement on the content of the Programme under practically every heading. Major disputes came over social policy, nationalization, and defence. In May the PCF was pressing for an increase in the French minimum wage in line with CGT demands (2,400 francs at April 1977 prices). The Socialists were prepared to concede this, but not before April 1978. In line with this demand Communists also called for a reduction of salary differentials to 1:5 although Socialists argued that 1:7 was the only practical possibility, and whilst the PCF wanted to increase family allowances by 50 per cent the Socialists were prepared to see them rise by only 25 per cent. Higher taxation on personal wealth above 1 million francs and on capital were proposed by the PCF; the Socialists, to some extent, went along with this although they wanted a progressive annual tax on large companies and on personal wealth above 2 million francs. A further series of propositions concerning the management and running of the nationalized industries were grouped by the PCF under the previously reviled heading of *autogestion*. In using the term the PCF was making an attempt to snatch the Socialist battle flag, but *only* the flag; analysis of their proposals revealed merely traditional Communist demands. The Communists, anxious to build upon their shop-floor strength, wanted the workers' representatives on the administrative councils of nationalized firms to be chosen from lists drawn up by the unions. Such proposals were designed to produce a Communist majority or, failing that, at least an inordinately strong Communist presence in the state sector. Because of the PCF's organizational strength in the unions and the extension of Communist control over French society which the proposals could have entailed, the demands presented by the PCF were unacceptable.[22]

However, it proved even more difficult to determine the extent of new nationalizations, despite the flat statement in the Common Programme that only nine groups were to be nationalized. The Communists interpreted this to mean the complete nationalization of the main holding companies and all subsidiaries in which the main company held over 51 per cent of the stock; at a minimum this would mean about 730 companies. The Socialists, however, claimed that the number should not exceed 100 companies, interpreting the proposals to mean state ownership of the holding companies and only those branches 100 per cent owned by the major company, plus a financial share in other subsidiaries where stock was owned by the firm. The PCF believed that a large state sector was necessary to lift France out of the capitalist economy and to finance the Common Programme (through company profits) and they believed that minority votes would block the state management of public-sector companies. Furthermore, the Communists wished to add Peugeot–Citroën, CFP–Total, and steel to the list of firms to be nationalized. In the negotiations of September 1977 the PCF actually only insisted on steel, where there was considerable unemployment and where the PCF had large support. Rocard made the old social-democratic point that control could be exercised even if ownership remained private, but for the

[22] *Le Monde*, 17 May 1977.

most part the Socialists considered the PCF proposals simply too expensive.

Defence policy was another area of major disagreement, and this largely because on 11 May 1977 the PCF Central Committee approved the French nuclear force after having long opposed it. Such a nuclear force would be developed as a defence against all-comers ('*tous azimuts*') and without any pre-determined enemy—a sort of atavistic Gaullism. In early May 1977 Socialist policy was highly unclear and remained so even after a party conference on nuclear arms in January 1978. However, the Socialists wanted to remain in the Atlantic Alliance, refused a '*tous azimuts*' policy, proposed multilateral disarmament and a referendum to decide the future of the nuclear strike force. The referendum idea was contemptuously rejected by the PCF for what it was, a device to get the Socialist Party off the hook while it made up its mind on the matter. (The PS later accepted the *force de frappe*.)

From the Left 'rupture' to the 1978 elections

With the atmosphere poisoned and with PCF attacks on Socialist backsliding, the Communist press kept up the pressure through the summer of 1977. A Left summit meeting was scheduled for September, but nothing was done to relax the tension. The Socialists were in no position to concede under Communist pressure, a fact the Communists appeared unable to recognize. The Communists, likewise, had been driven into a corner; they had either to accept Socialist terms as a way out of their political isolation or to retreat into their ghetto. However, forcing one's partner into a corner is not a good negotiating tactic; the reactions of even the most rational, when cornered, can become unpredictable.

The debate on updating the Common Programme had continued since Easter 1977, but on 14 September came the end of five months of intensive negotiation,[23] as Fabre, the MRG leader, swept Marchais aside at a press conference and proceeded to read, on live TV, a Radical communiqué which flatly stated that the Left summit would not continue. The conflict over nationalization was the breaking-point. A week

[23] François Loncle, *Autopsie d'une rupture*, Simoën (Paris), 1979, pp. 13–47.

later, in resumed discussions on Communist demands, the talks finally foundered. This was *'la rupture'* of the Union of the Left. The initiative for the renegotiation had been Marchais's (on 1 April) and neither the Socialists nor the Radicals thought in terms other than of minor adjustments to a document, the PS and MRG reformist interpretation of which had increasingly diverged from that of the PCF. There was, against PCF demands, no question of a detailed costing being set out; perhaps there could be a series of dates for the applications of key measures, but no precise figures.[24] Faced with such deep dissatisfaction, there was no possibility of an amicable conclusion.

For the activists of the Socialist Party the impact of the failure to update the Common Programme was telling. Communist activists had been well prepared and well briefed by the party bureaucracy and therefore knew exactly what was at issue. The 'bourgeois' press, which has a limited impact in PCF milieux, made much of Communist discomfort during this pre-election period, but it was Socialist, rather than Communist, activists who were embarrassed. Socialists were bombarded with Communist attacks on the PS for its *'tournant à droite'* and it was some time before the PS was able to react by sending instructions from party headquarters. Thus the consequence of the dispute, as the Communists no doubt intended, was to chase away essential Socialist supporters—those needed to win marginal constituencies—and to lower the morale of party activists.

Although a pre-election atmosphere had existed almost continuously since the 1974 presidential elections, the campaign for the March 1978 elections was effectively opened when François Mitterrand, on his own initiative and against the advice of many in the Party, decided to make the minimum wage at 2,400 francs the basis of the PS campaign platform. This was in effect a concession to the PCF which had been calling for such a measure since April 1977. It was viewed with misgivings by the CFDT and by Rocard, who saw it as a wholly inflationary proposal. The PS also confirmed its support for a compression of wage differentials to something like 1:7.[25]

[24] Ibid., pp. 115–36.
[25] 'Quelle politique économique après mars 78?', *Projet*, Feb. 1972, pp. 219–39.

On 14 February Socialist economists produced their costing of the Common Programme, foreseeing an annual expansion of 4.9 per cent in 1978 and 5.6 per cent in 1979, a reduction of welfare costs (social security etc.) for industry, and government aid for imperilled businesses. They did not appear to expect increased wages to increase imports or to create a profits squeeze, investment decline, and a fall in output, followed by faster inflation (the classic syndrome of Left high-wage policies as pursued in Chile, Portugal, and the UK).[26] No thought seems to have been given to this problem, except in the CFDT, where they were particularly fearful about it, but the Socialists seemed to have envisaged *'temporary'* [*sic*] import controls on non-EEC goods to avoid an import consumer boom.

The quarrel on the Left continued up to the first ballot, with the PCF upping the bids in a 'soak the rich' campaign and, had it not been for opinion polls consistently affirming a big Socialist vote leading to a Left total of around 52 per cent, it would have been difficult to envisage a Left victory. Giscard appeared to take a possible defeat into account in a tactically adroit speech at Verdun-sur-le-Doubs, where he declared that, should the Left win, he would stay in office, but would be unable to prevent the application of the Common Programme—a threat as much as a promise. Meanwhile the Socialists and Communists were not even agreed on the reciprocal electoral pact which had been in force since 1967 and Marchais talked darkly of the need for a minimum national Communist vote of 21 per cent before the Party would agree to second-ballot withdrawals. The Socialists did not reply to such threats directly, but confirmed that they would enforce 'republican discipline' by standing down for the Left's best-placed candidate—a concept the Communists were now calling 'outdated'.

By some 100,000 votes the Socialist Party failed to displace the Gaullists and confirm the pollsters' description of the Party as the 'first party of France'. Nor did it reach the dizzy heights of 28–30 per cent predicted by the polls since 1977. The Party's share of the vote did, however, rise to 22.5 per cent (6.4 million votes) or if the Left–Radical vote is included, 24.5 per cent (7 million votes). The increase in the

[26] S. K. Kolm, *La Transition socialiste*, CERF (Paris), 1976.

Socialist vote was sufficient to achieve the one major significant gain of the elections both for the PS and for the Left
as a whole; the PS had at last overtaken the PCF (20.5
per cent; 5.8 million votes) as the largest party of the Left—
the absolutely essential precondition of eventual Left success.
The lead, however, was narrow and too recently established
to save the Left from defeat in many seats it had hoped to
gain in 1978. The long left-wing polemic had taken its toll
and many target (Catholic and middle-class) voters had been
scared off. The PCF had in fact managed to stop Mitterrand
and the PS in their march to power. It was not without some
cynicism that, despite the long polemic, the three Left
'partners' (PCF, PS, and MRG) agreed to observe the traditional Left discipline at the second ballot—till then put in
doubt by the Communists. At a meeting described as 'surreal'
the Left parties thus appeared able in a day to agree on what
had divided them for six months. A number of Socialist
policy suggestions were accepted on the nod by a blandly
smiling Marchais. An edge of bitterness was added to the
débâcle.

6
Discord, Victory and Office 1978–1986

Although the Socialists' electoral performance in 1978 represented a significant advance for the party, by failing to meet high expectations generated by the election results of 1974 and 1977 and the euphoric opinion polls of the same period, the result was reckoned a failure for the Party, the Left alliance, and above all, for Mitterrand personally. In these circumstances, the party leadership came under attack: until late 1980 the PS was divided by a dispute between Mitterrand and Michel Rocard for the soul of the Party, and —more pertinently—for the Socialist nomination for the presidential election of 1981, and by implication, the party leadership thereafter.

Rocard's campaign against Mitterrand was launched during the election-night TV coverage of the 1978 results (19 March). With the failure of the Left alliance having become clear and the difficulties of dealing with the Communists recognized by many activists, the essence of Rocard's criticism was that the special relationship with the Communists, cultivated assiduously by Mitterrand since 1971, had led the Party to an electoral dead end; that the Common Programme, defunct since 1977 and to which Rocard had never been sympathetic, was an electoral millstone serving to scare off middle-of-the-road voters; and that the PS should pursue a more distinct, 'autonomous' course, seeking the support of Communist voters through a reformist programme but without reference to Communist leaders or jointly agreed programmes. Although Rocard was careful not to challenge the strategy of the union of the Left *per se*, Mitterrand's supporters were anxious to present his challenge as a rightward swerve aimed at resuscitating the 'third-force' strategies employed by Mollet's SFIO before 1958. Rocard was to be categorized as *'travailliste'* and 'social democratic', not least because of his defence of the market and his scepticism about nationalization.

What made Rocard's assault more than a little local difficulty following a disappointing election result was the support accorded him in the media. Opinion-poll surveys from late 1978 showed him to be the most popular politician of the Left and more likely than Mitterrand to beat President Giscard d'Estaing in the 1981 presidential election. He was shown to have particular appeal to centrist voters who had played an important part in ensuring Giscard's narrow victory in 1974 and who were most put off from voting Socialist by the Party's alliance with the PCF.[1] By early 1979, moreover, the polls showed Rocard to be more popular than Mitterrand not only with the electorate at large, but with Socialist Party voters also. They also showed that of Socialist voters only 32 per cent supported a Common Programme.[2] Rocard was fêted by the broadcasters, being frequently accorded television interviews on such programmes as *Cartes sur table*, and it was for both his poll rating and the TV exposure that he was dubbed by Mitterrand's supporters as the media's candidate for 1981. Rocard indeed did have a carefully prepared and elaborate media campaign assembled by an influential back-up team.[3]

Mitterrand's reaction to Rocard's challenge was to defend his version of the Union of the Left strategy and to keep his options open about the 1981 presidential candidature, delaying the announcement of his intentions as long as possible in the hope that Rocard's fashionable star would wane. (It was equally possible that Mitterrand was genuinely undecided about his future intentions: even among his closest supporters, there were doubts about whether he really did intend to run in 1981.) His strategy was to stick close to the PCF in order to compete with it on its own ground for Communist votes. By reaffirming the commitment to the Union of the Left the PS could hope to attract the PCF's electorate and if this proved successful the PCF itself could be expected to be pulled by its own electorate back into the alliance. Having built his whole career in the Fifth Republic on the Left union strategy—*la ligne d'Épinay*—Mitterrand could scarcely do other than reaffirm his commitment to it. His problem, however, was that to do so and to rebuff the challenge from

---

[1] See J.-L. Parodi and I. Perrineau, 'Les leaders socialistes devant l'opinion', *Projet*, April 1979.   [2] *Le Monde*, 18–19 Mar. 1979.
[3] See 'Offensive Rocard', *Le Point*, 9 Oct. 1978, and H. Hamon and P. Rotman, *L'Effet Rocard*, Stock (Paris), 1980, pp. 317–18.

Rocard would require the break-up of the alliance of the Party's Centre and Right which had comprised its leadership since 1975. This became more inevitable an outcome with the emergence soon after the 1978 electoral defeat of Pierre Mauroy, *seigneur* of the Party's Nord federation, as Rocard's ally.

However, unlike Rocard, Mauroy did not want a split with Mitterrand if it could be avoided, preferring to preserve party unity. He kept his links with Mitterrand throughout this period, despite disagreements over a number of issues, including the internal running of the Party and the suggested publication of a party newspaper (to which he was opposed). He believed that Mitterrand should either declare his presidential candidacy or withdraw and leave the field to Rocard, and in the last analysis he was not prepared to allow Rocard to go into lonely opposition inside the Party.

The conflict between the Party's senior *caciques* was made worse by the enthusiasm of their supporters.[4] Mitterrand's current was particularly unfavourable to any accommodation with Rocard and in September 1978 thirty of them, under prompting of Pierre Joxe and Jacques Delors, issued the *Manifeste de trente* which, reaffirming the Left union strategy determined in 1971, was circulated round the federations to galvanize support for Mitterrand. Inside the Party, Mitterrand could in fact rely on support built up over eight years, for if Rocard's strength lay with the voters,[5] Mitterrand's lay with the activists. In the winter of 1978-9 Mitterrand toured the country ostensibly as part of a campaign for the cantonal elections of March 1979, but in reality to build up his activist power base prior to the 1979 party congress at Metz, where the confrontation with Rocard would come to a head.

As the Metz Congress (April 1979) loomed, the battle of words intensified. In September 1978 Rocard had obliquely attacked Mitterrand by employing the phrase *'un certain archaïsme'*.[6] In January 1979 when accused by Mitterrand of personal ambition, Rocard reflected that he had been in

[4] *Le Monde*, 11 Dec. 1979. Gilbert Baumont and Henri Darras asked Mitterrand for 'one last service' to the Party—his resignation.

[5] On Rocard's support see *L'Express*, 4 Apr. 1980, and Kathleen Évin, *Michel Rocard ou l'art du possible*, Simoën (Paris), 1979, p. 89.

[6] *Le Monde*, 19 Sept. 1978.

the Socialist movement for thirty years (i.e. four times as long as Mitterrand's membership of the Socialist party).[7] In March 1979, reacting to the accusation that he was moving to the Right, Rocard more provocatively asked 'who was it who was a minister during the Algerian war, and who was a student being pursued by the police?'[8] In January 1979 Rocard had directly challenged Mitterrand's leadership by declaring that Mauroy was a candidate for the First Secretary-ship, a ruse designed to commit Mauroy to his side and to prevent any hope the Mitterrandists had of winning him over. (An embarrassed Mauroy repudiated Rocard's suggestion.) At a meeting of the Comité Directeur in February, Colliard, a close supporter of Mitterrand, dubbed Rocard a 'Brutus'; prompting him, with Mauroy, to leave the meeting in protest.

The run-up to the Metz Congress was therefore bitter and divisive. It was a measure of this bitterness that the normally united Nord federation was badly split and that the Mitterrand majority included many of the federation's old 'Molletists' and those traditionally hostile to the Communists such as Arthur Notebart and Augustin Laurent.

The Metz Congress—April 1979

All the major figures in the Party had been 'campaigning' for the Metz Congress since the autumn of 1978. Pre-congress votes in the Party's federations suggested that Mitterrand's motion was likely to obtain 40 per cent of the votes at Metz, a vote which would have enabled him to govern the Party only with some difficulty. Defferre, his ally, had obtained 6 per cent, but as his federation was split, the prospect of a Mitterrand–CERES alliance was opened up. CERES, whose support, like Mauroy's had been eroded by the bipolarization of the Party around Mitterrand and Rocard, wanted to recoup their losses and re-enter the Secretariat which they had left at Pau in 1975. Rocard and Mauroy had 21 and 17 per cent respectively, a total lower than they had expected. Their continuing dispute with Mitterrand meant that they would have to leave the majority and thus the Secretariat.[9]

---

[7] *Le Monde*, 6 Jan. 1979.   [8] *L'Express*, 31 Mar. 1979.
[9] For the Metz Congress motions see *Le Poing et la rose*, No. 79, February 1979. For a summary of the issues which divided the currents at the Metz Congress see Appendix.

The highly personalized nature of the confrontation in the Party was reflected by a break with tradition at Metz, allowing the two protagonists to open the congress with speeches outlining their positions. The congress was also novel in another respect: that instead of the leadership having to rebut a 'maximalist' Socialist challenge from CERES as in 1975 and 1977, Mitterrand now found himself putting down an assault from the 'minimalist' Right. Already guilty of *lèse majesté*, Rocard in his peroration committed the additional offence of *lèse orthodoxie*—striking out at some of the more comfortable illusions of the Left (on centralized planning and administration, wealth creation, nationalization) and supporting the mixed economy.[10] Most heretical was his declaration that 'between the market and rationing there is nothing', to which Mitterrand's aide Laurent Fabius was to retort that there *was* something between the two, namely Socialism. Rocard further offended by referring to the traditional weakness of French Socialism—rarely in power and then unsuccessfully so; and suffering from weak social roots. He called too for a collegial leadership of the Party— with decision-making power located in the Bureau Exécutif (on which all currents are represented) instead of the Secretariat—an issue of importance for Mauroy who resented Mitterrand's leadership style.

All of Rocard's propositions were rejected one by one by Mitterrand and his supporters. Mitterrand posed as the *père fondateur* of the Party, the renovator of French Socialism, the heir to Jaurès and Blum, and the 'onlie begetter' of *la ligne d'Épinay*—whose sacrosanct status was questioned by Rocard. 'Épinay', Rocard suggested, had been 'overtaken by events'—by the crisis, unemployment, monetary disorder, growing international tension—and it was necessary to be flexible in the face of changing situations. Such 'realism' was not what was required and it was clear that Mitterrand had carried the congress. The argument was now to be taken to the public as Rocard tried to build up sufficient support to make his candidature inevitable.

After the Metz Congress, Mitterrand reincorporated CERES into the Secretariat, which was now dominated by an entirely

[10] *Le Monde*, 8–9 Apr. 1979.

new generation of Mitterrand supporters, notably Lionel Jospin, who had replaced Mauroy as the new Number Two in the Party, Laurent Fabius as press spokesman, and Paul Quilès as head of organization. More prominent figures, such as Mermaz, Estier, and Édith Cresson were moved out of high party office in preparation for the June 1979 election to the European Parliament in which they were to occupy high positions on the Party's list of candidates. In the event, this election was a major disappointment, with the PS vote reaching only 23.5 per cent, and the gap between PS and PCF reduced to 3 per cent, as Marchais was keen to point out. There was some criticism from Rocard and Mauroy of the Party's departure in the election from its traditionally strong commitment to the EEC—with CERES in particular mirroring the nationalistic attitudes of the PCF.

The establishment of the new power balance in the Party at Metz was reflected in the drafting of the party programme for the 1980s—*Le Projet socialiste*,[11] a task conferred by Mitterrand on CERES's leader Chevènement. Building on previous policy documents—the Suresnes programme of 1972, the Common Programme of the Left, and the 1975 '15 theses on *autogestion*'[12]—the new *Projet* was intended to redefine priorities and was accorded near-unanimous backing (85 per cent) at a conference at Alfortville in January 1980. It was, however, a document with many radical CERES-inspired components and as such designed to make it even more unsuitable for use by a presidential candidate such as Rocard. But the latter was wise enough to avoid offending the activists for whose consumption the *Projet* was essentially geared and whose support he would need if he was to become the Party's presidential candidate for 1981.

Marchais was not much impressed either with the incorporation of CERES into the Secretariat or with the *Projet*, for although it looked as if the Socialist Party had moved sharply to the Left and was continuing the search for Left unity, Mitterrand's position was forced upon him by Rocard's challenge. It can hardly have been by choice that the long-sought Socialist unity was disrupted and two of the Party's most politically attractive personalities ejected from the

[11] *Projet socialiste—pour la France des années 80*, Club Socialiste du Livre (Paris), 1980.   [12] Adopted at a Party Convention in June 1975.

Secretariat. Other than resign, it is difficult to see what else Mitterrand could have done, even if the outcome at Metz, rather than resolving the party split, allowed Rocard to keep it open.

As far as the presidential election of 1981 was concerned, the Metz Congress and the *Projet socialiste* had changed little, for although strong in the Party, Mitterrand was still weak in the polls. In January 1980 he rated only 29 per cent to Rocard's 58 per cent.[13] Thus Rocard could not be wished away by exclusion from the Secretariat or by a CERES-drafted party programme. Mitterrand's acknowledgement of this reality was reflected in his postponement (secured at a Party conference in April 1980) of the presidential nomination procedure until January 1981. It was reflected also in Mitterrand's perceptible move towards Rocardian positions on the Party governing alone, if need be, and on decentralization of power. The two men were also in close agreement on the international questions of the day (notably President Carter's intervention in Iran). Indeed, Mitterrand had more in common with Rocard than with many of his own allies. The difficulty was that both wanted to be President.

Rocard finally declared his candidacy on 19 October 1981 at his town hall in Conflans-Sainte-Honorine.[14] Three weeks later Mitterrand similarly declared himself a candidate, and Rocard promptly withdrew, suddenly ending a long confrontation. Rocard had always maintained that he would not seek nomination once Mitterrand declared his own desire to run. His 'defeat' was not surprising: he was seen by activists as right wing, externally imposed by the media, and, most important, a potentially destabilizing force in the Party, unable, like Mitterrand, to play the great unifier.[15]

The presidential elections of April–May 1981

Mitterrand's nomination duly took place at a special congress at Créteil in January 1981. He was the only candidate nominated and obtained endorsement from 84 per cent of the delegates—some Rocard supporters showing a little resistance.

[13] *Le Nouvel Observateur*, 21 Jan. 1980.
[14] See *Le Matin*, 20 Oct. 1980, and *L'Express*, 26 Oct. 1980.
[15] See H. Portelli, 'En attendant 1981', *Projet*, May 1979, p. 607.

On becoming candidate he resigned the First Secretaryship, handing the job to his protégé Jospin. The congress adopted Mitterrand's policy statement '110 Propositions', thereby adding to the range of statements on which the Socialist campaign might be based: the CERES-drafted *Projet socialiste* (1980), Mitterrand's recent book *Ici et maintenant*,[16] and the Socialist Manifesto (1981). During the campaign Mitterrand was to ignore all programmes generated by others in the Party and to stand on a platform consisting of his own *ad hoc* utterances (such as his 'Six measures for full employment' published in *L'Express* in April) and selections from his '110 Propositions'.

Early in February, in a unifying gesture, Mitterrand announced a campaign committee comprising all groups in the Party—even Rocard—and with Mauroy given a leading role as press spokesman. Outside experts, such as Claude Cheysson, who was to become Mitterrand's Foreign Minister, were also included. The advertising specialist, Jacques Séguéla, provided his services to promote Mitterrand as a *'force tranquille'* on posters in which the candidate was superimposed upon a rural background incorporating the national red, white, and blue colours. In February a daily newspaper, *Combat Socialiste*, was launched (only to expire after the elections).

Despite being a two-time presidential loser, and notwithstanding the divisive confrontation with Rocard since 1978, Mitterrand went into the campaign with a number of distinct advantages. First, he was a candidate of recognizably presidential stature, having for years personified the left-wing opposition, and thus being the focus for the hopes of all Socialist and Communist voters who earnestly hoped for a change of government. His stature moreover was soon reflected in a climbing poll rating in February, with Rocard no longer stealing the limelight, with party unity apparently restored, and with his former opponents playing prominent roles in his campaign.

Secondly, he was running against an incumbent President who was in substantial difficulty. Giscard d'Estaing was heading a deeply unpopular administration, under attack from all sides for the impact of the economic recession—notably for

[16] François Mitterrand, *Ici et maintenant*, Fayard (Paris), 1980.

high inflation and unemployment, for the failure to deliver the substantive reforms promised, to such electoral effect, in 1974, and for an arrogant and, to some, a semi-monarchical style of leadership. These deficiencies made it hard for Giscard to convince the electorate that the Right was entitled to a further seven years of power on top of the twenty-three unbroken years already enjoyed since 1958.

Finally, crowning Giscard's problems was the candidacy of Gaullist leader, Jacques Chirac, whose presence in the race bore eloquent testimony to the serious discord into which the governing *majorité* had fallen since Chirac had resigned the premiership in 1976. So strong was Chirac's appeal to conservative voters that his supporters were to claim at the end of the campaign for the first ballot that he would be runner-up to Giscard in the first round, thus ensuring a wholly destructive second-ballot confrontation between Giscard and himself. To contemplate such an eventuality was to gaze upon the ruins of the governing coalition.

Yet, despite all these minuses, it was still believed by most commentators—as by a complacent Giscard—that the Right's problems were still less serious than the Left's and that Mitterrand would be thwarted, as in 1978, by the antics of the Communist Party and its candidate Georges Marchais. Marchais's candidacy, formally announced in October 1980 (but effectively in place since 1978 when it became clear he would run in 1981) was an act of pure defiance. It was motivated by the desire to build up, as in the elections of 1978 and 1979, a Communist resistance to Socialist advance, and by a particular concern to establish a strong base from which to defend Communist positions in the municipal elections due in March 1983.

The Communist tactic was firstly to denounce the Socialists as potential collaborators with the Right, a possibility cited by Marchais to justify the PCF's refusal to confirm whether it would deliver its electorate to Mitterrand at the second ballot. In September 1980 the PCF had actually maintained its candidates at the second ballot in senatorial elections, thereby delivering some seats to the Right. Secondly, the Communists sought to outbid the Socialists, as in 1978, with an extensive slate of radical social policy demands; and thirdly they sought to trawl indiscriminately for protest votes through a combination of class-war rhetoric and xenophobia. (Hence the largely counter-productive campaigns against steel-mill closures, Spanish and Portuguese EEC entry, and immigrants, during the 1979–81 period.) The Party's hard line was backed up by the expulsion of liberal Communists favourable to co-operation with the PS—such as Elleinstein and Fiszbin in 1980.

The most insistent Communist demand made on Mitterrand during the presidential campaign concerned Communist ministers in a Left government, but Mitterrand's reaction to this, as to all Communist demands and attacks, was to make little or no response and specifically to reject any deal on ministerial posts until the PCF fell in line behind Socialist policies, particularly in the foreign-policy field where events in Poland and Afghanistan had opened up old sores. This conditional, ambiguous response probably served to reassure Communist and floating voters alike.[17]

In his own campaign Mitterrand concentrated upon President Giscard, and on his most obvious flaws at home (unemployment) and abroad (a conciliatory stance towards the Soviet Union). The attack on the home front was coupled with the promise of a wide range of reforms including longer paid holidays, earlier retirement, an increased minimum wage and a shorter (thirty-five-hour) working week. These proposals were popular not only with the Left's electorate, but with the supporters of the governing *majorité*.[18] In his attack on Giscard's foreign-policy record, Mitterrand harnessed the growing anti-Russian feeling, criticizing Giscard for being the first western leader to meet Brezhnev after the Afghanistan invasion, and seeking to embarrass him over the favourable report on his term of office in *Pravda*.[19]

Mitterrand's campaign was a rather low-key, but largely faultless performance, involving a new broadcasting persona appropriate for the *'force tranquille'* and a detached, almost Gaullian, style—appealing for a broad *rassemblement* around a programme of moderate reforms. The relaxed and reassuring style of Mitterrand's poster publicity and television interviews

[17] *Le Monde*, 16 Feb. 1981, and Claude Estier, *Mitterrand Président*, Stock (Paris), 1981, p. 81.
[18] *Le Point*, Survey, 25 May 1981.
[19] *Pravda*, 13 Mar. 1981, quoted in *Le Monde*.

was noteworthy, given the absence of a similar sureness of touch in Giscard's case. Complacent and 'monarchical' at first, but combative and aggressive at the end, Giscard was reduced to employing the perennial weapons of the Right: that a Mitterrand victory would mean, with Communists in power, either 'Socialist disorder' or 'Communist order', and would provoke a constitutional crisis, given the anti-Socialist complexion of the National Assembly (elected in 1978) which Mitterrand would inherit. It would, said Giscard in his final TV broadcast, mean the end of the Fifth Republic. Of these two traditional scares, the first—the red bogey—was neutralized by Marchais's poor performance at the first ballot. The second was disposed of by Mitterrand making it very clear that his first act, if elected, would be to dissolve the National Assembly in order that the Left might seek a parliamentary majority. The Right's two traditional foxes were thus effectively shot.

So it was that by his own astute campaigning and by a strong combination of negative factors comprising the defects of Giscard, the destructive impact of Chirac, and the non-acceptability of Marchais to many of his own party's supporters, Mitterrand emerged at the first ballot in a strong position with 25.8 per cent, to Giscard's 28.3 per cent, Chirac's 18.0 per cent, and Marchais's 15.3 per cent. Of greatest help to Mitterrand's prospects of victory were the low votes of Giscard and Marchais. A vote of 28 per cent for the incumbent President was almost humiliating, and, much more serious, Giscard could not count on Chirac's electorate moving to him at the second ballot. Chirac made only a formal appeal to his voters to back Giscard and in the event 16 per cent of his supporters deserted to Mitterrand. But the low vote for Marchais—5 per cent down on the usual PCF vote—was the crucial development of the election for the gap it opened up between Communist and Socialist electorates. Adding the 2.2-per-cent vote for the MRG candidate Crépeau to that of Mitterrand, the Socialist electorate at 28 per cent was 12.7 per cent greater than the PCF's 15.3 per cent. The widening of this gap from 4 per cent in 1978 to almost 13 per cent in 1981 destroyed the Right's most telling electoral weapon—that a Socialist-led government would be in hock to a dominant Communist Party.

The PCF's leaders might, of course, still have chosen to forestall a Mitterrand victory by calling on Communist voters to abstain: that they did not is evidence that they were accommodating themselves to the inevitable and acknowledging, in effect, the vote of no confidence that had been delivered by the 1.5 million Communist voters who had deserted Marchais for Mitterrand at the first ballot. Thus, with the Communists marginalized and the Right damagingly split, Mitterrand won the second ballot by 51.8 per cent to Giscard's 48.2 per cent.[20] He appointed Pierre Mauroy Prime Minister and, as promised, dissolved the National Assembly without delay.

Parliamentary landslide

Upon Mitterrand's dramatic victory of 10 May was built the Socialist Party's spectacular success in the legislative elections of 14 and 21 June. The PS vote at the first ballot of the legislative elections, 37.5 per cent, was 10 per cent up on the Mitterrand–Crépeau vote and 15 per cent up on the PS–MRG vote in the 1978 legislative elections. Between the elections of 1978 and 1981 the Socialist (plus MRG) electorate had inflated from 7 to 9.4 million. This huge leap, bringing the Party to its highest-ever share of the vote and, after the second ballot on 21 June, to a landslide in seats, was to be accounted for in two ways. First, the Party was riding in on Mitterrand's coat-tails and secondly, it was profiting from *la logique majoritaire*: the acceptance by the electorate of the need for concordance between presidential and parliamentary majorities, without which the Fifth Republic's constitutional stability seemed at risk. A vote for the PS in the legislative elections was thus a vote for constitutional stability and common sense—a response to President Mitterrand's request that he be given the means to govern.[21] Taking place immediately after a presidential election, and one in which power changed hands, and with opinion polls showing that almost half (47 per cent) the voters regarded the legislative election

---

[20] For a discussion of Mitterrand's victory see 'Après l'élection présidentielle', *Projet*, July–Aug. 1981.

[21] Mitterrand: 'Je souhaite que le pays me donne les moyens' (*Le Monde*, 9 June 1981).

vote as one for or against President Mitterrand, the June 1981 legislative elections were the most presidentialized of the Fifth Republic. And this time the electoral institutions of the Fifth Republic—so favourable to incumbent Presidents— were at last working in the Left's favour.

Novelty also played a part in determining the scale of the Socialists' victory: the novelty of Mitterrand's first acts as President—a new government under Pierre Mauroy, of new faces (Rocard, Cheysson, Delors, Fabius, Cresson, Questiaux, etc.), and with new ministries ('National Solidarity', 'Free Time' (Leisure), 'Interior and Decentralization'), and new policies (on welfare, women, ecology), many of them immediately put into effect in the space between the presidential and parliamentary elections, with an eye on certain target voters. All major ministerial posts, moreover, went to moderate Socialists, plus one to the Radical Crépeau and another to the ex-Gaullist Jobert.[22]

After the second ballot, in which the Left secured nearly 70 per cent of the seats (PS 269, MRG 14, PCF 44), Mitterrand shuffled Mauroy's government, bringing in four Communist ministers.[23] Given the scale of the PCF's drubbing in both presidential and parliamentary elections—its vote reduced by a quarter and its number of seats halved—there was no immediate political need to incorporate the Communists in government. It was, however, an act of magnanimity and prudence, following the conclusion of a short political agreement of slight substance, to offer four relatively minor ministries to the Communists Fiterman (Transport), Le Pors (Civil Service), Ralite (Health), and Rigout (Professional Training), thus ensuring against social disorder and implying a desire to sustain an appeal to the erstwhile Communist voters who had rejected Marchais for Mitterrand to such crucial effect in the presidential election.

From opposition to office

With the electoral triumphs of May and June 1981 and the appointment of the second Mauroy government (comprising

[22] For survey analysis of the election result see 'Un triomphe en microscope', *Le Nouvel Observateur*, 4 July 1981.

[23] See Appendix for a list of government ministers and biographies.

thirty-seven Socialist, four Communist, one ex-Gaullist, and two Left Radical ministers) in June, the Socialist Party moved into uncharted seas. Now that the peaks of power were transposed from the Party to the Government, the Matignon, and the Élysée, the relationship between Party and Government became a matter of considerable importance. Initially, and not unnaturally, the 1981 party congress, held at Valence in October, was seen as the opportunity for a harmonious victory celebration. No separate motions were presented by the rival currents, whose factional activity was formally suspended; only a single text was tabled with a few amendments from individuals. In these conditions the membership of the various organs—normally determined by competitive votes for rival motions—was determined by the out-going leaders after extensive bargaining. This process saw the Rocard group as relative losers, securing only one place in the Secretariat, whilst Mitterrand's supporters took nine of the fifteen seats. Some Mitterrandists had tried to get Rocard to submit a motion so that the strength of his support could be measured. Sensibly, he chose to avoid the trap of pitting his popularity as mere Minister of Planning against that of men standing four-square with the President of the Republic.

But in victory, magnanimity—of a sort—was shown to all the Party's currents by the Mitterrandist leadership. However if the Valence Congress willed a formal unity in the Party as it moved from opposition to office, it was quite unrealistic to suppose that the four main currents active since the Metz Congress of 1979 would not be reactivated in the quest for power and influence in government and for the longer-term contest for the presidential nomination.

In the early stages of government it was Rocard, at an uninfluential post, and the Rocardians who lost out because they presented the main long-term challenge to Mitterrand's leadership and because of their reservations about the strategy the government started to apply in 1981. Thus Rocard's supporters faced a period of difficulty as the party leadership worked to eliminate the possibility of a Rocardian surge from inside the government and the 'unified' party. Mauroy, although Prime Minister, faced similar difficulties. He did not at first have any philosophical objection to government policy but his group was reduced to two representatives on the party's secretariat and deprived of any real chance to exploit the Matignon in order to build up a base within the party.

It was some time before the distribution of power between the various outposts of Socialist influence settled into a permanent pattern. The new parliamentary group flexed its muscles over a number of issues, (such as immigration laws, local radio, penal reform, higher education, and the Constitutional Council's rejection of part of the nationalization bill) and the Government was soon obliged to take a closer interest in the 'parliament within a parliament', the Socialist majority. Difficulties between the Government and the parliamentary majority were not merely a reflection of traditional factional in-fighting for many issues cut across currents. As the going got rough and the Government began to apply austerity measures, figures of some influence (such as group leader Pierre Joxe and CERES deputy Michel Charzat) emerged within the majority and expressed their reservations with varying degrees of forcefulness.

Early in the life of the government indecision affected the Party activists: at the 1981 Valence Congress, there were those who called for the party to back the government and those who sought another role. A brief expression of 'we are the masters now' gave the Valence Congress a feeling of being a tribune for activist expression. Paul Quilès, for example, used unguarded allusions to 'Robespierre and revolution' and noted that if 'heads were to roll' amongst prefects, state corporation leaders and civil servants in order to prevent the sabotage of Socialist legislation, the party would have to say so and quickly. Quilès, or 'Robespaul', expressed the party's desire to push the government in a more radical direction despite the ministers, including Chevènement, who started to develop reputations for an unexpected pragmatism, upholding state authority and calm realism. According to *Le Monde* in June 1982, Socialist radicalism, as measured by the number of rolling heads, may have been too variable for some activists: all the senior officials in Communist-led ministries, such as Health and Transport, were replaced, and in certain Socialist-led ministries, notably Agriculture, Solidarity, Justice and Education, most senior officials departed. But in key ministries, such as Finance, Interior,

Defence and Industry less than half the senior heads 'rolled'.

Within the Party itself, Lionel Jospin, Mitterrand's successor as First Secretary, had to fight down the exuberance of victory and ensure that the Party performed as the President wished. Whilst lacking Mitterrand's authority, and with the party organization incompletely co-ordinated, Jospin enjoyed the confidence of Mitterrand and was thus able to make his view prevail on most occasions and to ensure amicable relations between party and government. His importance, and the care taken to maintain close relations, were reflected in the early institution of weekly breakfast meetings involving President, Prime Minister and Party leader. The desire to turn the Party into a loyal and co-operative agent of government was evidenced in the experiment of setting different tasks for the party activists. In the first year of office, the party was mobilized in defence of the nationalization bill which was blocked by the Constitutional Council, and in July 1982 it was decided at a meeting of Socialist Ministers and leading party officials that party committees would draw up proposals for tax reform, although they were, significantly, to be—in Jospin's words—'suggestions not plans'. As the government began to change course during the first two years, it was thought that there might be great potential for disunity in the Party and in the Government; in the event this did not occur.

The Socialists came to office in 1981 with the intention of reflating out of the recession but in mid-1982 this strategy was diluted and in March 1983 actually dropped. By that date the franc had been devalued three times. The tortuous path from reflation to deflation provoked some tension within the party and caused problems for the alliance with the Communists, but stronger dissent was voiced by the Socialist 'right'. Michel Rocard soon established himself as an advocate of 'rigour' (i.e. austerity) long before the Government moved away from its initial expansionist strategy in 1982; he even brushed with his old ally Mauroy on budgetary policy in the autumn of 1981. His concern about the consequences of reflation and its effects on the balance of trade did find an echo both with the Finance Minister Delors and the ex-Gaullist Trade Minister, Jobert. Neither of these men, however, carried weight in the Party—Jobert indeed was not even a member. More important, as well as more divisive of Left unity, was the support for Rocard's position that came from the CFDT unions and their leader, Edmond Maire. Rocard's advocacy of restraint and his use of the 1983 municipal election campaign to promote his belief that more belt tightening and a slower rise, or even a fall, in living standards were inevitable on top of the cuts already imposed in 1982, were resented as unhelpful by most sections of the party and made him the butt of criticism from left wing Mitterrandists such as the PS parliamentary leader, Pierre Joxe and the Chairman of the National Assembly Finance Committee, Christian Goux, as well, as from some of Mauroy's supporters.

Rocard, like Delors, also disapproved of Chevènement's stewardship of the Ministry of Industry after the amalgamation in 1982 of that department with the Ministry of Research and Technology, to which the CERES leader had been appointed in May 1981. Chevènement's attitudes reflected the 'lyrical illusion' of the election victory and, in particular, the view that there were no industrial sectors that need be 'abandoned', but that with sufficient state impetus old industries could be made competitive. This industrial expression of *'tout est possible'* was widespread at the time and ignored Mendès France's famous realistic maxim that 'to govern is to choose'—choices were being avoided. There was also, however, another side to Chevènement which made him much less of a radical force than his reputation before 1981 might have led observers to suppose; he did, for example, actually support the Finance Minister's call for a 'pause' in the pace of the reform programme in late 1981. Whilst ostensibly an interventionist minister who favoured directing nationalized firms, and notably the banks, in their investment priorities, (a position entirely contrary to the views of Rocard and Delors who favoured leaving such matters to be determined by conventional market criteria), Chevènement was a much less effective Minister of Industry than were other less publicity-conscious members of the Government.

Although still officially only a 'parenthesis' in Government strategy, the deflationary approach was confirmed by the third Mauroy Government formed in March 1983, but by that time two of the four original CERES ministers had departed: the

Solidarity (Social Services) Minister, Mme Nicole Questiaux, having resigned in June 1982 rather than adapt to the compromises of power when public spending was reined-in, and Chevènement himself leaving in March 1983 after a public reprimand from the president for speaking out of turn. However, CERES was given another junior post in the reshuffle of March 1983, and the main CERES personality remaining, Mme Edwige Avice (Sports, Youth, and Leisure) who had proved a competent junior minister, was duly rewarded with a slight promotion. But despite its 1981 complement of four ministers—two of whom of Cabinet rank—CERES, like the Communist Party, was not a major presence in government: its representatives showed us much keenness to make a success of their departments as to rock the boat, and CERES activists were accordingly quiet. But whilst Nicole Questiaux's resignation was not the occasion for a public blast from the left wing against the Government, Chevènement's departure in March 1983 was a more serious affair and his replacement as industry minister by the rising figure of Laurent Fabius who set out to reassure the business community, provoked the publication of *Le Socialisme et la France*, a defence of Chevènement's position by Jacques Mandrin (a pseudonym for CERES spokesmen). This book established the lines for a Left-Right struggle, aiming barbs at all those who opposed the CERES brand of interventionist socialism.

As Prime Minister, Pierre Mauroy sought to perform the task of holding the ring as the (supposedly suspended) factions engaged each other and to apply Mitterrand's programme. This role made for a certain incoherence as squabbles spilled out into the popular press and was rather weakly defended by Mauroy in an April 1982 *Le Monde* article entitled *'gouverner autrement'*. He was first forced to defend the Government's reflationary policies against the attacks of Delors and Rocard, and then after the change of gear in May 1982 to argue the case for deflation against the president's advisers and the Cabinet's left wing. This process ensured, by early 1983, a low popularity rating for Mauroy who found himself carrying the can for government mistakes. His position was not made any easier by the knowledge that certain Mitterrandists, notably Joxe, had never entirely forgiven him for deserting Mitterrand at the Metz Congress in 1979, and wanted the Matignon to go to a closer ally of the President. As pressure on the Government built up whilst it negotiated its economic policy 'U'-turn in 1982 and 1983, so did Mauroy's position appear progressively weaker, with speculation about a change of Prime Minister becoming almost permanent from the beginning of 1983.

The municipal elections of March 1983 were billed as 'make or break' elections as much for Mauroy as for the Government, and since large losses were anticipated (between thirty and forty major towns were expected to move from Socialist control), so too was the Prime Minister's demise. In the event, however, after a vigorous campaign in defence of the Government, Socialist losses numbered only fifteen large towns, and one major town was actually gained, by Edith Cresson, Minister of Agriculture, from the Right. This limitation of anticipated damage reflected well on Mauroy, whose prestige was duly restored enough to enable him to survive and to preside not only over a third devaluation of the franc, but also over a third Mauroy government in which moderate ministers, notably Delors and Fabius, were significantly promoted; the Communist ministers did not depart at this point although Chevènement did, as also did Michel Jobert—something which was more ominous because it indicated the weakening of vital centrist support.

With the Communists still in government and with the party still behind Mitterrand and the government, CERES found little leverage. Unlike the 1970s, when it was the most organised current in the Party, the 1980s were not propitious for a left-wing ginger group. In May 1983 Chevènement launched an attack on the 'monetarism' of the Government in a move designed to stimulate factional debate in the run-up to the party congress in Bourg-en-Bresse in the autumn, but CERES was effectively cut out of the policy-making process and their reiteration of Communist pro-Soviet themes was easily brushed aside. Opinion in the Party became decidedly governmental by 1983 and the economic U-turn made no substantial difference, despite CERES' move into quasi-opposition.

After May 1981 the PCF maintained an ostensible commitment to the Government whilst using the CGT to probe the factory floors for any chance to make capital out of the unpopularity of the cuts imposed after mid-1982. The Communist Party, as distinct from the four Communist ministers, ran several campaigns against the interests of the Government, mostly around the theme that the platform of 1981 was not being applied with sufficient enthusiasm. The Communists thus laid down a trail of criticisms that could, if necessary, be retraced to show a consistent pattern of complaint and disapproval. In December 1981, after the imposition of martial law in Poland, the PCF and the CGT both refused to condemn General Jaruzelski, whilst the Socialists, and the Government, took a hard line, with (Mauroy ensuring that the four PCF ministers supported the Government's view. In late 1982 the leader of the Communist deputies, André Lajoinie, taking up the characteristic Communist cause of workers' defence, castigated the Government for what he saw as concessions to the *patronat* and the Right— a theme which became increasingly strident. After the new austerity measures of 1983, and in particular the cutting of aid to old industrial areas, Communist criticisms grew. This led to the Socialists demanding a 'verification' of the governmental agreement between the two parties in December 1983 and to a demand for a 'clarification' of the PCF position after Marchais joined a march of Lorraine steelworkers through Paris in April 1984. On these occasions, as with Communist anti-nuclear campaigns, it appeared that the PCF was trying to make capital out of its criticism of the Government whilst remaining unwilling to make the final break whenever it was challenged by the Socialists—a tactic similar to that employed in 1946–7. The four PCF ministers, on the other hand, much more inclined to present the acceptable face of Communist solidarity, largely avoided the limelight, with the exception of Health Minister Jack Ralite, whose public brush with the medical profession in 1982 presaged his move to a different post in 1983. Charles Fiterman, the Communist Minister whose reputation was most enhanced by his work in Government (despite the February 1984 road haulage strike which forced the Government to back down and which caused great inconvenience), remained the most popular Communist personality after 1984. The Socialists harboured no illusions about the PCF's entirely self-interested commitment to the

Government and anticipated a time when they would consider cutting loose but, since the advantages of quitting did not appear clear and since the onus for the break-up of Left unity could not be placed squarely on the Socialists, the actual date of the break was always difficult to predict.

Until the Spring of 1983, the PCF was especially preoccupied with the need to keep in step with the Socialists so as to stand a chance of saving its important municipal gains of 1977 in the March 1983 elections. In those elections the Left duly fought in harness in all but twenty-four of the 221 largest towns, a pattern very similar to that of 1977. Moreover, despite the wholly transformed balance of strengths within the Left since 1977, the Socialists let the Communists retain local leadership in many municipalities where they ought, on the basis of the 1981 Socialist landslide, to have made way for Socialist mayors. This was not, however, an example of Socialist magnanimity, so much as a calculation that if losses were to be sustained it was desirable for the Communists to carry their share (they duly lost sixteen towns), and a recognition that if the Communist electorate was to be properly mobilized in the Socialists' aid, the docility of the PCF's leadership was required. Thus a degree of mutual dependence existed and although the Socialists had been the predominant force on the Left since 1981, the Communists' electoral decline—down to 16 per cent in 1981, sticking at that figure in the cantonal elections of 1982, declining further in the municipal elections of 1983, and falling to 11 per cent in the European elections of 1984—was not entirely a matter for Socialist rejoicing as long as Communist votes were needed to elect Socialist mayors (or deputies) at the second ballot. Moreover, even if the PCF had been reduced to the role of supplicant after 1981, it was not reconciled to permanent inferiority.

Communist party criticisms of Socialist policy had steadily grown throughout 1983 (despite being pulled back into line by the Prime Minister) but the European elections of 1984 showed that the Socialists' and Communists' vote was still dropping (the Communists polled 11% and the Socialists 21%) whilst that of the Right wing National Front had risen to 11%. Matters came to a head with the collapse of the proposal to integrate Church schools into the state system and the resignation of the Mauroy government in July 1984. Mitterrand may have hoped for a change of government rather later in the year or even in 1985, but the events forced the pace and, in addition, provided the Communists with a difficult choice: they quit the government.

With the schools issue behind them, the Socialists looked to the new government of Laurent Fabius to redress the deteriorating situation around the theme of 'modernization'. The Fabius government benefited from a 'honeymoon' with public opinion and Fabius, young, a good communicator, and 'modern', emerged as the 'dauphin' to Mitterrand. The Government which once more included Chevènement, as Education Minister, and Pierre Joxe, as Interior Minister, presented a reassuring and technocratic front for a Socialist party which had decided to 'pause' in its pace of reforms (despite the heightening tone of PCF and CGT attacks) and to emphasise the theme of 'modernism'.

This stable state of affairs was not however to last. The first problem stemmed from Fabius' popularity: until 1985 the Mitterrand current had had its internal differences, but its battles were in reality struggles for influence with the leader. After becoming prime minister, however, Fabius emerged as potential leader of a current within the Mitterrandists. A side effect of the new position was that in March 1985 a quarrel over who should lead the coming election campaign opened up between Jospin and Fabius, and was only settled in June by Mitterrand's direct intervention.

There was also Rocard's resignation as Minister of Agriculture in April 1985, ostensibly over his objection to the introduction of proportional representation, and in July came the 'Greenpeace affair'. The sinking of the ecologist ship in Auckland harbour by French agents was first denied, then investigated and only, after the resignation of Defence Minister Hernu in September, admitted. The handling of the whole affair was debilitating for the government and left a series of unanswered questions. In October 1985 Fabius performed badly in a televised debate with Jacques Chirac, and in December dissociated himself from the president's decision to meet Polish Head of State General Jaruzelski. These events led to an eclipse of the prime minister and, in consequence, a move by Mitterrand more directly onto the centre stage for the important parliamentary elections of March 1986.

Despite these difficulties, and Rocard's challenge from outside the government, the party's October congress in Toulouse was uneventful. The leadership's language was restrained and governmental as the party prepared for the elections but the 'Bad Godesberg' (the overt denial of a Marxist past) heralded by the press for the Toulouse Congress was not evident. Before Toulouse there had been talk of a Rocardian split, but if this were ever a serious possibility, the threat was removed by Rocard's large share (29%) of the delegates' vote—a share big enough to hold out hope for the eventual presidential nomination, yet small enough for the party leadership to accommodate.

The Socialist 'campaign' for the 1986 elections opened in the autumn of 1985 with announcements of good news (including a Disneyland for the Paris outskirts and new TV channels and the Channel Tunnel project) and with a series of poster campaigns commended for their 'humour'. Ministers began to devote themselves increasingly to electioneering but by early 1986 the party campaign had become very much Mitterrand's, putting into effect the strategy announced by Mauroy at a December meeting of the party's directing committee: that of 'following in the President's furrow.' During the campaign Fabius, by undertaking an extensive round of party rallies, began to work his passage back with both Party and public opinion, whilst Rocard, who stood aloof from the hustings and refused to address such meetings, did his own cause considerable damage. In betting on a Socialist humiliation at the polls so that he could step forward as the party's only hope, Rocard was being too obviously self-serving.

In the event the Socialist party's creditable 32% vote in the March 1986 general election was insufficient to give the president room for manoeuvre and made it inevitable that Fabius's Socialist Government would be succeeded by Jacques Chirac's Gaullist-Centrist coalition which had won a small parliamentary majority. Nevertheless, Socialist party leaders, anticipating a bigger defeat, treated the 1986 elections as a quasi-victory. With the Party reaffirmed as the dominant party on the Left, and even in defeat, the largest party in the country, it looked to the future with some confidence. It had in its ranks enough *présidentiables* to ensure it a future and most ministers had left office with enhanced reputations. Despite Rocard's persistent and credible challenge since 1978, the party's presidential nomination was still Mitterrand's if he chose to run again, and the party was as available for use as his instrument during the difficult period of his co-existence (*cohabitation*) with the new right-wing Government and prime minister, as it had ever been. Moreover, the 'opposition mentality' diagnosed by many observers as a fatal malady of the 1970s was not a feature of the party in 1986 as it prepared a strategy for an early return to power.

Thus in the short space of five years, the Socialist Party had come of age as a party of government; it had learnt quickly and retained its new-found position as the most important left of centre party in the country. The dominance of the Communists had been broken, the PCF's participation in government from 1981–84 having failed to stem an apparently inexorable decline. The government's resort to a deflationary strategy, a course traditionally disorientating to socialist parties in office, was absorbed without difficulty by a party in step with a cautious electorate. The journey from the euphoria of 1981, through the 'realism' of 1982/3, to the honourable defeat of 1986, was more painless than might have been expected.

Part II
The New Parti Socialiste

7
Socialist–Communist Relations

The Union of the Left pursued by the Socialist Party after 1971 has involved it in collaboration with a party whose leaders it does not trust and whose apparently anti-democratic and pro-Soviet characteristics it has long denounced. For sixty years the history of relations between French Socialists and Communists has seen an alternation between long periods of confrontation (1920–34, 1939–41, 1947–62) and of fragile and ephemeral reconciliations (1934–9, 1941–7, 1962–77). The periods of confrontation have coincided with those of Communist Party isolation; the periods of reconciliation with phases of relative Communist integration into French political life. The two *frères ennemis* have been competing since the election of 1924, and up to and including the election of 1936 the Socialists were the larger party. From the first post-war election in 1945, and until 1973, the Communists were the larger party; but in 1978 the Socialists recaptured the lead they had lost thirty-three years before (see Table 7.1). In the previously quoted words of a Communist leader[1]–'l'union est un combat'–a fight not least, though in the Communists' case not only, for electoral dominance. The 'logical' and 'natural' progression towards the Union of the Left prompted by the changes described in Chapter 2 had been implied during the short periods when the parties had co-operated before, in the 1930s and 1940s. But whilst the political and institutional indicators all pointed, by the early 'sixties, to the strategic necessity of an alliance, there were many grounds for supposing that such an arrangement, even with the Socialist Party's uncompromising commitment to it, would be an alliance against nature.

At the Épinay Congress of 1971 the Socialist Party set down its clear commitment to an alliance of the Left, to an explicit exclusion indeed of all third-force (centrist) strategies. At the same time, however, the motion containing this commitment included reference to the need for the Communists to

[1] E. Fajon, *L'Union est un combat*, Éditions Sociales (Paris), 1975.

Table 7.1

Socialist and Communist Comparative Electoral Performance 1924–1986

Election	Socialist Party*			Communist Party		
	Votes	Percentage	Seats	Votes	Percentage	Seats
1919	1,700,000		68			
1924	749,647**	8.1	105	875,812	9.5	26
1928	1,698,000	20.9	107	1,063,943	11.3	14
1932	1,964,000	20.8	129	794,883	8.4	12
1936	2,017,186	20.8	153	1,473,734	15.2	72
1945	4,711,552	24.6	135	5,011,005	26.1	148
1946j	4,234,114	21.3	115	5,243,325	26.4	146
1946n	3,480,773	18.1	91	5,524,799	28.8	165
1951	2,894,001	15.3	95	4,939,380	26.0	95
1956	3,366,371	15.8	89	5,503,491	25.8	146
1958	3,214,789	15.7	40	3,870,184	18.9	10
1962	2,337,195	12.7	65	4,010,463	21.9	40
1967	4,308,507	19.3	117	5,035,120	22.5	72
1968	3,684,165	16.6	57	4,434,832	20.0	33
1973	4,939,603	20.4	102	5,156,619	21.3	73
1978	7,055,083	24.7	115	5,870,402	20.6	86
1981	9,432,362	37.5	283	4,065,540	16.2	44
1986	8,867,463	32.1	216***	2,873,234	9.8	35

(Third Republic: 1919–1936; Fourth Republic: 1945–1956; Fifth Republic: 1958–1986)

* Figures for 1967 and 1968 include Radical Party; those for 1973, 1978, 1981 and 1986 include Left Radical (MRG).
** An underestimation of Socialist strength (other Socialist candidates stood in alliance with Radicals).
*** 209 PS; 7 MRG.

Sources: C. Leleu, *Géographie des élections françaises depuis 1936*, PUF, 1971; J. Elleinstein, *Le PC*, Grasset (Paris), 1976; *Le Monde*, Dossiers et Documents 1973, 1978, 1981, 1986.

give 'clear and public answers to questions concerning national sovereignty, democratic liberties and . . . submission to the will of the people as expressed through universal suffrage'.[2] Convincing answers to these questions would be required if the Left alliance was to have electoral credibility. This short list of Socialist demands summarizes the essence of the problem involved in collaboration with the Communist Party; concern about its acceptance of liberal–democratic norms and values and its loyalty to French national interests. These were no mere academic debating points.

International links

Since the creation of the Communist Party in 1920 and the process of bolshevization that it underwent thereafter, and which turned it into a malleable instrument of the Soviet Union, its international loyalties posed an intractable problem. The writer Annie Kriegel[3] has referred to the *'double appartenance'* of the PCF, seeing the Communists as simultaneously part of the international Communist movement and of a national political system. Kriegel holds that when these two attachments conflict primacy is always given to international obligations over national (domestic) considerations and responsibilities. This is because it is in its attachment to the Moscow-based international Communist movement that the true essence of the Party lies, with the Russian Soviet model being venerated as 'the first Socialist state' whose foreign policy is seen as an expression of the world revolutionary strategy to which Communists are committed. The PCF's close ties with Moscow are what have most prevented its integration into the French system. (Democratic centralism—the other problem characteristic of the Party—has arguably had a comparatively slighter effect.) The status of the PCF, established by 1924 and reaffirmed in 1947, as a branch of an international movement, externally financed, its leaders externally schooled and supervised and taking their orders from Moscow, and in

---

[2] Motion d'orientation, Épinay Congress 1971, *Guide du nouvel adherent*, Parti Socialiste, 1976, p. 82.

[3] A. Kriegel, in O. Duhamel and H. Weber (eds.), *Changer le PC?*, PUF (Paris), 1979, pp. 178-95.

Thorez's case spending more time between 1940 and 1953 in the Soviet Union than in France, has been at the centre of PCF-PS relations. Effectively it has meant that collaboration between the parties could only occur if the foreign-policy interests of the Soviet Union permitted it. The four occasions on which the Communist Party has undertaken stark reversals in strategy (1934, 1939, 1941, 1947) were all a consequence of adjustments to the international situation by the USSR, as was the gradual growth of a Communist-Socialist entente after 1962. Since, however, the foreign-policy interests of the Soviet Union can hardly coincide with those of France (or the Western Alliance), the Party has suffered most severely from its dual loyalties during such periods.[4]

When such conflicts arise—when, for example, the USSR is criticized—the Party's most natural inclination is to defend the Soviet Union from 'bourgeois' attacks. Attempts by elements inside the Communist Party to de-Russianize it by moving back from an automatic endorsement of Soviet positions do not succeed. When the Party condemned the Russian invasion of Czechoslovakia in 1968 Thorez's widow resigned from the politburo, and the Party soon reverted to an orthodox view of events in Czechoslovakia. When the reformist-inclined intellectual, Jean Elleinstein, in 1978 attacked support of the Soviet model and fêted some dissidents, the matter was ultimately resolved only by his expulsion from the Central Committee of the Party. In Kriegel's view, although the Party has distanced itself from some abuses inside the Soviet Union (notably the treatment of dissidents) it has retained—in a world divided into two camps, the one 'socialist', the other 'imperialist'—a clear allegiance to the former.[5]

Democracy

The Communists' commitment to pluralistic democracy has always been in doubt, given the Party's traditional veneration of Russia and of the Soviet system, which accords no place for pluralism. Socialist reservations about the Communist Party, as has been seen, have largely centred on the absence

[4] See R. Verdier, *PS-PC une lutte pour l'entente*, Seghers (Paris), 1976.
[5] Kriegel, in Duhamel and Weber (eds.), op. cit., p. 182.

of democratic credentials. Formally, the Communist Party is a Marxist–Leninist revolutionary party, and it is the Leninist part of that formula that Socialists have particularly resisted, and indeed refused to endorse at the Tours Congress, which split the Left in 1920. In May 1975 the Jospin Committee, set up by the Party to monitor relations between the two parties, listed five areas of divergence mostly concerning the PCF's commitment to democracy, notably the conception of the vanguard role of the Party; the evaluation of the experience of the Eastern European regimes; and the concept of the dictatorship of the proletariat.

Whilst the Communist Party has, during the past twenty years, come to endorse the conventional liberal–democratic values (party pluralism, acceptance of election results, etc.) it has never fully admitted that they are not operative in the Eastern Block countries. The doctrine of the Party as the vanguard of the proletariat is a core element in Marxism–Leninism and is used to justify a further central feature of Communist politics—democratic centralism. This last, of course, involves much 'centralism' and little 'democracy' (in the sense of pluralistic debate), and the orchestration of a unanimous view around texts issued by the leading organs of the Party. Democratic centralism and the vanguard of the proletariat are thus two sides of the same coin: to fulfil its vanguard role—of leadership of the proletariat—the Party requires structures, forms, and rules that give it maximum effectiveness. This rules out excessive internal discussion which, according to Marchais, leads to 'paralysis of decision and action': the Communist Party is not, said Marchais, 'a debating society'.[6] Thus the most important concession to electoralism made by the PCF in recent years—dropping the theory ('and the fact') of the 'dictatorship of the proletariat' —was decided at the 1976 congress after an announcement before the congress and a brief debate in the party press. Again, in 1977, a similar volte face on the French nuclear deterrent (endorsing it) was effected by the Central Committee with only slight debate. Policy in the PCF is revealed, not discussed. This is not to say that dissent does not exist; there was a loud chorus of it among the activists of the Paris region after the March 1978 election. But there is no mechanism in

[6] *Le Monde*, 29 Apr. 1978.

a Leninist party for seeking compromise—let alone permitting
the organization of minority opinion. Dissent, if persistent, is
resolved only by expulsion.

The Socialist Party could not be culturally more dissimilar
to the Communist Party. Its structures positively reward
factionalism, giving seats in the leading bodies of the Party
(Bureau Exécutif and Comité Directeur) to representatives of
all groups who can secure more than 5 per cent of the votes
cast at biennial party congresses. Rival motions to be debated
at the congress are debated in the federations of the Party
beforehand, without imposition from party headquarters.
This pluralistic state of affairs has met with the approval of
the dissident Communist Jean Elleinstein.[7] Whilst the leadership at the congress will seek unanimity or 'unity', as the
Socialists would prefer to call it, it is frequently denied, as at
Metz in 1979 where the delegates' votes were spread over
five rival motions in the ratio of 40:21:17:15:6; reduced
finally to 60:40. From its origins the PS has been an in-
tensely factionalized party (as was the SFIO of Blum and
Mollet), if held together out of a sense of mutual self-interest
by a leader, Mitterrand (until 1981), whose prestige allowed
him considerable leeway in imposing his authority. But
Mitterrand's authority was as nothing compared to the power
at the disposal of the Communist Party's politburo to purge
and to expel. The list of senior Communists who have fallen
to this process since the War is long: Lecoeur, Marty, Tillon,
Servin, Cassanova, Garaudy, Elleinstein . . .

Class

The cultural incompatibility of the two parties is further
highlighted in the *ouvriériste* and anti-intellectual traditions
of the Communist Party which confers a privileged role on
the working class, around which other exploited groups may
gather, but which are certainly not accorded the same status.
Intellectuals are not revered; they 'lack firmness, are more
susceptible to bourgeois influences and understand nothing
of the need for proletarian action.'[8] Intellectuals indeed do

---

[7] J. Elleinstein, in 'Le PS', *Regards sur*, no. 3, 1977, pp. 32-3.
[8] A. Barjonet, quoted by S. Tarrow in D. Blackmer and S. Tarrow (eds.), *Communism in Italy and France*, Princeton (NJ), 1976.

not play an important role in the Party's internal life; few reach the politburo, and one of the last to do so, Roger Garaudy, was expelled in 1970. Of the twenty-one-man politburo elected in 1976 two were farmers, six were teachers (four *professeurs*), two were white-collar employees, and nine workers.[9] In reality most of the nine (including Marchais, Leroy, Fiterman, Séguy, etc.) were party apparatchiks who had long since left the shop floor—but what they certainly were not was intellectual. Meanwhile in the Socialist Party intellectuals abound: *énarques, universitaires, professeurs*—a veritable '*parti de professeurs*'—as reflected in the factional life of the Party. In sociological terms the PCF deliberately seeks to project itself as a working-class party, with candidate selection monitored to ensure that the manual, routine clerical, and (primary) school-teacher categories comprise an overall majority; in 1978 nearly 60 per cent of all Communist parliamentary candidates were drawn from these groups.[10] It seeks to stress at all levels its *enracinement populaire* and whenever a stick is needed with which to beat the Socialists the assault frequently takes the form of attacking the number of *cadres supérieurs* amongst the Socialist Party's leaders: 'technocrates formés dans le giron de la grande bourgeoisie', as Marchais put it in 1977.[11]

It must be stressed that the collapse of the Left alliance in 1977 came when the Communists realized that their party's vanguard status was threatened by the Socialists, whose growing appeal was wooing working-class votes away from the PCF and undermining its claim to represent all manual workers. The wide margin that existed in 1973 between Communist (37 per cent) and Socialist (27 per cent) proportions of the working-class vote is revealed in Table 7.2. Opinion polls in 1976 and 1977 were, however, showing the two parties level, each with 32 per cent of the working-class vote. The Communists' 'soak the rich' campaign in 1978 was designed to fend off the Socialist threat to the Communist constituency by reaffirming a distinct identity, returning to its sources and reasserting its image as *the* working-class party

[9] J. Elleinstein, *Le PC*, Grasset (Paris), 1976, p. 114.
[10] P. Broyer *et al.*, 'Les candidats communistes aux élections législatives de 1973 and 1978', *RFSP*, 1979.
[11] G. Marchais, *Parlons franchement*, Grasset (Paris), 1977, p. 146.

The New Parti Socialiste

Table 7.2
Proportion of Social Categories Voting Socialist and Communist 1973-1986

	PS (+MRG)				PC			
	1973 (%)	1978 (%)	1981 (%)	1986 (%)	1973 (%)	1978 (%)	1981 (%)	1986 (%)
SEX								
Men	22	25	39	30	25	24	17	12
Women	20	25	38	32	18	19	19	7
AGE								
18-24		25	44	35		28	18	6
	23				22			
25-34		24	46	39		26	17	12
35-49	24	25	37	31	25	19	19	10
50-64	19	24	42	74	20	20	18	9
65+	19	25	27	21	17	15	10	10
OCCUPATION								
Farmers	17	17	32	11	13	9	6	7
Shopkeepers and self-employed	23	23	35	19	10	14	10	5
Upper managers and liberal professions	7	15	38	29	6	9	7	4
Middle managers and white-collar workers	23	29	45	39	17	18	16	9
Manual workers	27	27	44	36	37	36	24	20
Inactive and retired	20	26	29	37	20	17	16	15
ALL	20	25	38	32	21	21	16	10

Source: SOFRES surveys cited by G. Le Gall, 'Le nouvel ordre électoral', *Revue politique et parlementaire,* July–Aug. 1981, and G. Le Gall, 'Mars 1986: des élections de transition?' *Revue politique et parlementaire*, No 922, March–April 1986, pp. 6-13, and Bull–BVA poll, *Libération*, 18 March 1986.

for the poor and under-privileged, in contrast to the middle-class reformist picture presented by the Socialists. The election outcome was a satisfactory one for the Communists. The Socialist vote—though it moved, crucially, above the Communist share for the first time since 1936—only did so by four percentage points and not by the 8 per cent heralded by the polls. More important still, there was a 5-per-cent swing back amongst manual workers at the last moment from the PS to the Communists leaving the latter's working-class dominance intact.[12]

To have held working-class ground whilst losing in all other categories (except the under-thirty-four-year-olds) was a relief—but the overall long-term trends were extremely worrying for the PCF. It was becoming increasingly incapable at successive elections of outrunning the Socialists at the first ballot in the constituencies, a crucial requirement under the arrangement for mutual withdrawal. In 1973 the Socialists had led in 276 seats, the PCF in 197; in 1978 the figures were 321 and 153 (see Table 7.3). If 1978 showed the warning

Table 7.3
Relative Strengths of PS and PCF in the Constituencies

In the lead on the Left	1967	1968	1973	1978	1981
PS	212	217	276	321	429
PCF	258	253	197	153	45
Total number of metropolitan constituencies	470	470	473	474	474

Source: G. Le Gall, 'Le nouvel ordre électoral', *RRP*, July-Aug. 1981, p. 17.

lights, 1981 saw the crash, with Marchais in the presidential contest and the Party in the legislative election suffering a bigger haemorrhage of votes than in 1958. The Party was buried everywhere, in all regions and in all social categories, by an avalanche of Socialist votes. Most critically, almost twice as many (44 per cent) workers voted Socialist as Communist (24 per cent), and the ominous phrase 'hegemony of the Socialist Party' came into use to describe the relationship between the two parties. Half the sitting Communist deputies (44 out of 86) were overtaken by the Socialists and thus had to step down, including six members of the politburo. In the presidential election, Marchais's vote had been ahead of Mitterrand's in only four departments; in the general election the Party led in only two. Most damaging was its symbolic loss of dominance in the Paris region, the

[12] J. Jaffré, *Projet*, June 1978, p. 742.

heartland of the country and the heartland of the Party's proletarian base since 1936: the PCF was decaying at its core. Nor were the losses purely electoral: many activists were disengaging from party activity, a development posing a grave threat to the Party's organizational superiority.

The trend of events that culminated in the Communists' electoral disaster of 1981 suggested that the PCF was either at last declining or—the two processes are not unconnected—succumbing ineluctably to integration in the French political system. First, institutional imperatives had long pointed the way (the electoral system, presidentialization, etc.) drawing the Communist Party into the mainstream, obliging it to adapt in order to maintain its all-important presence as a vanguard party in a political system that otherwise threatened it with a rapid slide into the margins. The result of the 1958 election, echoing the results of the elections before the construction of the Popular Front alliance in 1934 when the PCF was reduced to a handful of seats (ten in 1958 and twelve in 1932), was not one which such a party (enjoying a dominant position on the Left which it was anxious to retain) could sensibly ignore. Thus from a patchy start in 1962, when the Communist and Socialist parties had agreed the tactic of mutual withdrawal of candidates in certain constituencies as part of an indispensable mutual seat-saving exercise, a national agreement became the norm at all legislative elections thereafter.

Secondly the PCF has long been—to paraphrase the analysis of Georges Lavau—a channel for the orderly expression of protest. Despite its self-proclaimed vocation as a revolutionary party committed to overturning the existing political and social system, it is in fact a party that organizes protest in a country where the force of class consciousness and the traditions of the working-class movement have led to habits of conflict rather than compromise. In such a context the Party performs a necessary role as a 'tribune of the people', diverting 'waves of discontent and class struggle towards the safer ground of legal, political conflict'.[13] Such an analysis sees the PCF as effectively serving the function of a non-revolutionary party of working-class protest. It is a view sustained by findings from surveys into the motivation of Communist

[13] G. Lavau, in Blackmer and Tarrow (eds.), op. cit., p. 93.

voters and, more important, by their voting behaviour. In 1958 a quarter (1.5 million) of those who had voted Communist only two years before deserted to parties which backed the new Gaullist regime. In 1981 a further 1.5 million voters who had voted for the Party in 1978 and 1979 deserted the Party's own leader in the first ballot of the presidential election in order to support a moderate Socialist candidate. These major desertions from the PCF imply non-ideological reasons for voting Communist and, in the latter case, a desire to cast a *vote utile* (or non-wasted vote) prompted by an institutional environment which undermines the role of purely protest parties.

Whereas, in the multi-party parliamentary system of the Fourth Republic, mere protest articulation sufficed to deliver a regular 25 per cent of the vote to the Communist Party, in the streamlined system of the Fifth Republic it is not enough merely to perform a 'tribune' role, for the Communists now have to pose, in alliance with the Socialists, as an alternative government with credible and electorally convincing proposals. It is not a role for which the Communist leaders and activists appear to be temperamentally or ideologically suited, but it is one they are obliged to play. The idea, suggested by Maurice Duverger, of the Left alliance as a 'forced marriage'[14] imposed not only by systemic constraints but by the traditional habit, particularly strong among Communist voters, of ensuring the victory for the Left through republican discipline at the second ballot, gave the Party little option: even if the parents might be estranged, it was necessary to stay together for the sake of the children. The evidence of 1981—when the Communist Party, in the wake of its leader's humiliation at the first ballot of the presidential election, dropped everything and more or less meekly followed in Mitterrand's wake to the ministerial participation they achieved in the second Mauroy government—was that increasingly, in the Fifth Republic, the Communist Party, 'vanguard of the proletariat', is obliged to follow its voters.

Furthermore the obligation is reinforced by social changes threatening the class base on which the PCF has traditionally relied.[15] The more important changes in French social

[14] M. Duverger, *Le Monde*, 6 Apr. 1979.   [15] A. Kriegel, op. cit., p. 189.

structure have not helped a party which has as its prime vocation the leadership of a numerically declining working class.
From inside the Communist Party dissidents such as Jean
Elleinstein made great play after the 1978 elections of the
need for the Party to extend its electoral appeal. Pauperiza-
tion of the working class was clearly a defunct concept, and
there was strong evidence of resistance to the *ouvriériste*
tradition in a society where working-class affluence had
become a fact. Elleinstein was particularly critical of the
Party's populist electoral tactic in the 1978 elections, when
in an effort to combat the competition from the Socialists,
it ran a pugnacious, 'class-war' campaign. His complaint was
that French workers are no longer poor and that they, and
the white-collar workers, are increasingly interested in
pressing qualitative rather than quantitative demands; that
the issues of urban decay, excessive bureaucracy, regionalism,
feminism, ecology, and democracy at work (*autogestion*) are
now interesting them more and yet the party leadership
shows as little interest as it can in such matters.[16] The
politics of old-fashioned working-class defence thus no longer
caters to the voters' needs, and the voters' desertion of the
Party at the elections of 1981 strongly suggested a ground-
swell of the workers' determination to leave the ghetto in
which the Party had traditionally sought to enclose them.

There was evidence too in 1981 that substantial numbers
of Communist voters specifically disapproved of the Party's
recently adopted positions on Poland and Afghanistan[17] as well
as of the controversial actions taken in the winter of 1980-1
in Communist municipalities against immigrant workers—a
particularly unattractive example of the Communist quest
for protest votes.[18] (In the elections of 1978 and 1979, and
in the presidential campaign of 1981, the Communists
campaigned hard for the 'protest' votes of redundant steel
workers in Lorraine, threatened farmers in the south, and
then, by their action at Vitry in December 1980, campaigned
for the protest votes of anti-immigrant whites.) Communist
voters' disapproval of the party's reversion to pro-Sovietism
over Afghanistan and Poland (evidence to Elleinstein of

[16] J. Elleinstein, *Le Monde*, 13, 14, 15 Apr. 1978.
[17] R. W. Johnson, *The Long March of the French Left*, Macmillan (London),
1981, p. 281.　　　　　　　　　　　　　　[18] See poll in *L'Express*, 11 Apr. 1981.

the Party's *'virage à l'Est'*)[19] implied that the PCF's enduring sympathies for the Moscow line were losing it support among its own electorate, and that the Party's international loyalties were still serving to isolate it in the French polity.

Whilst Socialist-Communist incompatibilities over foreign policy matters were lessened in the 'seventies by the relaxation of international tension, and with Communist endorsement òf Soviet actions being set against certain criticisms of Russia, the atmosphere of the 1980's was quite different. In 1978 and 1981 the PCF, faced with the need to drop the Left alliance which appeared to be threatening to take it to power only as a weak junior partner in a Socialist-dominated administration, could respond to Moscow's call for a united and hostile front to western capitalism. The deterioration of US-Soviet relations and the Russian offensive over the installation of Cruise and Pershing missiles in western Europe evoked an immediate response from the PCF: the party hosted a conference on 'peace' with the Polish Communist Party in 1980 and ran campaigns against nuclear arms. Unlike similar campaigns in the past however, those of the 'eighties evoked no response in public opinion; and worse, from the PCF's point of view, was the emergence in the 'eighties of an inter-party consensus in France on questions of nuclear arms and alliance strategies quite inimical to the Communist Party's international loyalties.

The relationship of the PCF to Moscow is nevertheless open to variable interpretation. That it is perceived by French public opinion, and not least by Communist supporters, as too close, is not in doubt.[20] The image of the party has always been best when it was co-operating with the Socialists, and making few demands, as during the so called 'Eurocommunist' phase in the 1970s, which coincided with Mitterrand's PCF-supported presidential bid in 1974. But that links between the PCF and CPSU are ambiguous was suggested by the contacts between the Soviet ambassador and Giscard d'Estaing during the election campaign of 1974, and the

[19] See J. Elleinstein, *Ils vous trompent camarades*, Belfond (Paris), 1981.

[20] G. Le Gall, 'Radiographie de l'image du PCF: double divorce avec la société et les sympathisants', *Revue politique et parlementaire*, Jan-Feb 1985, pp 16-27.

article in *Pravda* in February 1981 which, as quoted in *Le Monde* adjudged the Giscard presidency as *'globalement positif'*; such incidents were taken as evidence of Moscow's tacit endorsement of the conservative status quo in France. The potential for international destabilisation of Communists sharing in power in Western Europe plays some part in Soviet thinking, as does concern that left-wing coalitions of the sort being offered France by the late 'seventies, involved the difficult prospect of Communist tails unable to wag social democratic dogs.

Conflicting objectives

Seeking to unravel the Communist enigma is a major spectator sport and can become as frustrating as trying to negotiate the Hampton Court maze. Lavau, in his most recent re-examination of the Party[22] concluded that it continually hesitates between three options or activities: the first, the performance of the tribune role of protest mobilization; the second, the pursuit of electoral success; and the third, the declaration of revolutionary objectives. He argues that it is in the conjunction of these three contradictory preoccupations that lies the explanation of the Party's strength and also of its isolation. One might add that conflict between these objectives is ensured by the difference of emphasis within the party leadership, with Marchais responsible for the 'liberalization' and popular-frontist bonhomie of the early 1970s, rivalled by more orthodox figures such as Leroy and Krasucki. In fact the course steered by the PCF since the early 1960s has been neither revolutionary nor fully electoralist: it is pursuing the peaceful road to socialism, though that does not mean a fully parliamentary road, for whilst it values the maximum parliamentary representation it can get, it uses other channels—notably the CGT and its own party apparatus—to promote its interests. It is clear

~

---

[21] A. Kriegel, in Duhamel and Weber, op. cit., p. 190, and R. Tiersky, in Duhamel and Weber, op. cit., p. 222.

[22] G. Lavau, *A quoi sert le Parti Communiste français?*, Fayard (Paris), 1981.

above all that because the PCF is not primarily, or solely, a job-oriented, office-seeking party, controlling relations with it can never be an easy matter. For the Socialists, entering alliance with such a party involved the shedding of all illusions; the alliance was seen, on both sides, as an inherently conflict-ridden affair, each there for what they could extract from it.

Mitterrand's objective, as stated as long ago as 1969, was to create 'a political movement [i.e. the Socialist Party] able to balance, at first, and then to dominate the Communist Party and finally to obtain a majority on its own.'[23] It was believed that a common programme with the Communists, with the economic section negotiated for the Socialist Party by the Marxist, left-wing, CERES leaders, would serve to affirm Socialist good faith and enable the Party to become attractive to Communist working-class voters. Mitterrand's speech to the Socialist International meeting in Vienna in June 1972 (shortly after he and Marchais had signed the Common Programme) made clear enough that he was out to show that 3 million of the 5 million Communist voters could vote Socialist. Lionel Jospin's deliberations on the state of PS–PCF relations and the evolution of the PCF in the general direction of 'Eurocommunist' liberalization, concluded that the PCF was changing only because of the pressure from the revamped Socialist Party; it was evolving because it was forced to by the facts and not because it had positively decided or wished to do so. The Socialist response to the Communists' verbally aggressive reaction to signs of Socialist dominance after 1974 was to avoid returning much of the fire, in the belief that a break with the Communists would threaten all the ground made by the Socialist Party since 1971. It would destabilize its enlarged, pro-unity activist base and threaten to close the access to the Communists' electorate gained by the alliance and the Common Programme. Writing in 1980, Mitterrand prophetically envisaged the dramatic shifts of votes that were to wash him into the Élysée in 1981. Whilst acknowledging the PCF's powerful apparatus—of which he had gained some knowledge during the Resistance —he disputed its capacity to be the 'master of the hearts and consciences' of its voters, arguing that Communist voters

[23] F. Mitterrand, *Ma part de vérité*, Fayard (Paris), 1969, p. 120.

were not following the lead of the Party in the attacks being launched against the Socialist Party and himself after 1974.[24] This was an analysis that prefigured the substantial desertions of the PCF by its voters in 1981, which by reducing the Communist vote made possible Mitterrand's victory. Thus Mitterrand correctly anticipated that the Communist Party's veto over the Union of the Left would be overturned by the Communist voter's desire to see the election of a left-wing government.

For the Communists the alliance initially offered hope of growth. Previous alliances between the parties had always been accompanied by an expansion of Communist support. It was the Popular Front alliance in the 1930s that saw Communist penetration of the working-class electorate and the unions, and the post-war period of tripartism that saw the Party establish its status, after 1946, as the French party with the largest electorate. Communist hegemony on the Left was thus established through those early exercises in left-wing unity. In 1971 the PCF had no reason to suppose that this pattern would not be repeated. At the time the Socialist Party had only a meagre poll rating of 10 per cent and offered no threat to Communist dominance. When that dominance did come under threat the decision was taken to destroy the instrument—the Union of the Left—that had apparently been transformed into a vehicle for Socialist growth. Two specific reservations lay behind Communist wrecking tactics in 1977. First, the existence of a conservative President (in office until 1981) implied the threat of an accommodation between President Giscard d'Estaing and Mitterrand (as Prime Minister), which could reopen the centrist strategy which had served previously to confirm the isolation of the PCF. Secondly and specifically, the Communists, Mitterrand believed,[25] did not want to take power in an economic recession and have 'to manage the crisis'.[26] To do so would be to compromise the Party's specific commitment to a precise and detailed economic programme of Eastern European-style bureaucratic socialism,

[24] F. Mitterrand, *Ici et maintenant*, Fayard (Paris), 1980, p. 49.
[25] Ibid., p. 50.
[26] See C. Ysmal, 'Parti communiste—les raisons d'un durcissement', *Projet*, Jan. 1978, pp. 45–54.

involving extensive nationalization, which had been worked out by Communist economists.[27] More important, because 'managing the crisis' could involve, under Socialist leadership, a policy of economic 'realism' of the sort favoured by the conventional economists influential in the Socialist Party (Delors, Attali, Rocard), it would threaten to disappoint Communist voters and thus jeopardize the Party's performance of its 'tribune role'.

All this might seem like yet another Communist excuse for hesitation between its various objectives. Since the time when the Communists first started seriously seeking to work with the non-Communist Left in the mid-1930s, there have been a number of celebrated examples of what might be called opportunities left unseized. Thorez in 1936 had spoken of the need 'to know when to end a strike'; in 1944 he had ordered the disbandment of the Communist militias; and at the time of the May events of 1968 it was decided that a revolutionary situation did not exist, and that the workers should return to work and settle for a pay rise. Thus the decision that 1978 was not an opportune time for the Communists to participate in government was of a piece with the Party's previous caution.

'Autonomy' and centrism

The impact on the Socialist Party of Communist behaviour from 1975 to 1978, which culminated in the 1978 election defeat was severe. Factional conflict in the Socialist Party in the 1970s was almost entirely taken up with differences in emphasis over the conduct of the alliance with the Communists. In 1978 Rocard led the way by arguing that the Communists were neither revolutionary nor pro-Soviet nor democratic, and simply did not want to win.[28] Rocard, though acknowledging that some sort of alliance with the PCF was necessary, given the Communist Party's large presence, argued for an 'autonomous' strategy. For two years after 1978 debate inside the Socialist Party—cloaking essentially a struggle for the 1981 presidential nomination between Mitterrand and Rocard—took place around Rocard's analysis (made at the

---

[27] See P. Boccara *et al.*, *Capitalisme monopole de l'État* (2 vols.), Éditions Sociales (Paris), 1976. [28] R. W. Johnson, op. cit., p. 253.

1977 Nantes Congress) of the cultural conflict within the French Left. He identified two cultures; the one Jacobin and centralist (incarnate in the Communist Party), the other pluralistic, decentralist, and *autogestionnaire*, represented by the Socialists. Behind Rocard's analysis—which was effectively rejected at the Metz Congress in 1979—lay the implication that the two parties were culturally too dissimilar; and to some it seemed that his recommended solution of an 'autonomous' Socialist position was a euphemism for a return to a third-force strategy, in short a proposal for succumbing to *la tentation centriste*.

Because the Socialist Party formally rejected third-force strategies at its 1971 congress, centrism was no longer taken to be a serious option. The case against centrism usually involved a negative analysis of the record of the governments in which the SFIO participated before 1958. Centrism had come to possess an exaggeratedly bad reputation—a spectre requiring to be exorcised at Socialist feasts. The third-force coalitions of the Fourth Republic were seen as wholly negative in achievement and dismissed in the word '*molletisme*'. Meanwhile Mollet himself goes unmentioned at party gatherings: there is a gap in the Socialist Panthéon where his effigy should stand. It is as if, to adapt Malraux, between Blum and Mitterrand there was nothing. Pierre Guidoni, a CERES deputy, alliteratively dismissed the SFIO's record in the Fourth Republic with the words: 'Suez, CRS et centrisme'.[29]

It is, however, difficult to see how the Party in those years, given the international and domestic complications of the period, could have done other than it did. Moreover it is untrue to suggest that the Party lost electorally because of its involvement in the centrist coalitions of 1947–58. The Socialist vote fell between 1946 (the last election during tripartism) and 1951 (the election which came at the end of the SFIO's first four-year period of 'third-force' government) by only 2.8 per cent. In 1956 is rose slightly and remained stable in 1958, after two and a half years more of centrist coalitions, including the eighteen months of Mollet's own government. This is a picture of stagnation, not of decline; whereas it was precisely during the period of tripartist government (Socialist plus Communist plus MRP: 1944–7)

[29] P. Guidoni, *Histoire du nouveau parti socialiste*, Tema Action (Paris), 1973.

that the Party's vote fell by 6.5 per cent between the election of 1945 and that of November 1946. It is thus clear that whilst the Socialist Party's performance in government with centrist allies in the late 1940s and 1950s was unpopular with Socialist activists (whose disaffection was shown in a persistent decline in membership), it did not significantly dismay the voters. Mollet was an acute political weathercock who reflected public opinion in his anti-communism, his tough policy on Algeria, and, not least, his support for de Gaulle in 1958. The dismissive references made to the SFIO of the Fourth Republic are those of the earnest party activist rather than of the objective observer. Nevertheless, after the mid-sixties the centrist option *à la quatrième* ceased to be available to the Party.

The party system that necessitated centrist coalitions disappeared by 1967, as the centrist parties with whom the SFIO collaborated (Radical, MRP, Independents) lost their voters to the Gaullists. Since 1967 the only election in which the Centre registered strongly was the presidential election of 1969, when the centrist, Poher, got through to the second ballot to confront Pompidou. Poher's candidacy, however, did as well as it did only because of the temporary vacuum existing in 1969 on the non-Communist Left, and his first-ballot vote of 23 per cent was unremarkable, given that it relied considerably on Socialist voters. After 1969 the Centre was drained by Pompidou, and again after 1974 by Giscard, with both Presidents incorporating centrist leaders into the presidential *majorité*. A centrist alliance option cannot exist for the Socialist Party unless the bipolarizing trends of the past twenty years are reversed.

The surprising election results of 1981 made all such deliberations superfluous. The Socialists won a majority of seats in the National Assembly, and did so after pursuing precisely the autonomous strategy that Rocard was castigated for advocating after 1978: running without a programmatic agreement with the PCF; ignoring Communist demands for a promise of ministerial posts; and bidding for the support of Communist voters over the heads of Communist leaders. A Socialist parliamentary majority in 1981 meant a secure Socialist administration for at least five years, with four rather minor ministerial bones thrown to a demoralized

Communist Party in order to restrict, at least for a while, its freedom of manoeuvre. The electoral basis of Socialist success must also be noted. The social group that moved most heavily from the Giscardian–Gaullist camp over to the Socialist was the professional and managerial one, 38 per cent of whose voters voted Socialist compared with only 15 per cent in 1978 (see Table 7.2). Adding also the 45 per cent of the large and expanding white-collar class that voted Socialist, it can be seen that the Party had the sort of middle-class support base not uncharacteristic of 'centrist' governments.

Social democracy

The governments of Mauroy and Fabius were those in which socialists of reformist, social democratic inclination predominated, and yet they did not, nor could they, openly espouse such an identity without inviting a torrent of Communist abuse and, it was assumed, provoking a threat to the industrial peace which Communist involvement in government was intended to secure. Here one reached the nub of the Socialist Party's deficiency: its lack of a trade unionized working class base.

Social democratic parties may be defined by reference to two distinguishing characteristics: first, a working-class base provided through organizational links with the trade-union movement; and secondly, a commitment to the constitutional status quo and rules of the game, a preparedness to govern, and usually an experience of government. The French Socialist Party does not comply with the first condition. Since the 1930s the Party has suffered from its lack of trade-union support, for this has meant that it lacks a mass membership, an effective organization, money, and most important, an industrial working-class clientele, without which it has had no serious representational function, and consequently little clout. The great upsurges of union pressure in 1936 and 1968 were movements over which the Party had no control. As Portelli has observed, Prime Minister Blum in 1936 was able to extract the Matignon Accords from the employers only after factory occupations and strikes organized by others.[30]

[30] H. Portelli, *Le Socialisme français tel qu'il est*, PUF (Paris), 1980, p. 169.

Gilles Martinet has pointed out that whilst the SFIO participated in coalition governments, even leading some of them,
the division of union strength and the balance of forces
created by this division never allowed the Party to appear as
the chief political expression of the labour movement.[31]

By the beginning of the 1980s Socialist trade unionists
were scattered across a number of union confederations and
not concentrated in one, as are Communist workers in the
CGT. The highest concentration of Socialist members is in
the FEN—the teachers' union confederation—which is, of
course, a middle-class organization. Socialist workers are
distributed across the CFDT, the FO, and the CGT. The CGT
is a Communist preserve. The FO is a conservative-inclined
organization, of anti-Communist and anti-clerical tradition,
and thus somewhat out of step with the present-day Socialist
Party. The CFDT is closer to the Socialist Party—it has a
Socialist leader, and many of its members joined the Party in
1974—but its leadership is strongly attached to radical causes,
such as *autogestion* (to which it sees the Socialist Party's
commitment as slight). Its membership, many of whom have
Catholic associations, are not at ease with the laicist elements
inside the PS. The possibility of the Socialist Party being able
to encourage an amalgamation of non-Communist-controlled
union federations into a broadly Socialist-inclined organization is remote. Apart from the traditional syndicalist posture
dating from the rejection of partisan links (at Amiens in
1906), there are conflicting interests and ideologies at stake
sufficiently important to resist unification. The attempt by
the PS in the 1970s to rival Communist shopfloor strength by
setting up *sections d'entreprises*—workplace branches—has
not succeeded either. About 1,000 existed, but they did little
to rival the Communist presence and were in any case not all
affiliated to the same union federation: half were in the CGT,
a third in the CFDT, and a few in the FO.[32]

Dissipation of Socialist union strength and the absence of
direct union–party links has reinforced in the Party the
other social democratic characteristic—the propensity to
govern and to seek office. Without a significant working-class
component the Party has been more influenced by middle-class

[31] G. Martinet, in M. Rocard, *Qu'est-ce que la social-démocratie?*, Seuil
(Paris), 1979, p. 68.   [32] H. Portelli, op. cit., p. 187.

leaders and activists than, say, the British Labour Party or the German SPD. As it was projected by structural imperatives towards government in the 1970s the Socialist Party developed a power of attraction for the politically ambitious Parisian intellectual middle-class *énarques* and *universitaires*—highly intelligent people of technocratic and élitist bent—who have little personal knowledge of working-class life or access to it. A party as top-heavy with these elements as the Socialist Party cuts itself off even further from the trade-union and working-class world. Thus, paradoxically, as the Party's eagerness and—given the calibre of its élitist leadership— competence to govern increases, its capacity to do so is impaired by its social exclusiveness.

The working class roots denied the Socialist Party have traditionally been in the control of the Communists. Each party thus possessed one of the traditional characteristics of a large mass social democratic party, and in declaring in 1980 that 'nothing will be accomplished in society without the renewed rallying together of the forces of labour and production',[33] Mitterrand was acknowledging what had long been seen as the veto power of the PCF–CGT. Equally the Communists, in order to retain control of a working class electorate, needed to respond to the deradicalizing nature and contracting size of that class: a self-consciously working class party requires self-consciously working class workers. Furthermore, to retain its representational function in work-ing class districts, not to mention the financial gains derived by the PCF from possession of municipal power, the Com-munist party had to keep in step with the Socialists in order to milk the best results from the electoral system. There existed, in short, a mutual dependence. Crucially, however, in the 1980s this balance of interest was disturbed by a sharp decline in Communist support both electorally and on the shop floor, so that, in 1986 only one in ten of all voters supported the PCF and only one in five blue collar workers. With such marginalisation of the Communist party, the Socialists had nothing to lose but their chains.

---

[33] F. Mitterrand, *Ici et maintenant*, p. 46.

8
Socialist Policy
1981–1986

French politics is remarkably introspective and theatrical. Analyses of voting intentions, by-election and election results, and an obsession with opinion polls all serve to elevate political life to the status of major spectacle. Conflict, victory, and defeat are the subjects of unremitting speculation on the part of political commentators. The focus is upon the form rather than upon the substance; strategy is exalted to the detriment of policy; the game of politics—who wins and who loses—takes precedence over its programmatic content.

This is not to say however, that the Socialist Party is the innocent victim of misrepresentation in the various media. In the French Socialist tradition—as in that of the French Left as a whole—the contributions that gain acclaim are those dealing with philosophical or, to a degree, strategic problems, and not those that focus on mere policy concerns. This meant that although the broad commitment to 'socialism' has been assumed for years, the particular nature of the policies envisaged were not fully propounded, or even considered. Blame for this lay largely with the style and content of Socialist debate: Socialist rhetoric relied heavily on a series of concepts and terms derived from Marxism. The political analyses that were the currency of Socialist debate were characterized by an excessive devotion to theory —a preference for intellectual frameworks and philosophical principles—and a declaratory, somewhat discursive type of oratory.

Nor were such tendencies much discouraged by the fact that the Party suffered after 1958 more than two decades of political powerlessness. Characteristically, opposition parties, especially those in permanent or continuous opposition, are inclined to cater more for the emotional satisfaction of their party workers than for more ordinary material satisfaction of the voters. It is perhaps somewhat surprising that this tendency had not itself been counteracted by the excessively electoral nature of the Fifth Republic with major national elections recurring virtually year on year. Such a process, it might be assumed, would have caused the Party to depart from its indulgence in theoretical, windy rhetoric. That it did not do so may be, in part, attributed to the strategic need to treat constantly with the Communist Party, an association requiring debate around theoretical questions rather than policy formulation. The active presence of the Communist Party, in effect, acted as a barrier to the Socialists openly embracing a north-European, policy-oriented, social democratic style.

In Chapter 7 it was seen that the Party in some significant respects—notably its social base—cannot be regarded as a conventional social democratic party. And yet its objectives, in reality, do effectively fall within the confines of a pluralistic social democratic tradition comprising a belief in the virtues of the mixed economy and of representative democracy. The 'radical' government elected by the French in 1981 was thus one that would not abolish the free market or reverse the country's traditional alliances. In many respects its objectives were comparable to those of the British Labour Party in 1964 and many of the measures proposed were ones that either had been promised by, or had miscarried under, previous conservative governments. Substantial elements of the Party's rank and file of course take seriously the commitment, formally enshrined in its declaration of principles, to be seen in some unspecified way a revolutionary party with an objective of 'breaking with capitalism', but in the hands of President Mitterrand and the moderate figures prevailing in the Socialist governments, such expressions are purely declaratory, serving to provide a certain ideological ballast of the sort supplied, in Britain, by Clause IV of the Labour Party's constitution.

Whatever its formal billing, the French Socialist Government's programme was reformist in essence.[1] A social democratic policy would be expected to lean heavily on Keynesian

---

[1] Daniel Blum *et al.*, *Histoire du réformisme en France depuis 1920*, Éditions Sociales (Paris), 1976, 2 vols. The opposite view—that the PS is socialist—can be found in *Socialisme à responsabilité limitée* by Jacques Rougeot, France Empire (Paris), 1981.

methods of regulating the economy, whilst paying particular attention to redistributive reforms.[2] Such was the approach of the 1981-6 governments. Likewise such a party, with a concern for pluralism, would be expected, in the context of the Fifth Republic, to pay special attention to loosening the grip of administrative control through the extension of legal rights and the decentralization of power. Whilst the Socialist Party made its main objective the reduction of unemployment through reflation, the decentralization measures were by no means seen as secondary.

But the 1981 victory was neither the victory of a radical form of socialism, nor, arguably, was it a victory for a radical policy. Unemployment, for example, and the voters' reaction to it, was only one contributory factor in Giscard's defeat. More important in ensuring the Socialist success in 1981 was the deradicalization of the Left accomplished through the substantial defeat of the Communist Party at the first ballot of the presidential elections. It was this marginalization of the Communists that provided the necessary reassurance for an electorate disillusioned after long years of conservative rule. Furthermore, in contrast to the famous Popular Front victory of 1936 there was in 1981 no comparably great influx of members into the Socialist Party or the unions: no evidence in fact of a strong commitment to radical change. (In 1936 SFIO membership doubled, but in 1981 Socialist Party membership increased by a mere five per cent.) It is against this background that an examination of Socialist policy in government must be set: the rest of this chapter discusses the broad strategy of the Socialist government as it developed in the five years until the electoral defeat of 1986.

Economic policy, 1981–1983

From 1981 to March 1983 French Socialist economic policy pursued the primary objective of reducing unemployment using Keynesian means, rather than the containment of inflation through monetary policy (as under Giscard). Although

---

[2] See H. Machin and V. Wright (eds) *Economic Policy and Policy-Making under the Mitterrand Presidency: 1981–84*, Pinter (London) 1985. Introduction.

this ran counter to the prevailing orthodoxy, the main intention of the policy was to increase demand and the first
eighteen months of Mitterrand's presidency constituted a
reflationary 'dash for growth'. Increasing demand would, it
was argued, increase investment, production, and profits and
spread labour costs over a greater volume of output. In order
to make this work, the Government had hoped to stabilize
the rise of real wages and maintain the competitiveness of
industry, a competitiveness severely compromised by the
initial refusal to devalue. Jacques Delors, the Finance
Minister, tried to control inflationary wage rises by lowering
expectations.[3] French salaries were indexed to inflation which
some believed, created, or at least did not restrain, wage-push
inflation. Thus the proposal was made to change the indexing
of salaries from the end of the quarter to the beginning, with
a compensatory top-up adjustment if the calculated rate of
inflation proved incorrect. However, the policy pursued in
the first two years did not lead to a fall in unemployment,
inflation remained higher than OECD averages, whilst a
second devaluation of the franc in June 1982 (after the first
in October 1981) led to a four-month wages-and-prices freeze
and after a third devaluation a much reduced projection of
government spending.

As is well known, the new government was originally more
worried about unemployment than about inflation, but its
intention was not to abandon the attack on inflation—rather
that control of prices had to be undertaken within the context of reducing inequalities and putting France 'back to
work'. From 1981 to 1983 the broad strategy to end inflation was to seek to reduce inequalities (and hence to restrain
wage push) with low interest loans (to encourage investment),
an increase in wages and benefits for the poorest, and the
whole resting on the assumption of faster growth. By contrast, although the Socialists envisaged the possibility of a
'flight of capital', no specific measures were foreseen to
deal with it. A few prices, however, were frozen when the
Government came to power and some price controls were
extended after the four-month freeze in 1982.

So far, so Keynesian, but Keynes was not a Socialist and
there were specifically social democratic (egalitarian and

---

[3] Jacques Delors, *Changer*, Stock (Paris), 1975, pp. 125–30.

redistributive) aspects to the French Socialist policy.[4] During the election campaigns of 1981 the Socialists denounced the Giscardian government's fatalistic approach to unemployment: this was the main battle of the new government, the reason for the 95-million budget deficit, and its own criterion of success.[5] The prime need was felt to be the increased expansion of the economy (which was zero in 1981), but other measures were to be taken in parallel: for example, the reduction of the working week and the lowering of the retirement age. In this initial priority the new Ministry of Solidarity was important, as it was created to co-ordinate social policy—bringing together everything that touches on social services, unemployment benefits, and state assistance and handling a massive budget which was financed from taxes on those in work and on employers, but was in considerable deficit because of the demands made on it by the 2 million or so unemployed.

The French system of social security, unlike the British, is not financed out of general taxation, but at 4.5 per cent of GNP it is the country's special 'second budget'. At the beginning of the presidential term deficits of some size existed.[6] To bring in the money to pay for social security a levy on workers and business is pooled and paid out to claimants. This levy amounts to a third of the French employers' wage bill. Consequently, as the number of unemployed increases, so does the burden on other people, and a reform of the system was felt to be imperative. The right to welfare, as Solidarity Minister Nicole Questiaux commented, 'is not a matter of balance sheets', but nevertheless the Government became seriously worried about the deficits of the various public social-security organizations in the autumn of 1981, and in June 1982 Mme Questiaux was replaced by a more cost-conscious minister. The Government sought initially to appeal to a sense of 'national solidarity' and increased

---

[4] Anthony Crosland, *The Future of Socialism*, Cape (London), 1964, pp. 123 ff., and also Raymond Plant, 'Democratic Socialism and Equality', in David Lispey and Dick Leonard, eds., *The Socialist Agenda*, Cape (London), 1981 ch. 8, pp. 135-55.

[5] Prime Minister's 'Address to the National Assembly', Matignon press office, 8 July 1981. See also Pascal Petit, 'Reflation and Industrial Policy in France', *Cambridge Economic Policy Review*, April 1981, pp. 27-32.

[6] Vincent Merle, 'Politique de l'emploi', *Esprit*, Oct.-Nov. 1981, pp. 37-40.

payments to the social-security fund from workers, civil servants, and, despite the Finance Ministry, from business. These contributions were intended to dispose of the 33-billion-franc social security deficit, but in order to avoid 'punishing' small firms the Government took more from the big industries with high wage bills, exempted small industries to some extent, and contemplated a reform of the whole system, which would include various economies and an attack on 'waste'.

Mitterrand's election programme proposed an increase in the minimum wage (SMIC), an eventual reduction of the working week to thirty-five hours, the creation of 150,000 public sector jobs, a reduction of charges to businesses, and in-service training programmes. The Government also decided on the creation of 65,000 jobs in the postal service and in education and 37,500 additional civil-service posts, and hoped to use expansion of the public sector in general to soak up unemployment. Other measures were introduced concerning the rights of workers, the reform of employers' rights, and the reduction of the working week to thirty-nine hours, a fifth week of paid holiday, and early retirement schemes. Given the problems of technology which suggest a reduced need for labour, the Government added two corollaries to simple early retirement; increased use of plant and negotiated compensation for job losses. But, according to Nicole Questiaux, three early retirements produced one job; the same may have been true of the shortened week. Unions, however, were mostly dubious about early retirement, introduced without much regard to its impact on wage-costs: the CFDT believed that it would bring little and cost much. The right to retire at sixty with a full pension came into force in April 1983, though not all the 360,000 entitled to benefit chose to do so.

The Communist Minister of Health, Jack Ralite, was also involved in a new series of measures, encouraging France on its way towards a north-European 'welfare state' with the abolition of some prescription charges, an effort to supply wider health care, and an assault on private provision in public hospitals (a measure which provoked anger amongst doctors). The Government put 'preventive' medicine at the head of the list of priorities, created 2,000 jobs in 140 hospitals, provided equipment for researchers, reaffirmed workers' rights in the health services, and decentralized hospital administration. However the postponement of decisions on the very old problems of over-recruitment of medical students and the reform of doctors' careers stoked up resentments which burst out in the form of near-riots in 1983.

Energy policy was an issue over which Giscard's crash nuclear programme had met ecological and CFDT (though not CGT) resistance. The new government temporarily froze the power-station constructions at Le Pellerin, Chooz, Civaux, Golfech, and Cattenom 3 and 4, abandoned nuclear-waste dumping at Saint-Priest-la-Prugne; investment in coal and gas was initially increased though it was subsequently cut back sharply. For the CFDT and the ecologists the freeze on construction was not enough, because nothing much had been started on these sites. The Government also dropped the idea of a referendum on the nuclear issue and on local control of planning decisions. Meanwhile Research Minister Chevènement and the CGT saw ecological policy as mortgaging the country's future energy independence and creating unemployment. These forces came into conflict over the Hague nuclear-waste-reprocessing plant in Brittany, which was claimed to be essential, because it would render France the only country capable of dealing with the entire nuclear cycle. Since the scheme was already paid for, it went ahead despite protests. The Super-Phénix reactor posed similar problems: there were pressures both for the extension of this method and for a pause in decision-making on the issue. The main Socialist innovation was increased research into new energy resources. Ecologists, in any case a declining force, were bitterly disappointed by this policy, as it evolved, because the Party had appeared to promise something rather different from a continuation of the nuclear programme.

Mitterrand's election programme placed great emphasis on the need for a white-hot technological revolution generated through basic research. Investment in research was originally intended to increase to 80 billion francs by 1985, the equivalent of 2.5 per cent of GNP compared with about 1.8 per cent during Giscard's presidency. Chevènement, as Minister of Research, was delegated to co-ordinate research development, to divert funds to competitive industries, and to organize a national scientific debate on research priorities, but his liking for *dirigiste* policies brought him into conflict both with industry and with other government ministers. Chevènement had made his acceptance of this seemingly apolitical ministry conditional on control over all ministerial research budgets but this was difficult to put into effect, and the ministry's scope was not entirely clear. Despite the fact that technological research was one of Mitterrand's particular interests, Chevènement's interventionist approach and his unwillingness to tackle the restructuring of declining industries (such as steel) led to his departure in the reshuffle in March 1983.

Laurent Fabius, who took Chevènement's place, in the 1983-4 government, was still committed to these ambitious research objectives but by the time he had become Prime Minister the momentum had slowed. Nevertheless the promise to increase the research budget was kept: it rose by 8.9% over the legislature. Industrial and basic research were promoted and the programme enabled France to move up to fourth place in the OECD's ranking of research expenditure. Mitterrand's idea for a co-ordinated European research programme (Eureka) also had some initial success. However, other more specific objectives which the Socialists had set for research were not quite attained: only 2.3% of GNP was devoted to research in 1986 (not 2.5% as promised), not as many new posts were created as planned and the job mobility of researchers was not increased.

In industrial policy the Government was initially forced to take rapid *ad hoc* decisions to deal with collapsing enterprises in textiles (such as Boussac-Saint-Frères), machine tools, linen, etc., at the same time as it was trying to formulate a long-term strategy. However, machine-tool industries were examined in order to find 'centres of excellence' on which to concentrate (350 million francs were invested); and in paper-making the difficulties of Chapelle-Darbly in the north forced the same kind of rationalization—regrouping and regional specialization. But for small industries the situation was more delicate: because the Government hoped to use them to end unemployment, measures—such as the easing of credit—were taken quickly to ensure their health. It had been intended to create a giant Ministry of Research and Industry

modelled on the Japanese Ministry of Industry and Technology which was reckoned to have played a major part in
post-war recovery. Mitterrand noted that electronics were to
be 'our weapon for the future' and a big investment of (140
billion francs in five years) was implemented in that area.
The main companies were state owned (50 per cent of manu-
facture and 90 per cent of research) and a 3-9 per cent
growth rate was projected. In addition to this banks were
instructed to direct half their profit for 1981-2 into the loss-
making steel industry, and the Industry Ministry scheduled a
restructuring of the chemical industry to concentrate production into three nationalized groups. As Industry Minister
Fabius, did not increase the interventionist aspects of industrial policy (nor would his government after 1984 direct
capital or augment the subsidies for 'lame duck' businesses).

Many of the Socialist government's measures were insti-
tuted to press home the egalitarianism of the party programme.[7] These concerned taxation in particular, but also
education, housing, culture, health, and many other areas.
Giscard had been unable to pass an effective wealth tax
through a reluctant Assembly, but the Socialists had both
more determination and a favourable parliamentary majority.
A comprehensive tax reform was undertaken from 1981-6 and
the budget for 1982 had introduced a wealth tax, albeit one
exempting (as a result of industrial protests supported by
Delors) art and business assets. The Government also ended
the anonymity of gold transactions (25 per cent of the gold
in France is in private hands). Wealth taxes were started at
a level of about 3 million francs and were progressive. They
affected some 200,000 households and brought in an estimated 5-8 billion francs (1 per cent of state receipts).

Socialist attitudes to the economy should not have come
as a shock to business, for they were well known and had
been suitably publicized.[9] Nevertheless business fears seem
to have led Finance Minister Delors to call for a 'pause' in
the rate of reform in November 1981, thus fatefully echoing
Léon Blum as the Popular Front Government ran into trouble

[7] This is extensively mocked in F. Aftalion, *Socialisme et économie*, PUF
(Paris), 1978, Ch. V, pp. 86-114. [8] *Le Matin*, 3 Sept. 1981.
[9] Jean Boissonnat, *Les Socialistes face aux patrons*, Flammarion (Paris), 1977,
esp. Ch. 4 by Jacques Delors, 'Pour une véritable politique de l'emploi'.

in 1937. (This call was supported by others in the Party, although not by the President.) In 1977 when the Socialist Party seemed to be on the brink of power, a conference had been organized to demonstrate Socialist friendliness towards business, and the 1981-3 policy accurately reflected the reflationary stance. But reflation in the teeth of international monetarism was always a gamble. World demand could not be guaranteed, and this the Mauroy government appeared to recognize in its various diplomatic initiatives to reactivate expansion. Reflation also involved the dangerous tendency to suck in imports at the same time as other countries were cutting real wages, and hence effective demand, within their own economies.[10] This international deflation would have posed a threat to the French balance of payments even if the government had been able to maintain output—something which it proved unable to do.

The U-turn of March 1983

By the end of the first year, after two currency devaluations within eight months, the Government's economic strategy already looked somewhat battered. The first devaluation in October 1981 was largely a result of the over-valuation of the currency by the Giscard–Barre government which had used a high-value franc as a means of keeping down inflation. But the second devaluation, at the end of June 1982, was more complicated. Inflation during 1981-2, at 14 per cent, whilst comparing favourably with the previous year, contrasted unfavourably with falling inflation rates elsewhere, and particularly in France's partners in the European Monetary System (EMS)—the West German inflation rate, for example, was 5 per cent. A deterioration in French competitiveness over the year was therefore marked. Finance Minister Delors and Prime Minister Mauroy blamed this situation on the failure of the world economy to emerge from its stagnation, on lack of investment in France, and on particularly high US interest rates. But there were also tacitly recognized government failings mirrored in a shift in policy to re-emphasize the need to fight inflation, and it was this that implied a reversal in policy. The Government decided in June 1982 to

[10] *Le Monde*, 9 Jan. 1981.

control spending more carefully and to impose a wages-and-prices freeze for four months to break inflationary expectations. With the aim of reducing inflation to single figures, a package was put together to cut the budget deficit by 20 per cent and to cut spending by 20,000 million francs which, with extra savings made on social security, was intended to lower the growth of money supply from 16 to 13 per cent. The social-security cuts were the occasion for the departure from the Government of Nicole Questiaux who had become identified as a big spender (although there were other reasons too for her leaving office). Her replacement, Pierre Bérégovoy, could be relied upon, as a very close aide of Mitterrand and having spent the first year of government running the presidential secretariat, to rein in the social-security budget. A further contributory factor to the change of course and devaluation in mid-1982 was the Government's maladministration of the reduction of the working week: the introduction of an additional week's holiday without loss of pay became a policy for shedding labour rather than of job-sharing, as was the original intention.

Economic growth in 1981–2 at about 2 per cent was short of the expected 3.3 per cent and unemployment remained obstinately around 2 million (7 per cent). Meanwhile the balance of payments deteriorated as imports were sucked in and inflation did not fall at the expected rate. Thus, after the 'go' policy of the first two years, came the 'stop' of March 1983, imposed—after weeks of hesitation—by Mitterrand. Finance Minister Delors negotiated a 2.5-per-cent devaluation of the franc within the EMS and, as a *quid pro quo* for European support, the Government introduced a deflationary package. The ten-point package, designed to deal with the 90-billion-franc trade deficit in two years, included forced loans from all but the lowest wage earners, increased social-security contributions, introduced higher charges for telephones, gas, electricity, drink, and cigarettes, and imposed foreign currency restrictions. Government spending was also restricted (although the budget deficit was then maintained at 3 per cent), state enterprises reduced their vast deficits, and there were hints of protectionism. Mauroy's confirmation as Prime Minister, but with a slimmer 'war cabinet' to apply these measures, was an implicit rebuff to his earlier bullish views that the economy was 'on course'. It is difficult to see what else the Government could have done, given the international constraints on the French economy and the need for European co-operation: the Mauroy government had to go along with the measures its EMS partners demanded. It was left to the Government to apply a real 'U-turn' in the teeth of union opinion and to rebuild its reserves in a hostile world environment. As it was, there remained, even on the Government's optimistic assumptions, a gap between French and German inflation rates and a large trade deficit which still had to be financed.

Nationalization

To a large extent the passage of the Nationalization Bill was meant to show the Government's commitment to deep-seated change and it was used to argue that French Socialism differs from social democracy.[11] Despite an objection from the Constitutional Council, which ruled that the proposed compensation for owners was inadequate, the Nationalization Bill had been passed by mid-1982.[12] The effect of the measures was to bring industries employing 845,000 people into state ownership along with thirty-six banks. As a result, about 16 per cent of French GNP would now be produced by public enterprises.

The industries nationalized were: Rhône–Poulenc (chemicals), Thomson–Brandt (electronics), Pechiney–Ugine–Kuhlmann (metals), Saint-Gobain–Pont-à-Mousson, Compagnie Générale d'Électricité (all these from the Common Programme), Usinor and Sacilor (steel), Dassault, and Matra (space and arms branches) plus thirty-six banks and insurance companies (excluding small, foreign, and co-operative banks and finance companies), which brought much French

[11] François Fejtö, *La Social-démocratie quand même*, Laffont (Paris), 1980, and B. Manin and A. Bergounioux, *La Social-démocratie ou le compromis*, PUF (Paris), 1979, pp. 153–93.
[12] The Assembly passed the nationalization bill, but only after it had been referred back by the Constitutional Council; see *Le Monde*, 19 Jan. 1982.

banking into the state sector with only some sixty-five small banks remaining 'independent'. Although nationalization was rapidly pushed through the Assembly, the rationale for these measures was never entirely clear, nor was their future role and operation. Nationalization originally featured in the Socialist programme essentially as the price of Communist support, but it seemed unlikely to transform the mixed economy into a socialist one. The lack of prior thought given to the running of these industries indicated the tactical, rather than fundamental, reasons for the take-overs.[13] For example, in the much-cited case of Renault, management is free to act as it thinks best without civil-service or political interference (though subject to the test of cost efficiency). Renault hardly differs from private industry and ultimate ownership matters little in its case. As a model for public sector innovation the Renault company was unexciting, for there was little government interference in the running of the firm, and it was not insignificant that the first Socialist Industry minister was the former Renault head, Pierre Dreyfus. The nationalization programme was essentially political in origin and only in the event was it turned into a means of industrial restructuring, or rationalization through nationalization.[14]

Internal management of the nationalized industries posed another problem when the Government came under attack for 'statism' from Edmond Maire, head of the CFDT. This reflected the worry that the trade unions (particularly the pro-Socialist ones interested in *autogestion*) were not going to be given an adequate position in the new power structure. One of the dilemmas faced by Minister Jean Le Garrec (responsible for nationalization policy) was how to give workers a say in these industries without handing power to the Communist CGT. The solution was to introduce direct elections to cut out union intermediaries, but workers' representatives were promised considerable weight in the committees, something which prompted a struggle for power between unions.

[13] See Chapter 4.
[14] For further discussion see R. Holton, 'Industrial Politics in France: Nationalization under Mitterrand', *West European Politics*, January 1986, pp. 67–80.

The Plan

To many observers the Plan sets the French economy in a category apart from both the capitalist economies and the Russian-style Gosplan.[15] The Socialists were committed to a revitalization of the Plan after its conspicuous neglect by Giscard and Barre. In Mauroy's 1981–3 government Michel Rocard was Minister for the Plan (with Ministre d'État status) and an interim so-called mini-plan was introduced for 1982–3 to bridge the gap between the arrival of the Socialists and the next five-year plan. However, in this area, as in others, the exact nature of the changes envisaged was unclear and, notwithstanding Socialist Party publications on the subject, neither the practice of planning nor its relationship to self-management was mapped out beforehand.[16]

There are a number of theoretically useful tasks that the Plan could perform in an economy of the free-market type, but the Socialist Government did not seem to see it carrying out any of these tasks.[17] Moreover it was intended to make public choices explicit by bringing diverse and scattered choices made in different parts of the Government to the notice of the ministries concerned. It also played the role of co-ordinator, much needed in any bureaucracy, although in the Socialist Government, the Prime Minister's office claimed this particular role. In effect, the Plan has been limited to the detailed exposition of the economic policy already decided upon by the Government and to providing a further rationale for the Government's strategy as decided by the Prime Minister and the Ministry of Finance, although the provision of information was still the Plan's principal role.

Thus the essentially expository role of the Plan remains its primary function despite reorganization under the leadership of Hubert Prévot (of the CFDT). DATAR, the regional planning office, was amalgamated with the Plan and the establishment increased contacts with all the ministries at that time associated

[15] See Peter Holmes and Saul Estrin, 'The Performance of French Economic Planning 1952-1978', Southampton University Economics Department, Discussion Paper No. 8008 January 1980; and S. Estrin and P. Holmes, *French Economic Planning in Theory and Practice*, Allen & Unwin (London), 1982.

[16] This is despite the 'Quinze thèses sur l'autogestion', *Le Poing et la rose*, 1975.

[17] M.Schonfield, *Modern Capitalism*, Oxford University Press (London), 1965, Ch. VII.

with the Plan's work. Regional planning was reinvigorated through a systematic census of local needs by local authorities who set out their resources and their hopes, to be studied by Plan experts and ministry representatives.[18] However, the Force Ouvrière and the business confederation, the CNPF, felt it necessary to add an appendix to disassociate themselves from the 'Socialist' plans, just as the CGT and CFDT had distanced themselves from Giscard's plans. Reorganization of the Plan did not, therefore, make for appreciably greater industrial consensus than under previous regimes. Moreover, further reorganization replaced the Plan's specific public spending targets and an inter-ministerial committee was set up to monitor the development of the Plan particularly in the weaker sectors of the economy.

Michel Rocard's interim plan, published in October 1981 was above all the expression of an 'ardent obligation', and set out the Government's social and economic strategy. Although it went into considerable detail in some sectors it did not tackle or try to suggest solutions to undecided issues such as those of failing and backward industries.[19] The interim plan set out Socialists' hopes for the future direction of the economy and identified areas where some decisions had yet to be taken—on workers' control for example—but it remained an indicative plan with no binding force on the contracting parties. When Michel Rocard was moved to Agriculture in 1983 an important political prop was removed and the Plan slipped onto the sidelines although it remained an important way of publicizing economic action.

Foreign policy

The Fifth Republic is virtually synonymous with an active foreign policy and, like previous presidents, François Mitterrand almost made it a virtually 'reserved domain'. Futhermore, like de Gaulle, he had a *'grand dessein'*, albeit a Socialist one.[20] Socialist foreign policy was intended to combine Atlantic solidarity, a new Europeanism, a contribution to North–South dialogue, a rejection of indiscriminate

---

[18] *Les Socialistes face aux patrons*, Ch. 6.   [19] *Le Matin*, 2 Nov. 1981.
[20] Richard Gombin, 'Le Parti socialiste et la politique étrangère', in *Politique étrangère* (Paris), 1977, No. 2, pp. 199–212.

arms sales, a concern for political refugees and an increased 'cultural role' for France, particularly in the Third World.[21] Morally commendable as some of these goals were, they were unattainable with French resources. Hence the constant tension in French foreign policy between ambitious principles and restricted means continued.

Mitterrand departed from previous Fifth Republic precedent by developing a new firmness towards the USSR whilst cultivating Atlantic links, something not widely foreseen before the 1981 elections.[22] Socialist diplomats made Bonn and Washington their first targets with the intention of reassuring allies on France's place within the Atlantic Alliance. On 24 May 1981 Mitterrand was visited by Chancellor Schmidt. A few days later Foreign Minister Cheysson went to Bonn and then the United States to prepare for the visit of Vice-President Bush to Paris.[23] In contrast to Giscard d'Estaing, Socialist diplomats argued that negotiations on the withdrawal of Russian SS20 missiles had to be achieved through the installation of Pershing and Cruise missiles by America in Europe if need be, a course which Mitterrand urged on Schmidt against the protests of the SPD's left wing. France, not being a NATO member, would not have to accept American missiles, but the Russian SS20s posed a threat to France which she could not combat alone. Withdrawal, as a result of super-power negotiations, would have been a valuable aid to an independent policy.

But Socialist foreign policy did not mean a loss of independence *vis-à-vis* the United States and a clash quickly came over Third World issues: the Socialists disapproving of the American preference, as they saw it, for corrupt regimes over those with reformist or left-wing tinges. Mitterrand said without extravagant novelty: 'It is the misery and exploitation of these [Latin American] countries under the political domination of merciless dictatorships, that sparks off revolutions when the western world appears as an enemy on account of its support for oligarchies. I should like to break that logical chain. That is France's policy'.[24] This

[21] 'Tiers-Mondisme? Atlantisme?', *Esprit*, No. 58-9, 1981, pp. 69-80.
[22] Simon Serafty (ed.), *The Foreign Policies of the French Left*, Westview Press (Colorado), 1979, Ch. 1, pp. 1-20.
[23] *Le Nouvel Économiste*, Paris, No. 304, 28 Sept. 1981.
[24] *Le Figaro*, 3 Aug. 1981.

implicit criticism of the United States and the *simpliste* Reaganite vision of the world in terms of Communism and anti-Communism was underlined when Mitterrand declared that friendship towards the Americans would not lead him to support all the dictatorships in the world that happen to be supported by the USA. The French government believed that the Sandanista regime in Nicaragua should have been helped (with arms amongst other aid) by the Europeans, to avoid the American mistake over Cuba and to encourage democratic development. Likewise the Socialists wished to aid Costa Rica (to remain democratic), and Honduras (to enable it to move towards democracy) and publicly supported the El Salvador guerrilla movement. All this was within a zone regarded by the United States as its own backyard and was an affront to Reagan's policy of cutting economic aid to Honduras whilst giving it to the military regime in El Salvador.

Limits to the Franco-American 'rapprochement' were further underscored in 1982 over the issues of the Russian gas pipeline and international economic policy. The Government was particularly angry at the American attempt to prevent French branches of US companies exporting machinery for the Siberian gas pipeline. Cheysson maintained that America could have cut grain exports and that the policy forced on France (which would cost jobs) would be ineffective; the French view was that American action was high-handed. Mitterrand was also disappointed by the results of the Versailles summit of July 1982 where it was believed that joint action on interest rates—a particular target for the Socialist government—had been agreed. Similar problems were raised by Reagan's threats to limit European steel exports to the US. On this, as on the other issues, France worked for a united European response. However, Mitterrand maintained an attitude critical of the USSR and, although it found itself in increasing differences with the Reagan administration, the Government hosted a meeting of Nato Ministers in Paris in 1983—the first since 1966.

The Socialist government also declared itself in favour of a 'new international order', increased North–South understanding, and had increased aid to 0.6 per cent of GNP by 1986. In September 1981 UNCTAD held a North–South conference in Paris at which Mitterrand made the opening speech. He noted the growing gap between rich and poor and argued that help to the Third World was in effect help for industrial countries to overcome the crisis. French spokesmen expressed their opposition to bilateral, and their preference for multi-lateral, aid, and argued that the Third World should define its own objectives so that aid donors did not impose a view on recipients. There were other areas where the new French Socialist diplomacy came into conflict with 'Reaganism', but the Third World and Latin America were the most obvious. These clashes arose from a different, less manichean, view of the world and a different international economic policy. However, the lack of change, and in particular the Government's tolerance of human rights violations in French Africa, led to the resignation of J.-P. Cot, Minister for Co-operation and Development, who, like many others, was exasperated by the continuing close relations fostered with the regimes of Francophone Africa.

In defence too, there was continuity: the Socialist government started neutron-bomb development and continued the nuclear-submarine programme, planning to build one more. Over the last few years Socialist defence policy had evolved rapidly. The 1972 Common Programme envisaged the abolition of the French nuclear-weapons system—the *force de frappe*—and the destruction of weapons stocks. However, in 1977 the Communist Party suddenly decided to accept the independent deterrent and the Socialist Party was then obliged to come round to this view if it wished to maintain the Left alliance. Thus the Socialists eventually accepted the French nuclear deterrent,[25] the groups most insistent on the retention of the *force de frappe* being CERES and the new Defence Minister Hernu. Although the French deterrent is minor compared to super-power arsenals, the memory of the war and the political pressure of nationalist opinion meant that policy on this issue did not change.

The new government prepared to develop the neutron bomb as a continuation of, as Mauroy said, 'de Gaulle's policy of military independence' whilst remaining faithful to allies, with the 'United States in the first rank'. Mauroy made it clear that the nuclear policy was a counter-city strategy

[25] *Le Monde*, 31 Dec. 1981.

and that if the American strategy of graduated response was accepted, Europe could become a mere rung on the ladder of escalation policy—a location for a super-power battle rather than the primary consideration in defence policy. For this reason the government was prepared to build a neutron bomb which it was argued could increase the capacity of both French and European deterrence policy. Public opinion in France was not much affected by the European nuclear-disarmament sentiment evident elsewhere. The Communist Party was an exception to this, but Communist campaigns focused exclusively on American policy and had little resonance outside PCF circles. Although French defence policy could only make sense inside NATO and although integration with the Atlantic Alliance was taken more seriously by the Socialists, there was no pressure for France to rejoin the military alliance.

High principles also came into question in the field of arms sales—a 65-billion-franc industry employing 300,000. To what extent was the former arms sales policy being changed and could France afford to sell arms only to those countries that respect human rights? The Mauroy government did not, it said, intend to provide arms to world tension areas such as Guatemala although it showed day-to-day pragmatism about arms sales in general. In the end the policy was not examined and the morality of arms sales was rarely taken into account; in particular the competition in sales with Britain, Italy, Brazil, Taiwan, and Indonesia was not to be slackened. The nationalization of the Matra and Thomson-CSF arms firms did not, according to the Government, increase uncertainty for clients: on the contrary, the State guaranteed the 'made in France' label. Arms sales policy was from 1981-6 at the declaratory level and, despite strong words, the pressure to change to a moralistic policy was weak.

The Socialist government seemed aware that in some areas France alone could make only a limited impact: hence the Government's attempt to create a European consensus on reflation, cruise missiles, Atlantic policy, etc. In the European arena the Socialist Party had long desired to 'get Europe moving again'. Mitterrand's first Community policy-making initiative came at the end of June 1981 with proposals for a European-wide stimulation of growth through increased public

demand. The proposals had four aspects: (i) to help key industrial sectors through Community or joint-European loans,
(ii) to increase efforts to give computer and technological
research and energy-saving industries a European dimension,
(iii) to create concerted European-wide economic policies,
and (iv) to move more rapidly towards European-wide reduc-
tions of the working week and changed working conditions.
There were also proposals for a common approach to the
United States about its high interest rates, proposals to deal
with the closed Japanese market, and suggested North–
South initiatives. The French approach underlined the
'priority of priorities', the fight against unemployment,
something which ran counter to the approach of other EEC
states and which thus stood little chance of implementation.
(It was viewed even less charitably after the resignation of
the SPD's Chancellor Schmidt and the election of the conservative Kohl.) The same went for the French hope of a
general European reflation and North–South policy: whilst
Schmidt came round to Mitterrand's side at the Ottawa
summit in July 1981 against Reagan's monetarism, no common European view emerged. French protectionism in
certain areas, until 1983, remained a possibility, but measures
under this heading were not at all extensive despite Trade
Minister Michel Jobert's spectacular 'non-tariff' barrier
(a re-routing of video electronic appliances through a small
customs post at Poitiers) on some Japanese imports in
late 1982.

Mitterrand had made it clear at a meeting with Chancellor
Schmidt in July 1981 that a new series of French proposals
for the EEC would be tabled. These came in October and,
although they were conservative about much of the common agricultural policy, they attempted to breathe new
life into the EEC and its unemployment, industrial, regional,
energy, and social policies. André Chandernagor, the staunchly
pro-EEC Minister for European Affairs, accepted a change
in the price system to discourage over-production by large
farms, but there was no question of a concession to the
British idea of fairness—the *juste retour*. The Government
took up Mitterrand's four points and tried to use them to
combat unemployment through EEC borrowing to finance
investment, an extension of the European Monetary System,

a European economic policy, and community protection extended over agricultural and some other products. Through greater use of the European Social Fund the Socialists tried to help medium and small sized firms to create jobs and reduce working hours. They had hoped to increase consultation with labour, to increase worker participation, and to remove obstacles to the expansion of new technological industries through co-operative research, energy development, and Community expansion. The Government was not, however, able to push the European Community in these directions.

In European Community matters, as in others, the government's original high principles were eventually considerably watered down. The original intention to seek an understanding with Britain, for example, gave way to the re-establishment of the Franco-German special relationship. Likewise in African affairs, the close relationship with 'Francophonie' continued and it was difficult to detect change, notably in respect of the French intervention in Chad. Whereas Giscard had been reluctant to commit France to what could be a very long-term support for Chad against Libyan encroachments, the Socialist government was unable to resist a similar appeal and sent troops. This, operation 'Manta', was in fact circumspect, avoiding direct engagements and merely protecting areas over which the Chad government retained authority.

The Socialist's early imposition of a distinctive voice in foreign policy, which included a break in the Vth Republic's closer relations with Russia and support for the deployment of Cruise and Pershing missiles, was more a continuation of established objectives in a different form than anything specifically Socialist. The determination to continue nuclear testing in the Pacific was the major element in the sinking of the Greenpeace ship 'Rainbow Warrior' in Auckland harbour in 1985: Greenpeace had intended sailing into the exclusion zone to prevent further testing. Charles Hernu, the Defence Minister, resigned over the affair but his popularity was raised to unprecedented heights by it.

Mitterrand, like de Gaulle, had an exalted view of France's place in the world, but the tension between this vision and the relative poverty of resources meant that foreign policy was continuously over-reaching itself. The Socialists discovered that France was not able to influence world affairs in isolation, but sometimes continued to act as if it could.

Civil liberties

The Socialists were particularly insistent on the human rights aspect of their programme, a desire underlined by the appointment of the liberal Robert Badinter as Justice Minister. The 'new citizenship' of Socialist France, to use Pierre Mauroy's phrase, involved the promise to repeal several much-disliked laws and to ensure the guarantee of immigrant rights. The Socialists had serious objections to the 'Security and Liberty' Law of February 1981 (introduced by Giscard's Minister of Justice Alain Peyrefitte) which was intended to clamp down on street crime and contained numerous stringent provisions including extensive stop-and-search powers for the police. As an expression of a distinctly liberal approach Mitterrand, in one of his first acts as President, invoked clemency for a condemned murderer, and the abolition of capital punishment followed quickly.

Mitterrand promised that judicial independence would be ensured, that there would be a prison amnesty and that Peyrefitte's 'exceptional' measures would be ended (so that criminal charges would go before ordinary assize courts). Under Peyrefitte the prison population expanded to 40,000 (an increase of 33 per cent in two years), but by August 1981 it was down to 31,500, because in addition to the usual categories of amnesty there was the releasing of press-law breakers, permit breakers, those accused of state-security infringements, and imprisoned trade unionists. These generosities were not popular with public opinion and by 1986, chiefly under the impulse of Defferre and Joxe, the prison population had risen to 47,000.

As far as law reform was concerned, it was expected to take a legislative term to see Socialist good intentions come into effect because of the long process involved in drafting laws. Even the Peyrefitte Law could not simply be repealed: the penal parts dealing with habitual criminals, remission, and penalties were to be abolished, but the code of procedure would have to be rewritten, to which end the Léauté Committee was set up. Moreover, divisions over law-and-order policy came to the surface in the spring of 1982 with disagreements between the liberal Justice Minister, Badinter, and the Interior (i.e. Police) Minister, Defferre. The Socialist government had hoped to make France more hospitable to political refugees. This policy led to difficulties with the Spanish government (over Basque terrorism) and was severely tested by an outbreak of terrorism in 1982. After twenty deaths in four months and after an attack on a Jewish restaurant in August 1982 on top of persistent terrorist acts carried out by Corsican separatists there was a security clamp-down, and a Junior Minister for Public Security was appointed—Joseph Franceschi, himself a Corsican by ancestry.

François Autain, the Minister for Immigrant Workers, never had much room for manoeuvre, but he nevertheless sought to end the twilight world of immigration law. There was a need to regularize the position of many immigrants (some 200,000 workers) though they were not enfranchised for the 1983 local elections, as was once expected, and measures of immigration control were actually tightened. Three principal measures were taken in this latter area: a number of clandestine immigrants already in France were given legal status, but frontier controls were stepped up and the number of entry visas was to be restricted (except for families), and associated problems of education and culture were examined with the relevant home country. There was also increased government help for professional training. A further aspect of the Socialist government's civil liberties activity was the creation of the Ministry for Women's Rights run by Yvette Roudy. The Ministry, despite its small budget, kept up a constant pressure for egalitarian legislation.

The question of liberties arose also in the field of education where the Socialists were committed to the integration by consent into the state system of all, mostly Church-run, private schools. The issue of Church schools (*écoles libres*) had long ceased to be a burning issue on the Left, but a minority, strongly represented in the Socialist parliamentary group, half of whom were teachers, and in the pro-Socialist teachers' union, the FEN, persisted in gnawing at the issue, and in 1981 Mitterrand's campaign platform had included a commitment to a 'unified and secular' school system. Alain Savary, Minister of Education from 1981 to 1984 sought to achieve this in such a way as to retain state aid to private institutions and to maintain the 'plurality' of schools; he sought to balance the competing claims of teachers' unions, private school parents and the Church hierarchy.[26] An acceptable compromise might indeed have been reached had not other factors intervened.

The confirmation of austerity as a permanent policy in 1983 led Socialist leaders to accelerate the integration of the schools system doubtless in the hope that anti-clericalism was an issue with which to raise morale and mobilise the Left; in the event it was the Right's mobilisation that brought thousands of people onto the streets to defend 'free schools' in the Spring of 1984 in some of the biggest demonstrations since the Liberation. For the Socialists this reaction had the doubly unfortunate effect of depriving them of their reputation as principal defenders of civil liberties and threatening considerable electoral damage in Catholic areas where large gains had been made in the 'seventies; whilst only 15 per cent of children attend private schools, in parts of the Catholic West the figure reaches 40 per cent. Thus, after the demonstrations Mitterrand abruptly back-tracked and disowned the Savary bill. The mishandling of this sensitive, if peripheral issue prompted the fall of the Mauroy government, the departure of Savary, and the end of Communist participation in government in July 1984. Although Mitterrand then tried to wrong-foot the Right by proposing a referendum on the question of whether there should be more referenda on civil rights issues, the political initiative was never thereafter really regained; the proposal for a referendum on referenda was, in the event, turned down by the Senate. The new Education Minister, Chevènement, returning to office with a wish to promote his presidential ambitions, devoted his time at the Ministry to public relations, reassuring parents about educational standards and stressing traditional values. Administration replaced ambition: much was made of the 360 educational priority zones (ZEPs) where a pupil-teacher ratio of 25:1 was envisaged and resources increased, but other

---

[26] Alain Savary *En Toute Liberté*, Hachette (Paris), 1985.

reforms were neither completed nor pushed with vigour. In other areas, such as higher education, where reforms involved the abolition of status distinctions between staff, reforming zeal upset the institutions concerned. Although in 1981 the Socialists had enjoyed strong support in the education sector for policies of reform, by 1986 both credibility and the opportunity to push through much needed change had been lost. Thus despite tackling problems, some of which had been on the agenda since 1968 (such as student representation in higher education), the Socialists paid a high price for their miscalculations.

It could, of course, be assumed that like education, culture would feature highly amongst the preoccupations of any French Socialist government. The Minister for Culture, Jack Lang, took this symbolic sector in hand, with an unprecedented increase in the budget and a strong emphasis on decentralization. The increase in funds did serve to benefit disfavoured regions and to enhance career prospects for those working on cultural projects in the provinces. In the decentralization laws (examined below) Article 61 devolved responsibility for culture to the communes, departments, and regions, although the responsibilities of local government were lightened in respect of certain current expenditures (museums, libraries, etc.). Jack Lang was, by 1986, one of the most popular of Socialist Ministers. Partially this popularity was a result of spectacular projects (including the Bastille Opera and the Louvre 'pyramid' as well as new libraries), and partially the result of an increased share of the budget in more major areas, such as cinema, theatre, and publishing. In particular a law facilitating tax free investment in the cinema industry was introduced. Lang was also a very effective publicist; his polemic against 'American cinema', for example, did not have much practical consequence, though it did attract headlines.[27] The general intention in the cultural sphere was to decentralize, to widen access, and to seek to improve the *cadre de vie* or lifestyle of the population. Thus, under a President concerned about cultural life, France once more appeared to have a cultural policy.

[27] See J.-F. Revel's polemic, *Grace de l'état*, Grasset (Paris), 1981, pp. 145 ff.

The Socialist impact on Fifth Republic institutions

Although left-wing condemnations of the Fifth Republic's institutions have been toned down over the last twenty years, there were still criticisms in 1981. Root-and-branch objections to the presidential system were no longer evident, but the Socialist Party had frequently and untiringly objected to the National Assembly's lack of an effective role and to the 'undemocratic' constraints of the system as operated by the Right. Nevertheless, Mitterrand stated in his inaugural speech in May 1981 that he intended to use presidential power 'to the fullest'. This power had, from 1981–6, a distinctly Gaullist flavour, with the President determining the overall lines of policy and the Government dealing with day-to-day application of the programme. Moreover the Socialist Party in the National Assembly of June 1981 so swamped all other parties that the problem of respect for the parliamentary opposition, to which the Party had always drawn attention, became somewhat academic.

As far as relations between President and Prime Minister are concerned the 'super-presidentialism' of the Giscard years, which saw, at least from 1974 to 1976, the development of an active and minutely interventionist presidency and which pushed the Prime Minister to the sidelines, was not reproduced.[28] Although the area of foreign affairs was taken to be a Gaullist *domaine réservé*, the Prime Minister was active in most policy areas. The Matignon had a large team of some forty or so, responsible for the co-ordination and time-tabling of government action and although the President's representatives were present at inter-ministerial conferences (Jacques Fournier being responsible for Élysée/Matignon co-ordination) they did not intervene directly. The Prime Minister was responsible for these inter-ministerial matters (but was not in Giscard's time), and the compatibility of the Government's actions with the presidential programme, from which its legitimacy significantly derived, was assured by Mitterrand and the Prime Minister at their frequent meetings (usually in advance of each week's cabinet meeting).

The Élysée none the less intervened from time to time and did take unco-ordinated initiatives on its own; thus

[28] M. Duverger, *Échec au roi*, Albin Michel (Paris), 1978, pp. 141 ff.

Pierre Mauroy's authority over the Government of 1981–4 was not total. There were also Prime Ministerial lapses, public concern forced the President to be more active at times, and on some occasions when Mitterrand was abroad inter-ministerial disputes broke out inside the government which were only resolved on the President's return. It must be noted however, that there was very little conflict between President and Prime Minister. Mitterrand in 1981 had re-stated the essentially orthodox (Gaullist) view that the President can dismiss the Prime Minister, even though this is not a constitutional power. On most important matters the Prime Minister asked ministers to outline their proposals, which were then transmitted to the President, who (usually to only a limited extent) made recommendations on those aspects that concerned or interested him. Detailed announce-ments were left to the Matignon, with Mitterrand's public pronouncements rather rare and of a general nature—again in marked contrast to Giscard's practice. Rather than being active, interventionist, and the co-ordinator of policy, as was Giscard, Mitterrand returned to a Gaullist practice in which the Prime Minister applied the President's programme and was responsible for day-to-day running of the Government. The composition of the Government, of course, bore the unmistakable evidence of Mitterrand's wishes (with its careful balance of interests and inclusion of close associates) but both Mauroy and Fabius had some influence on the choice and the ranking of ministers.

But above all both governments made explicit reference to their role as the executors of the Mitterrand programme and the President also stressed that his 'engagements con-stituaient la charte d'action gouvernmentale'. Thus the Mitterrand programme constituted the 'general lines' of action for the governments. The Prime Minister was also responsible for arbitration between Ministers on disputed matters and for co-ordinating the work of government. The Prime Minister's role in promoting government harmony was more active than the Élysée's: the number of *conseils restreints* (meetings involving the President and particular ministers) was fewer than under Pompidou or (especially) under Giscard, and the number of *comités interministériels* (meet-ings involving the Prime Minister and certain ministers) was increased. Mitterrand, unlike Giscard, only rarely went behind the Prime Minister to deal directly with ministers or ministries, but some decisions were taken without the Prime Minister's knowledge and this led to a certain incoherence at times. Cabinet meetings were also upgraded because they became occasions for real decision-making, and not, as had been the case at times, the place for registering decisions taken elsewhere.

Mitterrand's desire to leave more of the centre stage to the Prime Minister, whilst he devoted himself to high politics in the *domaine réservé* of international affairs, led to difficulties. The President's view was not always clear and an impression of hesitation and indecision was generated which frequently placed the Prime Minister in an invidious position. Mitterrand also attempted to mark out the difference from Giscard who over-used the media and who dominated the political debate. Thus he sought to keep a weather eye on the Government and intervened only as a last resort, although this often allowed opposition to the government line to build up within the Party. A notable example was the application of the Mauroy–Delors austerity policy in March 1983: Mitterrand did not make up his mind or say what his policy was and eventually resorted to a television appearance (8 June 1983) to make his position clear and to impose his authority on the situation. Mitterrand sometimes allowed debates between ministers to thrive before imposing his point of view, and, through lack of presidential guidance, the Prime Minister was often unable to impose a solution. Mauroy found it especially hard to control strong-willed ministers such as Defferre (Interior) who clashed with Badinter (Justice) in 1982, and to cope with outspoken figures such as Delors and Rocard, who favoured less radical policies. Fabius was more successful in this respect.

Mauroy's third government of 1983–4 changed some practices but his retention as Prime Minister to oversee an austerity policy which he had explicitly repudiated in the run-up to the local elections of 1983, severely damaged his authority. The Finance Minister Delors along with Social Security Minister Bérégovoy emerged with enhanced stature. The third Mauroy government was smaller, dropped the leading left-winger Chevènement, and introduced a triumvirate of Mauroy-Delors-Bérégovoy to provide administrative coherence and a new sense of purpose. The new inner cabinet was to handle the most important matters except in the rare cases where economic policy was not involved. A more passive role for the Prime Minister was therefore evident: whilst he still tried to produce consensus in the govern-ment by acting as an arbiter in disputes, it was more up to the ministers to work out agreed positions than previously. Such a retreat into a more collective leadership of the Government served inevitably to reaffirm the predominance of the Presidency during 1983-4.

Thus by the spring of 1986, if Mitterrand's Presidency represented a scaling down from the visibly interventionist early period of Giscard's *septennat*, it was still staunchly in the Fifth Republic tradition. Government policy was based on Mitterrand's presidential campaign programme and on his strategic decisions thereafter; its timetabling was Mitterrand's prerogative; and international policy was firmly in the President's control, the more so with the replacement of Claude Cheysson by Mitterrand loyalist Roland Dumas as Foreign Minister in December 1984. Moreover, wherever domestic politics demanded, as the economic position declined, so presidential interventions increased. Thus the chief Élysée adviser, Bérégovoy, was put into the Cabinet in 1982 to cut social-security spending; the President ordered a quieter approach to the schools question after 1984; and the major government change of July 1984, which boosted the position of moderate (deflationary) ministers at the expense of the left wing, was clearly the President's doing. Moreover, the apparently irresolute manner in which the Government was reconstructed in March 1983—after a ten-day period of rumour, speculation, and negotiation—was more Machiavellian than incompetent, as Mitterrand took care to retain Communist support for a government that was slamming on the brakes and veering to the 'Right'.

Mitterrand predominated, as presidents have done since 1958, because of his majority in the Assembly—a majority moreover, elected on his coat-tails—and because, having attained the office and the means, he had no intention of renouncing the power. He had prevailed, also, because he was one of the only three members of the Government with any past ministerial experience, having served in Fourth Republic cabinets along with Gaston Defferre and Alain Savary. Otherwise, with the British Labour Government of 1964, inexperience of office was the prevailing characteristic of Pierre Mauroy's governments. All the Socialist ministers were, furthermore, only in office because Mitterrand approved of them, and had risen so high mainly on the basis of his patronage of their careers—first in the Party and then in the Government. This was true of Fabius, who was not leader of a separate current inside the Party, and was entirely beholden to Mitterrand for his elevation to the Matignon. In common with Gaullist prime ministers, Fabius lost no time in affirming his acceptance of presidential predominance and worked hard to avoid any disagreement between Élysée and Matignon. Moreover, whilst the Prime Minister had more responsibility for internal governmental co-ordination than in Giscard's time, interventions were made by the Élysée as and when Mitterrand desired (often to the detriment of government coherence). From 1981—6 regular weekly meetings at the Élysée between President and Premier before cabinet meetings have served to ensure both Mitterrand's superiority and the Prime Minister's authority over the Government as, at base, the bearer of presidential sanction.

Another sensitive area for Socialists was the relation between Government and Parliament. An enhanced role for Parliament was foreseen in Mitterrand's programme promise to forgo the use of Article 49 (clause 3), which allows the Government to pass measures on the nod by making them a matter of confidence, and to improve proportional representation on committees. In the event the RPR and UDF refused the offer of parliamentary-committee chairmanships, and article 49(3) was frequently invoked.

Despite a formal commitment to parliamentary rights and a past hostility to devices provided by the 1958 constitution designed to enable government mastery over the Assembly, the Socialists, between 1981-6 had recourse to the whole arsenal of powers to subdue opposition whether from the Right, the Communists, or even the majority's own backbenchers. Thus in 1982 Article 38 (the power to legislate by ordinance) was used to push through the Auroux laws on employees' rights in companies, and in April 1983 to deprive the Communists of the opportunity to state objections to the new austerity programme. Equally controversially, Article 49 was used in October 1981 to expedite the passage of legislation on energy against backbench Socialist hostility; in January 1982 to avoid the Right's campaign of obstruction to the Nationalization Bill; in June 1982 to circumvent the PCF's resistance to the prices-and-incomes freeze; and in October of the same year to pass over Socialist deputies' hostility, the bill amnestying rebel officers involved in seditious activities during the Algerian troubles of the 1960s.

Whilst such a record reflects badly on the Socialist Party, given its previously rather idealistic stance on parliamentary rights, it was to be expected. First, the demands of office required the transformation from poacher to gamekeeper; and secondly, a large, controversial programme had to be applied quickly, and it was probably prudent to get major legislation, such as the Nationalization Bill, through before the Opposition, demoralized by its dramatic defeat in 1981, had a chance to mobilize opinion. On the other hand, however, the Government also used all the weapons at its disposal to push through not only 'reforms' over the heads of the Right, but, in 1983, austerity measures in defiance of some of its own supporters. Given the overall Socialist majority, government legislation could be expected to be passed eventually; but the recourse to these constitutional mechanisms enabled the Government to move fast, to impart a sense of urgency and determination to some measures, and to avoid embarrassment (particularly to the Élysée where a reluctance to get involved directly frequently allowed disagreements to grow within Socialist ranks). Divisions among the Socialists were, however, far less serious than those between the RPR and UDF during the Giscard presidency.

Unlike Giscard, Mitterrand had a surer command of the National Assembly. The two important parliamentary posts (President of the Assembly and leader of the Socialist group) were, after May 1981, in the reliable hands of the staunch Mitterrandists Mermaz and Joxe, and from 1984–6, André Billardon. The parliamentary group did not, however, see its role as being simply a supporting one: in this respect the relation of Government to Party was not 'Gaullist', because the Gaullist Party, though independent, had less of an existence of its own, whereas the PS was not entirely the creature of the President, having had an existence that pre-dated the arrival of its leader in the Presidency—unlike both de Gaulle's UNR and Giscard's UDF. Negotiation between Government and Assembly was continuous and deputies brought about policy changes, notably on immigration, local radio and church schools. The Party's activists, its deputies, and the Government all represented different constituencies and responded to different pressures, even if Mitterrand, through First Secretary Jospin, had in mind a Party that was actively supportive rather than innovatory. Ministers too were still Socialist activists and, as is now habitual in the Fifth Republic, retained their constituency links. Even though they did not sit on the Executive Bureau or Secretariat of the Party, they still had their representatives there and a muted struggle for position took place.

The arrival of the new Socialist government also brought changes of personnel in the civil service, though these changes (under the direction of André Chadeau and Marceau Long at the Matignon) were not as far reaching as many in the Party would have wished, and there was certainly no 'witch-hunt'.[29] Even in broadcasting, where department heads, such as J.-P. Elkabach, were removed and most of the chairmen deposed, the replacements were not necessarily Socialist Party supporters. Thus Pierre Desgraupes (Antenne 2), Jacques Boutet (TF.1), Guy Thomas (FR3), and Michèle Cotta (RTL-political service), favourable to the Left, were in no-body's pockets, and the appointments as administrators of Maurice Sévens (PS) and Michel Cardoze (PCF) were symbolic rather than typical.

In some ministries changes of personnel were extensive, notably in the four Communist-run ministries and those of Education, Justice, Agriculture, and Solidarity, but in im-portant departments the changes were significantly slight, notably in Finance, Interior, Defence, and Industry. More-over, whilst 67 Prefects were moved in the first year, it was mostly by way of being a general post rather than a process of weeding out. (One—the first—Communist Prefect

[29] *Le Monde*, 30 June 1982.

did, however, emerge from this exercise.[30]) In an effort to reverse Giscard's policy of politicizing the education service nineteen of the twenty-seven regional rectors were replaced and some eight of the new rectors were certainly on the Left. But in the nationalized industries there was no evidence of an attempt to create a 'PS-state'. Out of twenty-six large banks and nationalized industries only half a dozen were administered by left-wingers and in the twenty-four small nationalized banks only ten or so were Socialist. Of 139 senior civil servants sixty-four were replaced; of the replacements only twenty were associated with the Left in some way or other, through union or party affiliation. Heads did not roll in substantial numbers. The Socialists did not pack the civil service, despite predictable charges from the Right to that effect.[31] What happened was that the Socialists used state power so as to promote *some* of their own people.

Decentralization

The decentralization policy of the government was described as the 'great affair of the presidential term'.[32] In fact, the proposals received no airing during the electoral campaigns of 1981, a tribute to the electorate's lack of real interest in the subject. The decentralization measures were however, inspired in theory by the Socialists' commitment to install greater democratic control over a system of local administration long characterised by bureaucratic domination rather than by democratic accountability. The proposals for enhanced regional government were also derived from a Socialist sensitivity to different linguistic or cultural traditions, whether Corsican or Basque. In practise however, the changes stemmed from hard-headed partisan calculation: the Socialists had long possessed a strong base in local politics, by 1981 controlling, in alliance with the Communists, the

[30] *Le Monde*, 29 June 1982.
[31] *Le Monde*, 30 Nov. 1981. J.-P. Soisson, a Giscardian minister, noted: 'We are not moving towards an occasional politicization [of the civil service] but towards the organized and institutionalized infiltration of the top of the civil service by the dominant parties.'
[32] Michel Philipponneau, *Décentralisation et régionalisation*, Calmann-Lévy (Paris), 1981.

great majority of the 230 largest towns and of the *départe-ment* councils, and the intention was, quite simply, to bolster the power of the Socialists' locally elected representatives, especially of big city mayors and *département* council chair-men. Significantly, the reforms were introduced by the most legendary of the Socialists' local *notables*, Gaston Defferre who was appointed Minister of the Interior *and Decentraliza-tion*. He typified the multiple office-holder: a parliamentarian since 1945; mayor of Marseilles continuously since 1953; a member of the Bouches-du-Rhône council and chairman of the Provence-Côte d'Azur regional council. He better than most represented the special interests of Socialist local chiefs and yet was, at base, a deeply conservative man who could be relied upon not to upturn any apple carts.

In essence, the reforms comprised a reallocation of powers between the prefect and the locally-elected politicians; the transfer of some powers from central to local government; the creation of directly-elected regional councils; a new system of devolved local government in Paris, Lyons, and Marseilles (with more administration run at arrondissement level); and the allocation of a central government block grant to provide the localities with the resources necessary to fulfill their enlarged functions. Some of the changes were introduced in a manner suggesting hasty or inadequate consideration. A rather crass plan for Paris local government was proposed, dividing the city into its 20 arrondissements, each with their own mayor: this had the double attraction of pushing administration down 'nearer the people', whilst at the same time balkanising what had been since 1977 the important power base of the Gaullist leader, Jacques Chirac, mayor of Paris. This florentine plan met with such resistance that the government retreated and returned with proposals to cover Marseilles and Lyons as well as Paris, and which combined a decentralization of administration with the retention of the authority of each city's mayor.

Were decentralization truly to have been the 'great affair of the presidential term', history would indeed have been made, for the record of the Fifth Republic on reforming local government was poor. Great inertia had been the watchword, with the communal map frozen into its 36,000 units and with governments uncertain about how much weight to give the regional units set up in the 1960s, relative to the traditional *départements*. In the event nothing important was done to disturb tradition in this respect. There were, however, in the words of one observer, some 'symbolic and spectacular gestures', such as the 'suppression' of the prefect.[33] Prefects, renamed *Commissaires de la République*, whilst retaining their function as representatives of the State in the *departements* and regions, were to cease to be the executives in these territorial units. They were to lose their supervisory power (*tutelle*) over the decisions of departmental, regional and municipal councils, as also were the local representatives of the Finance Ministry, the *trésoriers-payeurs-généraux*. Local authorities still had to balance their books but were to be subject to juridical control and given greater freedom over spending their income from taxes and grants. A transfer of resources from State to localities accompanied the transfer of functions.

But whilst symbolically important, these changes in part did little more than bring theory into line with practice, at least as far as the larger local authorities were concerned. In the big cities and the more important departments and regions, mayors and, in the latter cases, chairmen, had already established powerful bases and were well able to influence the prefectoral administration and the local agents of the Finance Ministry. Big local grandees, such as Defferre himself, had been far from powerless at the hands of the state administration and the new allocation of powers—affording 'less bureaucracy and more democracy' was as much a catching up exercise as it was an innovative one. Moreover whilst the extension of political control in local government did constitute an important change, the passage of a law limiting the number of elected offices which could be held by any one person could imply a weakening of local political control.

France is possibly unique amongst western democracies in its close government supervision of radio and television.[33] This was one area where pluralism and greater freedom of action were also keenly awaited. It is also an area where previous reforming intentions had not so much run into the sands as never been pressed with any enthusiasm.

[33] *Yves Mény*, 'Decentralization in Socialist France: The Politics of Pragmatism', *West European Politics*, January 1984, pp. 65–79.

In August 1982 the Government introduced a nine-member Broadcasting Authority which was intended to free television and radio from direct control and to ensure pluralism of expression in the media. The President, the President of the Assembly (a spokesman for the majority), and the President of the Senate (not a Socialist) each nominated three people to the Authority (these included a Communist and a Giscardian). The first head was the left-inclined, but independent, journalist Mme Michèle Cotta. Although none of the appointees was a career politician or party functionary most had a clear political affiliation and criticism tended to concentrate on this aspect. However, the Authority was not as powerful as the original plans had envisaged because budget control remained with the Assembly majority, and therefore ultimately with the Government.

But the 'liberalization' of the airwaves and the creation of the broadcasting High Authority did make a lasting impact. The measures, whether they stayed in place or not after 1986, changed the climate of thinking about broadcasting in France and made it difficult to go back to the old authoritarian practice. The Authority did take decisions not wholly approved of by the government, local radio was legalized and allowed to take advertising, and a fourth TV (subscription) channel was created. Finally the Fabius government established a fifth Channel conceded to the Italian Berlusconi who had previously been reviled for 'Americanization' of the Italian network; the station was on the air before the 1986 elections, although its reliance on films (the principal viewing and commercial attraction) was subsequently declared illegal, as was a sixth, popular music, channel.

If the decentralization measures were intended as a process of democratization, so too were the bundle of diverse measures known as the Auroux laws. These reforms harked back as a distant echo to the Socialists' 1970s theme of self-management (*autogestion*). One observer noted that the laws had four objectives: to strengthen worker representation in the firm, to provide new channels for employee expression, to give new rights of representation on the boards of state-run industries and to encourage collective bargaining.[34] The

[34] Duncan Gallie 'Les lois Auroux: the reform of French industrial relations?' in H. Machin and V. Wright, *op. cit.* pp. 205–220.

laws gave to work place committees the right to obtain information about the financial state of the company and to be consulted about changes in work practices; health and safety committees were also given extended powers, such as the right to call in work inspectors. The laws increased the rights of workers (in private sector firms with over 200 employees) to express their views on their work and on changes in the organization of their work by obligating negotiations and the creation of committees. In the state sector tripartite company boards (comprising representatives of the employees, the state and 'independents') were established, along with workshop councils and powers to call meetings in work time. Most importantly the laws tried to stimulate collective bargaining by obliging employees and unions to negotiate regularly over both salaries and work grading, and tried to ensure that a majority of the workforce was represented in such negotiations. Although the *Patronat*'s reaction was extremely hostile, the need for union co-operation and the long recognized failure of collective bargaining in France appeared to ensure the continuation of most of the legislation, for, as in Britain, the drive to direct employee expression and consultation did not necessarily make the task of management more difficult.

The Mauroy and Fabius governments: a pragmatic record

Where it mattered most—in economic policy—the Socialists' record was neither as good as they claimed nor as bad as their opponents alleged. The worst 'failure' was unemployment: Mauroy's promise in 1981 that by the end of 1982 there would no longer be a single unemployed person between 16 and 18 years of age was wildly optimistic. The rhetoric of the Socialist Party in the early 1980s inflated expectations and set the scene for later disappointments. Although the level of unemployment was held steady at around 2 million (7.3%) during 1982, the figure had increased by 1984 to 2.48 million (over 10%). Amongst the unemployed the number of long-term jobless also significantly increased and whilst the rate of unemployment was below European averages from 1981 to 1984, it had by 1986 reached the EEC average.

Thus the Socialist government's record on unemployment, though far from a disaster, was not regarded as the success story of the legislature, a fact exploited by the opposition, and indeed recognized by the government itself as it switched, in 1985, to defending its record on inflation.

Inflation, which stood at 13.5% in 1982, came down fast so that by 1985 it was below 5%; even if over the five years inflation stayed slightly above the EEC average and well above West German levels. One of the government's contributions here was to de-index salaries from the rate of inflation and by holding wage settlements more or less within government norms, bringing down the inflation rate and enabling companies to rebuild profit margins. Interest rates, by contrast, in 1986, were at 12.75%, the highest in the West.

Somewhat 'oversold' by the Socialists was the prospect of a rapid growth rate. French growth in 1982 (in real GNP) was 1.75% above the European average but fell back as the reflation policy was abandoned and by 1985 output was growing by 1% compared to an EEC growth rate of 2.25%. Although France did not experience a fall in real GNP in any year of the Socialist government, the policies managed to go against the international trend in 1982 (reflating in a deflating world) and in 1985-6 (deflating in a reflating world), so that the government risked missing any global recovery. According to the Ministry of Finance, purchasing power fell in two of the five years of Socialist government but over the period if grew by 5%, which was higher than in Italy or Britain but much lower than the USA (15.4%) or Japan (13.9%), whilst the Netherlands, West Germany and Belgium experienced falls over the same period.

Furthermore the balance of payments deficit (which prompted the abandonment of the reflation experiment) and public debt were bad by historical standards, although they were not excessive by international comparison. The balance of payments problem was met by cutting back imports, not expanding exports; the improving results were therefore less favourable than the government made out. The Government's budget deficit widened from 1.1% of GNP in 1980 to 3.3% in 1984; public debt doubled to over 900 billion Francs: long-term debt also rose from 187 billion Francs to 525 billion in 1984, though some of this was due to the increased strength of the dollar. Debt and borrowing are however largely technical matters; the amount a country can borrow is determined by the international market and France did not, of course, anticipate or experience repayment difficulties.

In terms of public debt the Socialists claimed success in turning round the nationalized industries. Notoriously loss-making, the Pechiney, Rhône-Poulenc and Thompson companies were in the black by 1985, but the nationalized sector as a whole continued to be a loss maker, due largely to catastrophic losses at Renault. Figures published during the 1986 election campaign owed something to creative accounting, but profit was back as a managerial target. Other improvements in company finance derived largely from holding salary costs down, and easing tax and social security burdens on firms, advantages enjoyed by public and private sectors alike.

Much gloomier were the results from industrial production and investment. In 1985 output was still at 1980 levels and investment had fallen by 1.3% (in all other industrial countries results had been positive over the same period). Moreover the rate of profit which fell to 1.7% in 1982 recovered to only 2.7% in 1984 (in the 1960s it had been between 6% and 7%) and the rate of return on investment was very weak by 1984. Thus although the volume of investment in manufacturing was higher in 1985 than in 1981 (and above EEC averages), total investment was lower and high interest rates were attracting funds away from industry. All this meant that there was much less room for manœuvre than the Socialists admitted and it was the inability of the government to expand the economy that became one of Rocard's targets after his resignation in 1985.

In the main, policy under the Socialists could be seen as a mix of good intentions, moderated self-interest, realism, orthodoxy and pragmatism. In the realm of good intentions, across a broad front idealism beat a retreat. Thus on immigration, tighter controls; on law and order, a special 'security' minister and boasts about the number of people imprisoned; on education, a major policy discarded. In all these areas conservative public opinion bore hard. In moral areas of foreign policy, such as Africa and arms sales, franco-centrism

—a single-minded defence of French national interest—came as ever to prevail. In ecological policy the same national interest dictated both a retention of the nuclear power programme and a defence of all but the violent, illegal aspects of the Greenpeace affair.

Evidence of partisan self-interest was present in the decentralization policy and in the Auroux laws, which boosted powers of Socialist representation in the localities and on the shop floor. But, the same was less true in the sphere of 'rolling heads': a 'socialist' government would have taken a surgeon's knife to the higher reaches of the state bureaucracy; the Mauroy government did not. Far from 'breaking with capitalism', which a rigorous pruning of the administration would have required, the aim was to reassure through sound financial orthodoxy and the rejection of alternative interventionist strategies.

Yet to see the record as somewhat compromised and meek is not to belittle it. There were substantial, if undramatic, changes made, not least in local government structures where greater democratic control was introduced; in nationalization, where changes were made for necessary industrial reconstruction; and in broadcasting, where a degree of distance was put between the state and the broadcasters. There were also important social policy gains, such as a shorter working week, earlier retirement, longer holidays and improved social benefits, and it was in defence of these gains that President Mitterrand threatened a defiant stand as the spectre of '*cohabitation*' with the Right loomed in 1985. On this, at least, the President had public opinion with him; indeed, at best, the Mauroy and Fabius governments were beholden to the weight of public opinion. The honeymoon with the voters in 1981 was short-lived; soon the government was unpopular for its economic 'incompetence', only to become, after the major U-turn of 1982–3, unpopular for its economic austerity. Thereafter the fragility of Socialist power was masked only by the large parliamentary majority elected in 1981 and guaranteed to endure come what may until March 1986, when it was predictably swept aside.

9

Voters, Members, and Leaders

Electoral performance

The electoral geography of French Socialism has retained
fairly consistent contours since 1905, although significant
modifications occurred between the two world wars and
during the ten years after the re-formation of the Parti
Socialiste in 1971. Before the split of 1920 the Party's
support was concentrated in the urban-industrialized areas
of Paris, the Nord, and Pas-de-Calais; in a string of rural
departments from Burgundy down across the north-western
flank of the Massif Central into Limousin; and in the Midi
area of the south. This map was essentially that of the
Radicals at the start of the Third Republic—on the one hand
urban, industrialized France (Paris and the Nord), and on the
other the predominantly rural, anti-clerical—and thus republican—areas of the centre and the south. At the first election
after the breach with the Communists in 1924 the Socialists
were pushed out of the industrial suburbs of Paris by the
Communists, and by 1928 the SFIO's centre of gravity was
displaced towards the south as it compensated for its loss in
industrialized areas of the north by capturing former Radical
areas south of the Loire. Thus began a long process of
'Radicalization' of the Socialist Party which characterized the
'thirties, 'forties, and 'fifties, and which involved the progressive petty-bourgeoisification of the Party's electoral base.
(Symbolic of this process was Blum's own election for Nar-
bonne in 1929.) In this way the Socialists began to suffer the
fate they had inflicted on the Radicals in the 1900s—displacement towards the political centre with the arrival of a
competitor on the Left. At the Popular Front election of
1936 the Socialist electorate further contracted in the Seine
and Nord departments, where more working-class support
transferred to the PCF (virtually all of it in Paris). The SFIO,
which had replaced the Radicals as the largest party of the
Left in 1932, significantly had a majority of its deputies

elected for seats in the ex-Radical rural centre and the Midi, where its role was simply now that of a *parti laïque*.[1]

1945. In the first post-war election (1945) the SFIO was further displaced by the Communists, not only in the industrial north, but also in the rural areas south of the Loire. The republican tradition of voting for the Left party *le plus avancé* was having a damaging impact on the Socialists, who continued to compensate for losses to the PCF by further gains from the Radicals. Having retained a stable vote in pre-war elections (see Table 7.1, p. 128) during the Fourth Republic the Party's electorate contracted steadily until 1956. In the post-war period SFIO strongholds, except the remaining industrial support in Nord and Pas-de-Calais, corresponded with the most secular departments. In 1951 the Party lost heavily to the Gaullist RPF and the Radicals, and this time the decline was most marked in the rural areas.

1956. The 1956 election saw a halt to the Party's decline, with its vote stabilizing around 15 per cent of the vote (3.3 million) by its association with the popular Radical politician, Pierre Mendès France. Its three regional bases remained intact—the industrialized Nord; the secular, rural, and poor centre; and the socially diverse but essentially republican south. But in 1956 the Party made slight gains in industrialized areas and some losses in rural areas, reversing the trend to 'Radicalization' of the previous thirty years. But in reality the SFIO of the Fourth Republic was characterized by a regionalized implantation which excluded it from the east, the Upper Loire, the Rhône, and the Paris region—areas accounting for about half of industrial France. Fourteen departments with large industrial populations did not figure in the list of leading Socialist departments in 1956.

1962. Four years after the 1958 elections, in which the Party held onto its traditional pockets of strength simply by associating itself with de Gaulle, the SFIO in 1962 (detached from Gaullism) reached its electoral nadir with 2.3 million votes (half the total obtained in the 1945 election). Its centre of gravity was now pushed squarely into the Radical south-west. Radicalization, the poaching of another

[1] R. Quilliot, *La SFIO et l'exercise du pouvoir 1944–1958*, Fayard (Paris), 1972, p. 767.

rapidly declining party's electorate, had resumed its inexorable course. Left-wing electors were shed to the Communist Party.

1967. The election of 1967 was both the first election of the Fifth Republic to take place in normal, i.e. non-crisis, conditions, and the first in which all the parties of the non-Communist Left (SFIO, Radical, PSU, CIR) pooled their resources as part of the FGDS (and amassed 4.3 million votes). The traditional zones of support were retained—south-west, centre, north—but some incursions were made into industrial areas, making the electorate less rural and *laïque*.

1973. After the crisis and panic election of 1968, in which decline was resumed, the first election under Mitterrand's leadership came in 1973. It was also the first election to be held since the signing of the programmatic agreement between the PS and the PCF, and, as in 1967, one that took place in conditions of calm. It was in this election that the spectacular advance of the Party in the 'seventies was heralded. The electorate of the UGSD (PS and MRG) rose to 4.9 million, its distribution reflecting the first move away from the regionalization of Socialist support. Whilst the vote rose by only 1.1 per cent nationally (compared with 1967) it increased in as many as fourteen of the twenty-one regions and by significantly large amounts in Brittany (+7.9 per cent), Lower Normandy (+5.6 per cent) and Pays de la Loire (+5.0 per cent), predominantly Catholic areas of traditional Left weakness. Half the UGSD voters in 1967 were practising Catholics (regular or occasional). At the same time support fell away in the rural *laïque* bastions (such as Limousin (−6.9 per cent)), where the traditional anti-Communist PS voters followed Socialist notables (such as Paul Alduy and Jean Montalat) out of the PS and into Centre parties.

This election saw the first real evidence of a working-class drift away from the Communists and towards the PS. In the proletarian redoubt of Seine Saint-Denis the UGSD vote rose from 10.9 to 15.5 per cent as the PCF's vote fell from 45 to 41 per cent. The Socialists were now at last advancing into the Communist heartland. The election saw the best Socialist performance since 1946—a doubling of its electorate compared with the rock-bottom vote of 1962. By moving into the Catholic regions and into the urban areas (with both middle- and working-class electorates) a new

Socialist electorate was emerging—much more urban than at any time since the War, socially cross-sectional, nationally distributed, and younger (two-thirds were under fifty-nine). Thus the 1973 election saw more than the restoration of the Socialists' strength lost in the freak Gaullist landslide of 1968. Most important, the Party was at last expanding in most of the areas of demographic growth forming an arc across the north of the country from Pays de la Loire and eastern Brittany, through Normandy, and down to the Rhine, and losing support in the depopulating regions of the south (notably Limousin).[2] In the process the Party was also dropping those parts of its electorate that tied it to the past—anti-clericals and anti-Communists. The de-Radicalization of the Party had been set in train.

Thus the 1973 election was a watershed. The significant gains and their geographical distribution were confirmed in a string of elections which followed in the 'seventies: 1974 (presidential), 1976 (cantonal), 1977 (municipal), and 1978 (legislative). The 'nationalization' of the PS electorate was reflected in Mitterrand's performance in the 1974 presidential election, where, in contrast to his first presidential campaign in 1965, when he relied on the traditional Third Republic Left zones of strength, he pushed into the west and the east (with support in Moselle up from 16.0 to 35.5 per cent; in Meuse from 17.2 to 35.4 per cent) and Paris. The more even distribution of the Left's support was shown in the decreasing gap between highest and lowest percentages of Left strength (in 1973 the gap was 35.1 per cent, in 1974 24.1 per cent).

1978. Socialist penetration of the Catholic east and west was reaffirmed at the municipal elections of 1977, when towns such as Rennes and Angers were captured, as a prelude to the anticipated achievement of a Left majority in the 1978 legislative election. In that election the Left's first-ballot aggregate reached 48.6 per cent and the Socialists overtook the Communists as the largest party of the Left— 22.6 per cent (+ 2 per cent MRG) to the PCF's 20.6 per cent. The PS was now the dominant Left party electorally in two-thirds of the constituencies (see Table 7.3, p. 137). The election saw a continuation of trends evident in 1973, notably

[2] See *La Population française*, INSEE (Paris), 1980.

the slackening grip of the Communists in their working-class strongholds, due partly to changing social structure and to the rival appeal of the PS. But although the Socialist vote was 40 per cent up on 1973, it was too well distributed to yield a harvest of seats. The PS vote increased by more than the national average (+4.3 per cent) in the regions of traditional weakness which had moved leftwards from 1973 on: Brittany (+7.8 per cent), Alsace (+7.7 per cent), Lorraine (+7.6 per cent), Loire (+6.1 per cent), Lower Normandy (+5.1 per cent), and Paris (+5.7 per cent). The trend in the Party's traditional strongholds was again, as in 1973, in the direction of relatively slight advance or stagnation, and actual decline in some cases: Languedoc (−1.7 per cent), Limousin (−0.9 per cent).

1981. The 1981 presidential election saw the best (first-ballot) Socialist vote since the War (25.8 per cent, plus 2.2 per cent going to the MRG candidate) and all the electoral trends of the 'seventies confirmed. The most significant electoral pointer to Mitterrand's second-ballot success was his marginalizing of the PCF candidate, Marchais, whom he outran in ninety-two of the ninety-six departments. Socialist decline in parts of the depopulating rural south continued—this time aided by the appeal of Gaullist Jacques Chirac in areas south of the Loire, notably in his own region of Limousin. The fact of Mitterrand's victory provides the explanation for the huge Socialist landslide in the June 1981 legislative elections, when the PS vote increased by 12.8 per cent (on 1978) to reach the unprecedented level of 37.7 per cent, or 9.4 million votes.

The scale of the 1981 victory was remarkable: the PS gained between 15 and 20 per cent in eighteen departments, between 10 and 14.9 per cent in fifty-nine, between 5 and 9.9 per cent in seventeen, and by less than 5 per cent in only two. Except in Poitou-Charentes (with the PS vote up by 16.0 per cent), south of the Loire the tide was less strong than to the north. Brittany (+14.1 per cent), Lower Normandy (+14.0 per cent), Lorraine (+15.3 per cent), Upper Normandy (+13.4 per cent) all registered PS growth greater than the national average of 12.8 per cent.[3] But although 2.5 million votes were added to the Socialists' 1978 total, it

[3] IFOP survey, *Le Point*, No. 455, June 1981.

was an election result from which few long-term conclusions could be drawn. From such dizzy heights the Socialists could only fall, as the results of 1986 were to confirm.

The dramatic shift in votes during the 1970s is summarized in Table 9.1. In the north of France in areas largely of

Table 9.1

Socialist Votes by Region 1967–1986

(percentage of first-ballot votes 1967–81)

	1967	1968	1973	1978	1981	1986
Regions of traditional strength						
North: Burgundy	30.0	25.6	26.0	29.6	43.0	34.4
Franche-Comté	26.8	23.0	27.4	30.9	41.5	36.1
Nord	28.0	24.6	26.6	28.1	40.3	31.8
South: Aquitaine	27.2	26.5	25.3	30.8	44.5	36.5
Auvergne	28.6	24.8	24.4	27.0	40.7	31.7
Corsica	29.3	30.5	27.5	29.0	37.1	31.4
Languedoc	24.8	24.4	27.0	25.3	38.1	32.0
Limousin	31.4	26.5	25.3	24.4	35.1	32.6
Midi-Pyrénées	30.2	29.7	31.3	34.3	49.5	37.8
Average regions						
North: Centre	21.5	17.0	18.7	24.0	36.8	32.5
Champagne	18.7	17.2	20.7	22.9	33.3	30.4
Picardy	19.4	13.5	18.6	21.8	36.0	32.2
Upper Normandy	15.2	12.1	16.8	22.6	36.0	34.6
South: Poitou-Charentes	18.5	19.1	21.1	27.9	43.9	36.6
Provence-Côte d'Azur	22.1	17.2	22.3	20.8	32.2	25.8
Rhône-Alps	16.6	13.8	20.8	25.1	37.4	30.9
Regions of traditional weakness						
North: Alsace	8.7	9.0	12.4	20.1	30.8	23.2
Brittany	9.3	7.3	17.1	24.9	39.0	35.8
Loire Country	13.6	12.1	18.5	24.6	37.4	32.8
Lorraine	10.2	12.1	18.5	26.1	41.4	30.6
Lower Normandy	12.1	9.6	17.7	22.8	36.8	32.5
Paris Region	12.4	8.4	14.9	20.6	32.8	30.9
France	19.3	16.6	20.4	24.7	37.5	32.1

Source: Adapted from J.R. Frears, *Political Parties and Elections in the French Fifth Republic*, Hurst (London), 1977, p. 122, with additions made for 1978, 1981, and 1986.

traditional Socialist weakness the Party's electorate had multiplied by a factor of 3 in some regions and quadrupled in the most Catholic regions of Brittany, Alsace, and Lorraine. In these regions the Socialist electorate had grown in the areas where Catholic observance had waned, and in the newer industrial areas especially around the expanding towns. Thus in capturing most of the 'rural' region of Brittany, the Party had done best in the urbanizing, economically dynamic parts of the region and not in its depopulating interior. Elsewhere, in the traditional republican territory south of the Loire, Socialist strength had not increased by anything like the same amount, and in one or two cases—notably in Limousin—it had all but declined. The party of the rural, small town, anti-clerical France of the 1930s and 1940s had become—whilst retaining a dominant position in its traditional southern fiefs—the party of the expanding conurbations of the 1970s and 1980s. What is demonstrated in Table 9:1 is that in both victory (1981) and defeat (1986) the party was now a nationally-pervasive force, with consistent strength in all regions: a geographically, as much as a socially, catch-all party.

Social composition

(1) Voters

The Socialist Party has been variously described as a *'parti de la bourgeoisie avancée'*,[4] as a *'parti des profs'*, and as a party of the new middle classes.[5] These are essentially descriptions of the Party's internal composition (its members, activists, and leaders), but they clearly imply something about its electorate. The Party has since the 1920s had a predominantly middle-class electoral base. In 1952 only 27 per cent of Socialist voters were working class and they constituted only about 15 per cent of the working-class electorate. The bulk of the Party's voting strength was provided by the salaried (as distinct from the self-employed) lower-middle class,[6] an embarrassing matter for a party with pretensions of being a working-class party.

---

[4] C. Ysmal, 'La Gauche française et les classes sociales', *Projet*, 7 June 1976.
[5] H. Portelli, *Le Socialisme français tel qu'il est*, PUF (Paris), 1981, pp. 119–41.
[6] P. Rimbert quoted in R. Quilliot, op. cit., p. 765.

Table 9.2

Composition of Socialist Electorate 1967–1978

	1967 (%)	1968 (%)	1973 (%)	1978 (%)	French electorate 1973 (%)
SEX					
Men	53	55	53	51	48
Women	47	45	47	49	52
AGE					
21–34*	30	57	31	43	35
35–49	27		26	25	25
50–64	27	42	22	18	20
65 and over	16		16	13	20
OCCUPATION OF HEAD OF HOUSEHOLD					
Farmers	14	18	11	5	8
Professions, Business, and Management	14	12	10	12	14
White-collar workers	18	16	22	29	19
Manual workers	33	34	36	34	32
Retired/no occupation	21	20	21	20	27
SIZE OF PLACE					
Rural communes	33	41	28	25	27
Towns of under 20,000 inhabitants	12	10	14	15	15
Towns of 20,000–100,000 inhabitants	17	18	17	14	13
Towns of over 100,000 inhabitants	22	20	27	29	28
Paris conurbation	16	11	13	17	17

* 18–34 in 1978.
Source: J. Charlot, *Quand la gauche peut gagner*, Alain Moreau (Paris), 1973; and *Le Point*, 13 Feb. 1978.

During the 'sixties and 'seventies the working-class voters accounted for about one-third of the Socialist electorate— somewhat more than in 1952. But the more important change in the composition of the Party's electorate was the increasing dependence on the votes of lower-managerial and white-collar workers. The proportion this group comprised of the Socialist electorate rose from 18 to 29 per cent between 1967 and 1978 (see Table 9.1). Moreover the 1978 figure of 29 per cent was significantly greater than that part (19 per cent) of the total electorate comprising the white-collar group. Data in Chapter 7 (see p. 134) show how uniform was the Socialist penetration of nearly all social categories by 1978. The 1981 landslide served mainly to deepen that penetration, and to do so in one highly important respect at the expense of the Communist Party: two-fifths of the working-class vote went to the PS, compared with a mere quarter to the PCF. Thus the PS achieved the double distinction of being a 'catch-all' party with a deeper penetration of the working-class than the country's leading working-class party.

The Socialist Party's electorate is socially cross-sectional, except in one or two respects. The youngest age group is over-represented and the oldest (65+) under-represented. The level of support for the PS provided by the two middle-aged groups is more nearly proportional to the size of those groups in the electorate at large (see Table 9.2). Traditionally the Party has always polled disproportionately strongly among male voters, and in 1978 men were still over-represented (51 per cent) in the PS electorate as compared with the electorate as a whole (48 per cent). The explanation for male over-representation, and female under-representation is that women traditionally have been more likely to resist voting Socialist for religious reasons; this resistance is now declining. These exceptions aside, by the late 'seventies the Socialist electorate was cross-sectional in respect of most of the occupational categories and notably so in all of the locational (size of place) ones. Where it was not cross-sectional it was healthily over-represented in the important expanding sectors: the young and the white-collared. The electoral picture is thus one of a catch-all party, and it is one that should be savoured, for an examination of the Party's internal composition reveals a rather different state of affairs. Internally, middle-class domination is the reality.

(ii) *Members*

With about 200,000 members by 1982 the Party had more than adequately reversed the membership decline that registered throughout the Mollet years. From a post-Liberation high point of 355,000 in 1946 membership fell to 279,000 (1947) and 132,000 (1948), levelling off to around 90,000 during the 1950s, 80,000 in the early 'sixties, and 70,000 by 1965. At the Épinay Congress of 1971, the figure, before the addition of the Mitterrandists and others, was 61,000. Thereafter the membership climbed to 100,000 (1973), 146,000 (1974), 164,000 (1977), and 170,000 (1979).

The enlarged membership, like the electorate, is more nationally distributed than it was before 1969: whereas the three biggest federations (Nord, Pas-de-Calais, and Bouches-du-Rhône) accounted for about half the total membership in the 'sixties and about 40 per cent at the time of Mitterrand's election to the leadership in 1971, they now comprise only a quarter. Areas of Socialist electoral growth north and east of the Loire are also areas of membership growth.

The social composition of the membership has changed slightly during the past thirty years. In 1951 working-class members accounted for two-fifths of the total; by 1973 only one in five members was working class, two-thirds were in lower-middle-class categories, and 20 per cent in business, professional, and managerial occupations (see Table 9.3).

Table 9.3
Social Composition of Membership 1951–1973

	1951 (%)	1970 (%)	1973 (%)
Business, managerial, and professional	3	15	20
Farming, shop keeping, lower managerial, and clerical	53	61	61
Workers	44	23	19

Source: M. Kesselman, 'The Recruitment of Rival Party Activists', *Journal of Politics*, February 1973.

This low level of working-class participation in Socialist politics compares with a working-class component in the membership of the West German SPD of 27 per cent; with 32 per cent in the Italian Socialist Party; and with 37 per cent in the Austrian Socialist Party.[7] A traditional feature of French Socialist Party membership has been not just middleclass over-representation, but specifically the over-abundance of teachers, who in 1973 comprised 13 per cent of the membership. The Socialist teacher is a legendary figure, but the Socialist teacher of the post-1971 Party is different from his predecessor: he is much more likely to be a *professeur* than a lower status *instituteur*, a change that reflects an expansion of the former category in the teaching profession in recent decades.

The relative unpopularity of the Party among female voters is much more evident in respect of party membership, although membership of political parties as a general rule is traditionally more a male than a female activity. In a variety of studies made in the early 'seventies only 21 per cent of the party members in the Rhône were women and only 26 per cent of those in Lyons. But the trend was upward; in the Isère the percentage of women members doubled between 1969 and 1975 from 10 to 23 per cent. In Paris the figure rose from 19 per cent in 1969 to 28 per cent in 1974. A certain degree of feminization is reflected in these figures.[8]

The general tendency in the composition of the party membership is a drift away from the 'popular' classes (blue- and routine white-collar workers) and a progressive *embourgeoisement*, involving the recruitment of the expanding new middle classes, credentialled, and frequently employed in intellectual occupations. The increasing preponderance of such people serves even more to colour debate in the Party and to marginalize further the dwindling working-class element. The trend is best demonstrated by an examination of the party activists.

(iii) *Activists, deputies, and leaders*

At the Grenoble Congress of 1973 51 per cent of the delegates were drawn from managerial occupations, 25 per cent were teachers, 8 per cent students, and only 11 per cent

---

[7] W. E. Paterson and A. H. Thomas (eds.), *Social Democratic Parties in Western Europe*, Croom Helm (London), 1977.

[8] J. Derville, 'La fédération socialiste de l'Isère depuis 1969', *RFSP* Vol. 26, No. 3, June 1976, pp. 568–99.

blue-collar or routine white-collar workers (3 per cent blue-collar workers, 8 per cent white-collar).[9] Eight years later at Valence, 50 per cent of the delegates were managerial, 31 per cent teachers, and 10 per cent blue- or white-collar workers (5 per cent of each).[10] Thus at both congresses four out of five delegates were in middle-class occupations, but even more notably, a third were teachers (or students) and more than half (60 per cent in 1981) had received higher education. It is at parliamentary level that the Party is most aptly seen as a *parti des profs*. Teachers provide 31 per cent of activists; 45 per cent of the Comité Directeur, 40 per cent of all (1981) candidates, 47 per cent of all deputies elected in 1981, and 56 per cent of those who made up the new intake of 1981—double the proportion of teachers in the National Assembly group in 1971 (see Tables 9.4 and 5). In 1972 nearly two-thirds of all Socialist mayors were also teachers, as were 47 per cent of all new Socialist mayors in the largest (30,000+) towns.[11] Fourteen of the Socialist ministers in the Mauroy government formed in June 1981 were teachers, half of them *universitaires*. This enormous over-representation of teachers at the top of the Party is demonstrated most simply by comparison with that proportion of the active population formed by teachers (5.6 per cent).

For comparative purposes it is worth referring to the British Labour Party, where teachers also play an important role as candidates and representatives. At the 1979 British election 26 per cent of Labour candidates were teachers (compared to 40 per cent of the 1981 PS candidates) and of those elected 21 per cent (as compared to 47 per cent at the French election) were teachers. Labour's comparatively slighter reliance on teachers is easily explained when comparing the proportions of manual-worker candidates in the two parties: 45 per cent of Labour candidates and 35 per cent

[9] *IFOP* Survey, 'L'identité des délégués et des auditeurs du Parti socialiste au congrès de Nantes des 17, 18 et 19 Juin 1977', *Sondages* 2–3, 1978.

[10] R. Cayrol, 'Les militants du Parti socialiste: Contribution à une sociologie', *Projet*, Sept.–Oct. 1974, pp. 929–40, and R. Cayrol and C. Ysmal, 'Les militants du PS—originalité et diversités', *Projet*, May 1982, pp. 572–86 (Cayrol's figures have to be treated with some caution given the size of his sample and response rate).

[11] P. Bacot, *Les Dirigeants du Parti socialiste*, Presses universitaires de Lyon (Lyons), 1978, p. 143.

Table 9.4

Occupational Background of Socialist Deputies 1956–1986

Occupations	1956 (N=89) (%)	1958 (N=40) (%)	1962 (N=65) (%)	1967 (N=93) (%)	1968 (N=44) (%)	1973 (N=89) (%)	1978 (N=105) (%)	1981 (N=269) (%)	1986 (N=209) (%)
farmers, merchants, employers	3	–	5	4	5	4	1	–	3
industrialists	4	2	2	6	9	7	7	3	–
higher admin. and management (including senior civil servants)	4	4	11	10	9	10	14	20	9
doctors/pharmacists	10	21	12	6	11	9	6	6	6
lawyers	14	9	8	9	7	4	8	6	5
journalists	7	4	5	2	–	3	4	4	3
engineers and other professionals	1	7	5	3	2	3	5	6	7
teachers and lecturers	33	32	28	33	30	37	44	47	49
executives, technicians, and lower management (including minor civil servants)	15	15	15	19	21	12	4	6	10
white-collar employees	3	2	3	6	5	8	1	1	5
manual workers	4	2	5	1	2	–	1	1	3
Total	98	98	99	99	101	97*	95**	100	100

* Excluding one (1 per cent) deputy whose occupation was unknown.
** Excluding six (6 per cent) who were retired or whose occupation was unknown.

Table 9.5
Occupational Background of New Intakes of Socialist Deputies
1973–1981

	New deputies		All deputies
	1981	1978	1973	1971
Higher managers, engineers, higher civil servants	12	26	23	18
Middle managers, employees	15	7	8	14
Liberal professions (doctors and lawyers)	12	11	12	21
Teachers	56	48	43	28
Shopkeepers, artisans, businessmen	1	0	4	9
Farmers	0	0	4	7
Others	4	7	6	2
Totals	100 (170)	100 (45)	100 (56)	100 (43)

of MPs in 1979,[12] as against a mere 1 per cent of both candidates and MPs at the French election in 1981. It is clear that the French Socialist teachers are filling a blue-collar void.

At the apex of the Party professional and managerial personnel predominate. In the Comité Directeur of 1977 81 per cent were in these categories, 12 per cent in the lower-managerial group, and a mere 3 per cent in the blue- and white-collar-worker categories. In the parliamentary group in 1981 working-class and routine non-manual deputies accounted for 2 per cent of the total, and of the 98 per cent drawn from the middle-class occupations, 32 per cent were drawn from the higher-managerial and senior professional ranks, with 47 per cent, as has been noted, from teaching. This sort of distribution has long been fairly standard in the PS (see Table 9.4), but the number of university teachers and *professeurs* (as distinct from *instituteurs*) and *grands corps* civil servants has perceptibly increased so that within the vast 'middle-class' category, the occupations represented are those of higher status than hitherto. Thus the lower-managerial category provided a decreasing proportion of Socialist deputies in 1978 and 1981 than in the 1960s.

[12] D. E. Butler and D. Kavanagh, *The British General Election of 1979*, Macmillan (London), 1979, p. 287.

At the new peak of the Socialist pyramid in 1981—the Mauroy government—the élitist composition was virtually complete. Among the thirty-seven Socialist ministers appointed to Mauroy's second government in June 1981, were eight *hauts fonctionnaires*; four lawyers; one doctor; seven university teachers; seven school teachers (five of them *professeurs*); three journalists; two company directors; an executive; a bank manager; a minor civil servant and a sales representative. Thus at the top the elimination of the working-class component was achieved. From the base of the Party's structure to its apex working-class representation comprises 35 per cent of the voters; 15 per cent of the members; 5 per cent of the activists; 3 per cent of the leadership; 1 per cent of the deputies; and none of the Government. But whilst the *'bourgeoisification'* appeared complete, two qualifications must be made. First, these 'bourgeois' were (at all levels of the Party) often the sons of workers. Thus much of the Party's middle-class personnel was provided by people who had experienced social mobility. By one calculation at least 28 per cent of the 1974 Comité Directeur were in this position, and at least seven (20 per cent) of the members of the Mauroy government were the sons or daughters of manual or routine non-manual workers. Of the graduates who sat in the 1974 Comité Directeur 27 per cent were from working-class families.[13] The occupational category that accounts for most of these 'sons of workers' is, not unexpectedly, teaching, the profession that has always afforded an avenue of mobility out of the working class.[14] Of the delegates at the Valence Congress in 1981 25 per cent were *professeurs*, and yet only 4 per cent were the children of *professeurs*. Only 30 per cent of the delegates had bourgeois origins (i.e. were the sons or daughters of businessmen, or professional and higher-managerial people, or *professeurs*).[15]

The second qualification relates to the nature of employment of the middle-class Socialist activists and leaders. The vast majority were graduates in public-sector employment, usually teaching or administration. Furthermore whilst some undoubtedly were to be numbered among the ranks of the

[13] Survey by M. Benassayag quoted in P. Bacot, op. cit., p. 184.
[14] See P. Bacot, 'Le comportement electoral des instituteurs: mitterrandistes et giscardiens', *RFSP* 1977, p. 878.   [15] Cayrol and Ysmal, op. cit., p. 578.

glittering prizewinners of the ENA, many more were rather less spectacularly meritocratic. Prime Minister Mauroy, for example, was a mere technical school teacher, and the Secretary General of the Élysée staff from May 1981 to June 1982, Pierre Bérégovoy, was a former manager with a state corporation and before that a worker—not quite the same pedigree as that possessed by the holders of the offices under Giscard's presidency.

Even allowing for these qualifications, however, a certain social exclusiveness does pervade and serves to underline how significant is the Party's lack of a trade-union base that could provide a means through which industrial workers might be recruited into leadership positions, as they are in the PCF and in the British Labour Party. Notably the only union federation that does afford entry to leadership positions in the Socialist Party (and government), is the white-collar teachers' union, the FEN, whose leader (André Henry) sat in Mauroy's government. There was, however, as befits a party in which trade-union membership is supposed to be obligatory, a perceptible increase in the proportion of trade-unionized activists between 1971 and 1981. Whereas in 1973 32 per cent of congress delegates had no union affiliation, by 1981 the figure had fallen to 15 per cent. In 1973, however, the FEN, with 24 per cent of the delegates, led the field, followed by the CFDT (18 per cent), but by 1981 the CFDT had taken the lead, with 28 per cent of the delegates to the FEN's 26 per cent, the CGT's 10 per cent, and the FO's 6 per cent.[16] These figures imply a certain diversification of the Party's activist base, with the traditionally predominant teachers being offset by the often Catholic, or ex-Catholic, members of the CFDT. There is, on the other hand, little evidence as yet of such people rising into the leadership of the Party, nor any indication that the Party has done anything to counter the dispersal of its unionized activists across the spectrum of union confederations.

If the under-representation of workers is going largely unresisted in the Party, the traditional under-representation of women certainly is not. Whilst women accounted for a small share (13 per cent) of the (1973) membership, a process of feminization is clearly under way. Between 1973 and 1981

[16] Cayrol and Ysmal, op. cit., p. 584.

the proportion of women congress delegates rose from 12 to 20 per cent.[17] Women have also come to comprise an increasing proportion of office holders at all levels, including the Party's leading bodies. This has been a direct consequence of the introduction, under Mitterrand's leadership, of a quota for women office holders—originally 10 per cent, but currently 20 per cent (Article 6 of the party statutes). Constituting only 4 per cent of the Comité Directeur in 1971, women occupied 11 per cent of the places in 1975, and 14 per cent in 1977 and 1981. In the Bureau Exécutif the proportion of women members has risen dramatically from zero in 1973 to 15 per cent in 1975; 19 per cent in 1977; and 30 per cent in 1981.[18] The proportion of women parliamentary candidates rose from 5 per cent in 1978 to 8 per cent in 1981.[19] In June 1982 it was decided that women should comprise at least 30 per cent of the candidates in towns with over 10,000 inhabitants in the municipal elections of March 1983. Between June 1981 and March 1986 women occupied 6 (or 14 per cent) of ministerial posts, and in contrast to a somewhat token promotion of women during Giscard's presidency, some of the posts were not those traditionally seen as 'women's' jobs. Thus, Agriculture and Industry were held in turn by the leading Socialist woman politician, Edith Cresson. Nevertheless, despite the introduction of a proportional representation system facilitating the placing of women candidates in high, winnable positions on party lists, only 10 per cent of Socialist deputies elected in 1986 were women.

To the ascension of women must be added an albeit less noticeable increase in Catholic participation. The movement of Catholic voters to the Left has been reflected in a slight increase in the numbers of practising Catholic activists in the PS. But they (10 per cent at Valence in 1981) constitute a very small minority confronted by the 25 per cent who are non-practising and the 59 per cent who have no religion.[20] In the Socialist electorate the declared non-religious account

[17] Cayrol and Ysmal, op. cit., p. 573.
[18] P. Bacot, op. cit., pp. 245–6 (for pre-1981 figures).
[19] A. Guédé and S. A. Rozenblum, 'Les candidats aux élections législatives de 1978 et 1981', *RFSP*, Oct.–Dec. 1981, p. 989.
[20] R. Cayrol, op. cit., p. 936, and Cayrol and Ysmal, op. cit., p. 581.

for only 14 per cent; the activists thus present a harder face to the Church than do the voters. Yet at leadership level changes are perceptible: the traditional pattern was for the majority of the Comité Directeur to have no religion, for a strong minority to be non-practising believers, and for a small minority to be practising. The new pattern which is emerging involves, still, a majority of non-believers, but a strong minority now of practising believers, and a decreasing minority of non-practising believers.[21] It is almost incredible that in a party once so impregnated with anti-clericalism and Freemasonry the proportion of leaders with religious beliefs should be slightly increasing.

In this development, as in all the others commented on in this chapter, the Socialist Party is very much the mirror of its times: a movement which has been the beneficiary of significant social changes which have, in turn, served to transform the internal life of the Party. Advancing more on the votes of the expanding new middle class than on the contracting industrial working class, and internally dominated by the new professionals in teaching and administration, the PS is the Party of the tertiary (largely public) sector, credentialled (not propertied) middle class. It is a party which assembled an unpredictable electorate in 1981. Popular (in 1981) with the working class, it lacks deep roots in that class. Capable also of taking 'protest' votes from the parties of the Right, it cannot rely on such support. It can hardly rely on its own, for, unlike the Right, which rests on the traditional bourgeoisie and the farming vote, and the Communists who rely on the industrial working class, the PS is essentially the party of a politically volatile new class which in 1981 voted for change, rather than for radicalism, but which has a certain vested interest in publc enterprise, given the nature of its employment in the public sector. It is, however, a class of too recent origin to make predictions about its long-term political commitment easy. Nor correspondingly is it easy to define the representative function of a party whose social roots are, comparatively speaking, so shallow and so recently put down.

Catch-all parties, of the sort that the PS has clearly become, rely on many factors for their health and well-being, and

[21] P. Bacot, op. cit., p. 167.

close attachment to a single well-defined traditional social class is not essential. But certainly all successful parties of this type on the Left in European democracies (Labour, SPD, etc.) have rested upon a rock of working-class support. The Socialist Party's drift away from its already slight attachment to such a class at activist and leadership level is admittedly mirrored in other socialist parties, and the slow decline of the political identity of that class is also evident throughout Western Europe. Moreover, assisting the Socialist Party in overcoming a traditionally weak organisational entrée into the working class is the decline of the Communist Party and of the CGT. Thus, whilst the PCF—with some two thirds of its vote drawn from manual workers—remained in 1986 an overwhelmingly working class party, its working class base comprised a mere fifth of the total blue collar electorate. By contrast, even when losing ground in 1986, the Socialists retained the support of a third of manual workers.

In an election in which a general displacement of the electorate toward the right appeared confirmed by the National Front's capture of some 10 per cent of the working class vote, it was likely that Socialist losses to the Right were compensated by Socialist gains from the PCF. This, given the overwhelmingly working class character of the Communist electorate, implied an accretion of blue collar support for the Socialists—a process likely to continue if the PCF's decline proved irreversible. However, given the finite size of the dwindling Communist working class vote and the static numerical condition of that class as a whole, it was from losses to the parties of the Right among the dynamic managerial and white collar groups that the Socialists had most to fear. Even if all Communist blue collar strength proved poachable, the Socialist Party was still dependent upon a politically fickle middle class to return it to power.

10
Structures and Currents

French Socialist Party organization is complex. Like the old SFIO, the Party has a structure which is pyramidal in form but which depends upon a continuous to and fro of consultations between levels and, in particular, between the activist base and the summit. Moreover, like the SFIO, the contemporary party is crossed by different currents of opinion—organized and semi-organized—which emerge from time to time in different guises: these factors combine to give it a rich inner life. The Party is, in fact, the most democratic —the most pluralistic—of the major French parties. It is the only party that gives proportional representation to competing groups in its executive bodies, and whilst a democratic intention may frequently give way to an oligarchic reality, the Party is still distinguishable from the Leninist centralism of the PCF and the leadership-supporting culture which pervades the larger parties of the Right.

Organization

The basic unit of organization is the section.[1] Sections are, in the main, geographically based, corresponding to the local administrative unit, whether commune or *quartier*. They are required to have at least five and not more than 250 members. In addition to geographical sections there are sections based on work-place (*sections d'entreprise*) and university sections. By 1981 there were only some 1,000 workplace sections against the (claimed) 8,000 Communist Party workplace cells —which the Socialist sections are supposedly seeking to rival. Most of the Socialist workplace sections are, moreover, in white-collar, rather than in blue-collar, businesses.[2] It is at

[1] For the party statutes see *Guide du nouvel adhérent (Parti Socialiste)*, pp. 51–63, P. Bacot, *Les dirigeants du Parti socialiste; histoire et sociologie*, Presses universitaires de Lyon (Lyons), 1979, pp. 336–51, or C. Hurtig, *De la SFIO au nouveau Parti Socialiste*, Colin (Paris), 1970, pp. 98–113.

[2] See K. Evin and R. Cayrol, 'Les partis politiques dans les entreprises', *Projet*, June 1976, pp. 633–48, and R. Cayrol, 'Le parti socialiste à l'entreprise', *RSFP*, April 1978, pp. 296–312.

section level that the member pays his dues and participates in electoral campaigning and political debate. A mandated delegation from the section proportionately represents the variety of its views at the federal congress which meets (biennially in each of the Party's federations (see Figure 10.1).

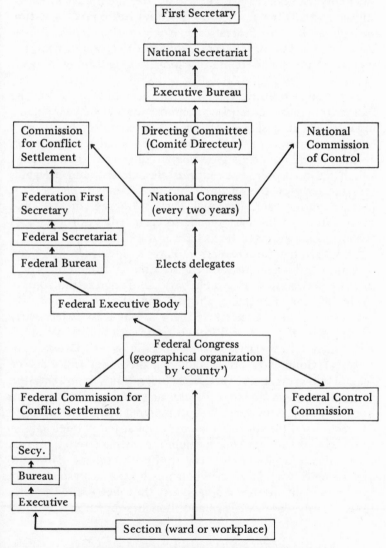

Figure. 10.1. French Socialist Party organization
(from P. Bacot, *op. cit.*)

The federation is the department (county) level of organization. It is the level that has formal responsibility for candidate
selection, although in fact the federation's role is usually to
ratify selections made at lower levels. Candidates for cantonal
elections, for example, are chosen by the locality; the National
Assembly candidates are chosen by the members in a constituency and then ratified by a special National Convention
as well as by the federation. (Where party membership is
below one in 500 of the electorate in an electoral district, the
section chooses a short list of candidates, and federal organs
can make the final choice.)

For representation at national levels of the Party, the
federation must comprise a minimum of fifty members
organized in at least five sections. Each federation has its own
executive committee, elected by proportional representation
at the federal congress. The federal congress is the forum in
which national policy resolutions are debated, and delegates
are selected for the biennial National Party Congress.[3] A
month before each National Party Congress the national
organization of the Party sends to each federation copies of
the motions submitted for debate at the congress.

The National Congress is the Party's electoral college and
determines the composition of the Comité Directeur, which
in turn determines after each National Congress the composition of the Executive Bureau and the Secretariat. (In
between National Congresses there are at least twice-yearly
meetings of the National Convention, with additional meetings called as necessary to decide specific issues.) Delegates to
National Congresses are elected by the federations at the
federal congresses, the size of a federation's representation
being decided on the basis of one delegate per 50–100 members, two delegates per 100–250 members, and one delegate
for every additional 250 members. Each federal delegate at
the National Congress has a minimum voting strength of one
vote, plus one for every twenty-five members. Thus the
departments with large memberships have a correspondingly
greater weight at the congress. (In the 1960s three federations—Nord, Pas-de-Calais, and Bouches-du-Rhône—wielded

[3] F. Borella, *Les Partis politiques dans la France d'aujourd'hui*, Seuil (Paris),
1973, pp. 158–62.

about half the votes cast; by 1979 their share had fallen to nearer a quarter.)

National Congresses meet to debate 'policy' and to elect the Comité Directeur. This is done through political motions to which lists of proposers' names are attached in rank order. In considering general political motions delegates are therefore deciding the leadership of the Party for the ensuing two years, as the seats on the Comité Directeur and Executive Bureau are allocated proportionately to the sponsors of the various motions, provided that their motion obtains more than 5 per cent of the delegates' votes. This system of proportional representation ensures that the Comité Directeur and the Executive Bureau comprise a representative sample of party opinion.

Before each congress the texts of the competing motions are circulated in the federations. The Comité Directeur will try at this stage to arrange a compositing of rival motions into a *texte de synthèse*. Such composite and non-composite motions are then returned to the federations and sections for discussion. The federal congresses will determine how their delegation will spread their vote over the various motions. Some departmental federations with a particular tradition or interest will often submit their own motion (as, for example, did the Bouches-du-Rhône federation in 1979) rather than split their votes over a variety of motions; and the Nord federation has usually sought to keep its vote together behind a leadership-supported motion so as to ensure that its leaders retain their position of influence within the Party.

As many as five significant motions may compete at National Congresses, though in the 'eighties with the Party in office and supporting President Mitterrand, unanimity — albeit a rather spurious one — came to prevail. This was first demonstrated at the post-victory Valence Congress in 1981 where a formally united party was seen to be preferable to the traditional pluralism. In effect, although motions to the National Congress are constantly discussed, their main function is the demarcation of competing leadership groups. Few activists read all the often weighty documents on which they are supposed to pass judgement; the nuances and inflections of motions are usually secondary to the identity of those whose names are appended to them. Thus, for example, 'Motion C' at the Metz

Congress in 1979 was a banner around which the supporters of its leading signatory, Michel Rocard, were being invited to rally. There are, however, sometimes real points of strategy, tactics, or policy at issue, but the difficulty comes in picking them out from the lexicographical morass. The Metz Congress clearly turned on the clash of ambition and personality between Mitterrand and Rocard, and yet underlying it there were also important issues concerning the nature of the Left alliance and of Socialism.

Because National Congresses shape the leadership for the subsequent two years and determine the broad lines of policy, they are key events in the Party's life and are usually referred to by the place where they were held ('Épinay' in 1971 or 'Metz' in 1979). However it would not be strictly accurate to say that the congresses 'decide' policy because delegates are normally already committed to one group or another. There can, however, be a 'floating vote' and surprises do happen at the National Congress: for example the 'coup' carried out in 1971 to bring François Mitterrand to the head of the Party involved the tactical but disguised co-operation of Mauroy, Defferre, CERES, and Mitterrand's CIR group during the congress, something which only just came off; and at Metz in 1979, against considerable counter-pressures Pierre Mauroy's speech kept his group together and maintained his own influence in the Party. The National Congress provides an environment in which plots and strategies can flourish like mushrooms in a dark cellar.

A principal focus for deals is the commission for the compositing (synthesis) of resolutions. This body, which meets during the congress, is made up of representatives of the different motions and seeks in theory to achieve a general composite motion. During this process everybody pays lip-service to the unity of the Party. More often than not disagreements within the Party prevent such compositing and sometimes a composite is refused for tactical reasons (for example to demonstrate the strength of a particular group). With Congress delegates traditionally calling for '*unité, unité*', the compositing committee can become an attempt to thrust the onus for refusing a composite motion onto one's opponents.

If no composite resolution is put together, the last day of

the National Congress votes a series of texts and the composition of the Comité Directeur (Article 34) is decided on the basis of the votes cast for those resolutions. The Comité Directeur has 131 members plus twenty-six 'substitutes' who stand in for full members when necessary. Members of other Party organizations (e.g. Mouvement de la Jeunesse Socialiste and some fringe groups) sit in attendance at Comité Directeur meetings. Article 38 gives the Comité superiority in determining party policy over the parliamentary group if the parliamentarians are out of step with it. The Comité Directeur controls the Party between congresses (Article 32) and is responsible for ensuring that congress decisions are carried out. It is also responsible for propaganda, control of activists, and elected office-holders (Article 33). It meets every two months (more if need be), and elects a twenty-seven-member Executive Bureau from amongst its number. Comité Directeur meetings are followed by the press with great attention and are often the occasion for spectacular debates.

The Executive Bureau (Article 39) is an administrative body whose (by 1987) forty members supervise different aspects of party activity. Within the Executive Bureau is a Secretariat of variable size (sometimes fourteen members, sometimes more) which comprises the Party's 'governing majority'. Those who have a majority on the Comité Directeur based on the votes cast for their text(s) at the National Congress are therefore in a position to control the Party by monopolizing all the places in the Secretariat. This indeed has been the position since 1971. Mitterrand's alliance with CERES after the 1979 Metz Congress, at which he did not quite achieve the 51 per cent needed, was required in order to secure the Secretariat. Positions on the Secretariat are highly sought after and can be used to push their holder to national prominence. They also allow—in fact demand—extensive contact with local activists for explaining, advocating, and sometimes imposing, party policy.

Each member of the Secretariat is a National Secretary for a policy area or function. National Secretaries have committees and delegates who are given specific tasks or who have been made spokesmen on specific issues. Some areas of activity of National Secretaries are extensive (e.g. local government), others less so (e.g. research), but the Secretariat makes somebody responsible for each of the main concerns from the press, through foreign policy, to the European Community. It is, however, at this point that party structure shades into the indeterminate.[4] Since Mitterrand's style of party leadership was to establish parallel organizations based on a private office staffed by people who had his confidence, a good deal of confusion arose between the formal and informal structure. For example, Jacques Delors, whose formal status in the Party was minimal, was extremely influential in policy-making before his appointment as Minister of Finance in 1981.

At the apex of the Socialist Party stands the First Secretary. This was not the original intention: the very name 'First' Secretary is meant to distinguish the post from 'General Secretary'—from the 'authoritarian' practice believed to exist in the SFIO. The description of the First Secretary (in article 39) is modest: he is 'the spokesman of the Party, responsible for *animation* and co-ordination'. There was in fact a form of collective leadership with the First Secretary as *primus inter pares* during Alain Savary's tenure from 1969 to 1971, but with the election of François Mitterrand in 1971 the position became quite different. Mitterrand established an authority and an ascendancy in the Party every bit as extensive as Guy Mollet's in the SFIO.

By 1978, when threatened by the rise of Rocard, Mitterrand's position was entrenched in years of party activity and bolstered by activists who had joined the Party in order to support him through one election campaign after another in the 1970s. Mitterrand used this influx of supporters to push back the challenge from Rocard at Metz in 1979, but his control of the Party had been established well before through a group of capable supporters who were executors in his cause. These people were rewarded, promoted, and pushed into positions in a manner expected of a good party manager. As a result Mitterrand was able to ground his control of the Party not just in goodwill, but in an extended network of supporters.

---

[4] Serge Quadruppani, *Les Permanents des partis politiques*, A. M. Métailié (Paris), 1979, pp. 102–8.

The press

French Socialists have a lively party press which caters for a variety of interests in the Party. Coming under the National Secretary for Propaganda, this included for about six months over the election period of 1981 the daily paper *Combat socialiste*, but it had a low circulation, never really looked workable, and ceased publication after the election. Most important of the other journals is the weekly *L'Unité*, which acts as the Party's official mouthpiece and has an agricultural version, *L'Unité agricole*. *L'Unité* was edited by Claude Estier, National Secretary for Press and Information until 1979. *Le Poing et la rose* is a journal for party activists, and *Le Combat socialiste* a monthly journal aimed particularly at workers in factories. There are also specialist journals such as *Armée nouvelle* (for military specialists), *Communes de France* (local government), *PS-Info*, etc. These journals are well written and in some cases detailed academic studies: the Party has a developed sense of the importance of theory, dissemination of information, and publicity.

The intellectual monthly *La Nouvelle Revue socialiste*, is intended to develop party doctrine on all matters and is devoted to theoretical argument. Associated with this side of the Party's activities is the Club Socialiste du Livre, a party publishing house which diffuses a large number of modestly priced socialist writings independent of a party view.

There are numerous local bulletins and journals, some like the Nord Federation's *Nord demain* being local and/or regional information journals for activists with additional articles, comments, and local or national news, while others are simply Socialist broadsheets. The Party has a sympathetic local press in some areas, for example *Le Provençal* which belonged to Gaston Defferre (with editions in Marseilles, Corsica, and the Côte d'Azur) and other local dailies. Some national dailies give the Party a very sympathetic press: *Le Matin*, in particular (although its circulation has fallen badly) is pro-Socialist, but has confirmed some misgivings with its strongly Rocardian stance, and *Le Monde* could not be accused of being anti-Socialist. There is also the pro-Socialist *Nouvel Observateur* which has played a big role on the Left as a French version of the *New Statesman*, though in a glossier format.

Although the Socialist Party benefits from a good deal of press support, its statutes still call for the acceptance of party discipline by journalist members of the Party (Article 80). François Mitterrand and others were known to be disgruntled with the Party's treatment (and Mitterrand's image) in the press. (This was in fact the original impetus behind the now failed *Combat socialiste*.)

Unions

As has already been noted in Chapter 7, the Party does not have a direct formal link with the unions (unlike the British Labour Party) and does not control a union federation in the way the PCF leads the CGT. Nevertheless many union activists in the FEN, CFDT, and FO are Socialists, even if the Socialist activist's obligation to join a union is not fully respected. French Socialists have very close historic relations with Force Ouvrière whose leader André Bergeron is a long-time Socialist; they are also close to the newer, more modern CFDT whose leadership is pro-Socialist. The FEN (teachers' union) is also close to the Socialists, although in this confederation the Communists constitute a sizeable minority.

The Socialist Party's flirtation with the CFDT unions has never led to a closer relationship than one of mutual sympathy, but it has benefited from Socialist success, and the Party gained numerous CFDT activists with the entry of Rocard in 1974. For Force Ouvrière the position has been complicated by Left union: though traditionally Socialist, the FO is anti-Communist and just as it is wary of the PCF, so have the Socialists been wary of its anti-Communism. Socialists do have sympathizers inside the Communist GCT and one Socialist has a token seat on the CGT executive, but even though there were strong currents of CGT opinion in favour of Left union in 1981, it is difficult to envisage a Socialist foothold of any size in the Communist unions. Thus a Socialist relationship with the unions similar to that of the British Labour Party is not on the agenda.[5]

[5] See J.-F. Bizot *et al.*, *Au parti des socialistes*, Grasset (Paris), 1976, pp. 284–310.

Divisions in the Party: currents, tendencies, and factions

Factionalism as such is condemned in the Party's statutes
(Article 4 opposes the existence of 'organized tendencies'),
and no group will claim to be factional. Currents of opinion
are, however, tolerated and form part of the Party's regular
functioning. As already shown, voting at congresses serves
two purposes: the determination of 'policy' and strategy, and
the allocation of leadership positions. Because of this dual
function of congress votes, aspirants for office whose names
do not appear on the lists attached to the rival motions stand
no chance of election. With the route to office-holding lying
in factional activity, there is no role for non-alignment; rival
groups are thus not so much tolerated as required.

Factional activity in the Party thus sees ideology, power,
and personality intertwined in an often confusing way. In
theory a spectrum of possibilities exists, extending from a
pure leadership contest on the one hand to a pure clash of
principle on the other. In the former case, personal ambition
has, however, to be cloaked in some ideological garb; no
group of aspirants to the leadership can afford to present
itself as merely power-orientated, and certain issues or ideologies have to be invoked to legitimate ambition. In the
second case—'the pure clash of principle'—the need for
motions to be accompanied by a list of sponsors ensures that
even ideologically polarized debate becomes associated with
the identities of particular leaders. Most battles in the Party
fall somewhere between the two ideal types described above,
but it must be acknowledged that the 'presidentialization' of
French politics in the Fifth Republic has had an important
impact upon the nature of conflict within the Party. No
longer is the Party merely selecting a leader to please the
activists, but a potential President of the Republic whose
appeal must extend well beyond the limited confines of the
Party. The presidentialized nature of French politics has
both increased the personalization of intra-party conflict
and decreased the force of purely ideological debate, as was
revealed in the competition after 1978 between Rocard and
Mitterrand for the 1981 presidential nomination. Whilst there
can still be conflict over motions espousing feminism or
ecology, which can hardly be represented as leadership

conflicts, the major confrontations at Socialist congresses have come to be between the battalions drawn up behind rival contenders for party, and now national, office. Even CERES, the most ideologically orientated of the Party's groups, has formed part—for all but four years since 1971—of the majority sustaining Mitterrand's leadership.

Discussion of factions requires some consideration of terms. *Faction* is conventionally taken to imply a group with continuity of existence, discipline, and stability of personnel over time.[6] Frequently such organizational permanence is underpinned by a distinct ideological coherence, and is expressed in the penetrative power of the group, with its members being found at all levels of the Party's operation: in the leadership (both parliamentary and extra-parliamentary), the activists, and the membership. A *current*, or *tendency*, on the other hand, is generally taken to be something rather looser: not necessarily permanent or well organized or well disciplined, and involving a more transient personnel (who may drift in and out of involvement with the group), and often lacking the ideological homogeneity of a faction. Sartori sees a current (or tendency) as 'a patterned set of attitudes', and a faction as 'a specific power group'.[7] In addition to factions and currents are what may be termed 'single-issue groups', formed around one specific theme, such as feminism or ecology, and normally lacking any serious leadership ambitions: such groups often cut across the more formal or permanent party groups.

If the above definitions are applied to the Socialist Party, one group—CERES—clearly qualifies for the term 'faction'. CERES has, in its time, been accused of being 'a party within a party', with its own headquarters, organization, subscriptions, and journal. It has, in fact, an existence that predates that of the present Party, and is, moreover, ideologically well defined and possesses a clear identity—and, importantly, a self-image—as the Party's left wing. Most other groups are closer to being currents than factions, essentially because they often lack the clarity of ideological

[6] See R. Rose, 'Parties, Factions and Tendencies in Britain', *Political Studies*, 1964, pp. 33-46, and D. Hine, 'Factionalism in West European Parties; a Framework for Analysis', *West European Politics*, January 1982, pp. 36-53.

[7] C. Sartori, *Parties and Party Systems* (Vol. 1), Cambridge University Press (London), 1976, pp. 71-5.

definition, have a much looser structure, and are more likely to represent either a specifically regional interest or identity (such as Mauroy's Nord or Defferre's Bouches-du-Rhône), or are formed around a personality, whether an attractive presidential aspirant such as Rocard, or an incumbent leader, Mitterrand. This latter presided for ten years over an extremely heterogeneous mixture of personnel of widely varying ideological stances, who were primarily united—it might be argued—in their quest for the spoils, patronage, and influence to be had from association with a securely established leader. Because the term 'faction' most accurately applies to only one of the Party's groups, it is more appropriate to use the term 'current', and for the purposes of this chapter the currents have been taken to comprise those groups that have had a definable influence on the Party's history since 1969.

The reconstruction of the Party in 1969 saw the unification of a heterogeneous collection of forces. Whilst the 'remaking of Socialist unity' in 1969 was not to be compared with that of 1905, which juxtaposed revolutionaries and parliamentarians, the Party was, like most Socialist parties, sufficiently diverse to warrant the reintroduction of the proportional representation of currents which had been abolished by Mollet in 1946. For like all socialist parties the PS inevitably enjoys a more or less incessant internal debate, both because of the reformist—and yet ill-defined —objectives of 'socialism' and because of the disputatious character of the (increasingly articulate) activists drawn to such parties. It is inevitable that factions, currents, and tendencies should emerge in such a context. Moreover, the Party has had to respond to pressures from without. Admittedly the pressures of the 1960s and 1970s were slight in comparison with the strains imposed on the SFIO by a series of crises during the Third and Fourth Republics (the Popular Front, the Fall of France, the Resistance, the ousting of the Communist ministers, the Cold War, German rearmament, the Algerian war, and the return of de Gaulle), but the contemporary party has had to confront the challenge posed by a *de facto* presidential system and has had to overcome its deep distrust of the Communists in order to build a consistent alliance strategy. Inevitably, such pressures provoke conflict, and so circumstance combines with tradition to ensure that the PS enjoys an internal life of some ebullience.

Of the various currents only CERES is comparable to the British Tribune group in longevity; others are, even in the perspective of the Socialist Party, more ephemeral affairs. For example, the Mauroy group only took on a separate existence before the 1979 Metz Party Congress (although the long-influential federation of the Nord provided its essential backing), and the 'Molletist' group based on the study circle OURS ceased to be identifiable to any real extent after the Grenoble Congress of 1973. The issues and personalities which separate the different currents are also impermanent and can be expected to change rapidly in the future. (A schematic classification of the currents at Metz in 1979 and Lille in 1987 is given in the Appendix.)

The Nord federation

From what has been said it will be evident that the 'Nord' as such is less a current than the base of support for the ex-Prime Minister, Mauroy, and has been his main base since 1969 when he replaced Augustin Laurent, then mayor of Lille, as the local Socialist leader. Most currents are more strongly represented in some federations than in others, and this is the case with Mauroy's. Based on the Lille area, the Nord federation formed one of the old working-class bastions of the non-Communist Left, with a history going back to the mid-nineteenth century.[8] With the Pas-de-Calais and the Bouches-du-Rhône, the Nord formed the troika of federations which dominated the SFIO in the 1950s and 1960s. Guy Mollet then presided over the adjacent Pas-de-Calais, and the SFIO was effectively managed by a Nord–Pas-de-Calais alliance, and it was Mauroy's decision to break this that made reform of the Party possible. The Nord is currently the largest federation, with an estimated 14,000 members in 1982, but its relative weight within the Party has declined.

Nord politics is often spoken of as 'Guesdist', after the marxist leader of the old SFIO left wing, Jules Guesde.[9] This is a term which evokes a narrow, bitter, jargon-ridden

---

[8] D. Bleitrach, *Classe ouvrière et social-démocratie: Lille et Marseille*, Éditions Sociales (Paris), 1981.   [9] Ibid., p. 273.

sectarianism with little or no concern for practical affairs. Nothing could be more misleading as a description of the Nord. Yet in a very specialized way the Nord is 'Guesdist' in the sense of being constantly occupied with the maintenance of the Party, its health, and the welfare of 'its' people (the Socialist voters), and imbued with a sense of identity, co-operation, and party solidarity. Thus the Nord, unlike the federations of Paris or the Bouches-du-Rhône, has a federation bureaucracy of some size, an impressive headquarters, a whole constellation of associated youth, welfare, and functional organizations, and a range of bulletins.

The Nord's other main feature is the vast network of Socialist local authorities around Lille and in the mining, textile, and industrial towns and villages of the Belgian border. A tradition of local-government administration which is both active and reliable has been established over many years. Local government is the Nord Socialists' principal area of activity and one which has maintained the Party in the area through good times and bad, so that unlike the rest of the Party outside the Pas-de-Calais and the Bouches-du-Rhône there is a genuine Socialist tradition and no abrupt discontinuity between the SFIO and the renewal of French Socialism under Mitterrand.

Activists have grown steadily in numbers since 1971, and the Party has conquered some new local authorities, it held its position in 1986 and retained control of the region (one of only two Socialist-controlled regional councils) although Socialist leadership of the powerful Lille urban district was briefly in doubt after the local elections of 1983. Big gains were unlikely, given that the federation was working efficiently enough even under the SFIO and the 'easy pickings' (in the form of newly captured municipalities) made in other, once moribund, federations were not available in the Nord, where further advances could only come at the expense of the well-entrenched Communist Party.[10]

The competition with the locally powerful Communist Party is indeed one of the main emotional issues. Even during periods of ostensible alliance relations between Communists and Socialists in the Nord had not been easy.

[10] G. Fillebeen, 'Les élections municipales à Lille sous la Ve République', mémoire de maîtrise Lille III.

During the Popular Front there was considerable resentment, after the Second World War there were brutal physical clashes, and more recently the mid-'seventies were marked by persistent local-government difficulties when Communists refused to vote for Socialist budgets. Both in the Nord federation, and in the neighbouring Pas-de-Calais, colourful anti-Communist figures are traditional; these include Arthur Notebart, head of the Lille urban district council and André Delelis (mayor of Lens), who refused the alliance with the PCF in the local elections of 1977 and 1983, and for the offence on the second occasion was sacked from the Government. The process of adaptation to the Union of the Left strategy at local level was hardest in those areas, like the Nord, where the Socialists and Communists had been locked in combat since the 1920s, for as in other areas where the Socialists had retained a working-class base after 1920, there was much at stake.

Within the Nord the major focus of attention is Lille, of which Pierre Mauroy was elected mayor in 1971. The council is one which prides itself on a long history of effective administration, having developed a series of expenditures on social services, housing, and transport. This is where Nord local government distinguishes itself; the management of the integrated Lille urban area (of about 1 million people) has been spectacular. Mauroy is the figurehead of the city council, but has always been more concerned with national than with local politics. This is possible because, unlike that of smaller cities, the management of business is a team affair, with the mayor being assisted by *'adjoints'*.[11] Mauroy came to the head of the Nord federation after Augustin Laurent, through Léo Lagrange groups, the small party in Le Cateau, and service in party work. This upward progression would have been impossible in the weaker federations where it would not have been easy for promising activists to be helped by the party organization. Pierre Mauroy is very much a product of the Nord federation.[12]

When the split between Mitterrand and Rocard in 1979 forced Mauroy to take a position (see Chapter 6) local contacts

[11] 'Choix de société ou élections de quartier? Les élections législatives de 1974 à Lille', *RFSP*, April, pp. 259–60.
[12] Pierre Mauroy, *Héritiers de l'avenir*, Stock (Paris), 1977.

were reactivated and a current was organized. The current included Robert Pontillon, Alain Savary, Francoise Gaspard, Jean Le Garrec, Roger Fajardie, Daniel Percheron (head of the Pas-de-Calais), and deputy Bernard Derosier, who led the Mauroy current after 1981. Study sessions were arranged from time to time and a small office was set up to produce the journal *Action Socialiste*. This expressed the group's position on party issues and maintained contacts between members.

Mauroy's 'Current B' at the Metz Congress in 1979 was focused on the personal and SFIO loyalties around Mauroy and brought in Marc Wolf from CERES in the Nord and the Vosges deputy Christian Pierret, who had broken with the rest of CERES over its nationalistic and sectarian views, and its over-sympathetic attitude towards the PCF after 1977. Unlike Rocard, Mauroy never broke outright with Mitterrand, for the current's view that party unity was the first priority implied the avoidance of an explicit break with the leadership. Mauroy and the group regarded the Rocard–Mitterrand squabble as ruinous and hoped that Mitterrand would either declare in advance that he would be presidential candidate in 1981 (in which case they would back him) or make way for Rocard. On other issues the Mauroy group were in favour of EEC enlargement and were pro-European in political-economic terms. The group, though not the entire Nord federation, also laid claim to a form of 'social democracy' and to a loosening of some aspects of party discipline to allow greater expression. Mauroy, unlike Rocard, favoured the Plan and wanted a more interventionist economic policy based on the nationalization measures foreseen in the Common Programme. However, his current, lacking a clear ideological focus, was characterized by an overall moderation and a concern for practical measures. It did not develop a strongly theoretical journal or much participate in the philosophical debates which are such a feature of Socialist Party politics. Mauroy himself, a technical school teacher, the son of a teacher (*instituteur*), and grandson of a worker, is not part of the Parisian Socialist élite of *énarques* and *universitaires*, nor an academic high flier. He lived before elevation to the Matignon in a council house close by the Lille *mairie*, and has always exhibited a mistrust for ideology and theory—

notably for *autogestion*. He is, with his large, pragmatic, re-assuring presence, the closest of the Socialist leaders to the north-European social democratic tradition, and reflects the more blue-collar character of Nord Socialism.

The Bouches-du-Rhône

Like the Nord, the Bouches-du-Rhône—centred on Marseilles —is a federation rather than a current, displaying, like the Nord, a distinct coherence in the political behaviour associated with the federation. This coherence is both greater and more regionally concentrated than in the Nord—not extending much beyond the region of Provence. It is a style of politics unique to Marseilles.[13] This is the area of Daly-style boss politics based on the control of the City Hall and a survivor of an earlier form of politics which no longer finds favour elsewhere. The controller of the federation, Marseilles mayor, Gaston Defferre, died in 1986 and was replaced by the less well-known Robert Vigouroux. The Defferre, or Bouches-du-Rhône, current was essentially one man's local power base, whose congress votes were deployed in a power-broking manner.[14]

There was some truth in Defferre's boast that, although people think Marseilles to be a left-wing city, in fact it was only his attention to municipal government that kept it in the hands of the Socialist Party. This, to some extent, explains the ferocity of the attacks from both Right and Left to which he was subject during his long tenure of the City Hall from 1953–86. Even a cursory glance at the Bouches-du-Rhône Socialist Party confirms Defferre's uncontested dominance, a dominance to which may be attributed the survival of Socialism in Marseilles.

Defferre, born of an old local protestant family, entered the Bouches-du-Rhône Socialist federation in the unhappy days of the 1930s. It was during the War as a member of the Resistance that he began to make his mark, emerging at the Liberation as the presumptive local leader of the Party and briefly as mayor of Marseilles in 1944, until the Communists won the council elections of 1945. Within the Socialist Party there began a long struggle in which Defferre fought, on the

[13] R. Bonnaud 'Que'est-ce qu'un Defferre?', *Partisans* (14), Feb.-Mar. 1964, pp. 1–14.   [14] Ibid.

one hand the old guard within the Party and, on the other the supporters of an alliance with the Communist Party. This was the period in which the distinctive features of the Bouches-du-Rhône federation were created: a wide popular support and fierce anti-Communism.

The Communists, like the Right, saw Defferre as the principal obstacle to their party's progress and the Marseilles Socialists had to fight both a series of extremist conservatives and a powerful Communist Party. Defferre's reformed Socialist Party, along with Centre allies, won the council elections in 1953 and proceeded to provide efficient government in a notoriously ungovernable city: this became the basis for national political prominence as well as the foundation of a local reputation. However Defferre's position in Marseilles always depended on help from Paris and his knowledge of the by-ways of power in the capital. When the Gaullists came to power in 1958 Defferre's links with national politics were cut, though his attempt to run for the Presidency in 1965 established him as a serious adversary of the Government.

Defferre's brand of Bouches-du-Rhône anti-Communism was, however, an obstacle to the development of Left unity on a national level. As the second city of France, Marseilles could hardly resist the national Socialist–Communist alliance, particularly when Defferre's national career depended on it. But it was not until 1983 that Defferre finally accepted a Communist presence on his council election slates (and even then he ensured that the Communists were in a small minority of nine to twenty-nine Socialists). The acceptance of the Communists in 1983 was probably responsible for the demobilization of many Socialist activists and the abstention of the traditional Socialist vote on the first ballot, something which almost cost Defferre the City Hall.

Over the years Defferre gathered around him a team of local Socialists who were both competent municipal administrators and yet posed no challenge to his personal position. These included Lucien Weygand, Jean Masse, Mme Irma Rapuzzi, and Émile Loo, all of whom established themselves as local figures and built up the Socialists' position on the basis of personal contact. Émile Loo, however, annoyed Defferre by declaring his choice for Pierre Mauroy at the Metz Congress in 1979 and was replaced as Federation

Secretary by the ambitious lawyer Michel Pezet. The political scene in Marseilles was never short of people who had crossed Defferre in one way or another, including an ex-ally, M. Jean-Claude Gaudin, who headed the Right's list against him in 1983.

Marseilles is a heterogeneous community, with a variety of local groups and interests which have to be accommodated in a finely judged municipal balancing act. The 1983 elections brought the question of Defferre's supposed liberality towards the immigrant population to the fore, but it also provided a reminder—in the form of an attack on a synagogue—of the nature of the Marseilles extreme Right and of Defferre's ability to reconcile the needs of a variety of ethnic groups: Jewish, Corsican, Armenian, Italian, and Arab.

The system of local administration, *le service rendu*, and popular Socialism depended on Defferre's continuing ability to keep control of the Hôtel de Ville. Were the Party's grip to weaken, the Socialist machine in Marseilles would be particularly difficult to sustain without the coherence currently provided by local-government responsibilities. Within Marseilles, a city of distinct communities, the city councillor is a key figure, in direct contact with the people of his district. *Comités d'Intérêts de Quartiers* (CIQ) form the point of liaison between City Hall and locality and are almost invariably staffed by Socialist activists. Personal loyalties are correspondingly great and the patrons of the city are flambuoyant figures (such as Mme Rapuzzi).[15] Defferre presided over the whole in an avuncular but firm manner, aided by his control both of the largest regional newspaper, *Le Provençal* and, significantly, of its conservative rival, *Le Méridional*.

At national level the position of the Bouches-du-Rhône federation in the Party can be explained by its peculiar politics.[16] Studies showed it to be the most united federation,[17] and yet a war for the succession to Defferre opened up in the 'eighties led by Pezet. Defferre and his allies (especially Sanmarco) fought back but at the time of his death in

[15] J.-F. Bizot *et al.*, op. cit., p. 170 ff.

[16] Georges Righetti, 'La social-démocratie dans les Bouches du Rhône', *Cahiers du Communisme*, April 1961, pp. 767–87.

[17] Roland Cayrol, 'Le vote de fédérations dans les congrès du Parti Socialiste', *RFSP*, Vol. XXI, Feb. 1971, pp. 51–75.

1986 the situation in the federation was one of acute factional rivalry.

On the Left the Bouches-du-Rhône Socialists are often caricatured as moss-backed conservatives.[18] Certainly Defferre was a full-blown conservative on the vogue issues of the 'seventies, notably *autogestion*. When asked why workers' participation was not part of the scene in *Le Provençal* offices Defferre replied that there was no reason for *autogestion* in his business, because if the workers had a say in running it they would choose him. (Collective control of the business was however, promised, after his death.) Defferre's record had its achievements: in recent years the cleaning up of gang-ridden Marseilles (with many of the malefactors transferring their attention to Lyons and Nice), and in the Fourth Republic, on the national stage, his decolonization law and a courageous hostility to the Algerian war. Local government remains the important consideration for the Bouches-du-Rhône, and it was not without significance that Defferre as Interior Minister was also given responsibility for decentralization—comprising measures to increase the powers of provincial authorities. On other matters the Bouches-du-Rhône has constantly supported Mitterrand in return for the Party's non-interference in internal federation politics. Rocard, for example, could never find a point of entry into the federation during his campaign for the presidential nomination in 1979–80. Defferre ran a tight ship in the Bouches-du-Rhône.

The Mitterrand current

The 'Mitterrandists' are, in effect, a constellation of mini-currents, some closer to the throne than others. At the centre is the king and his court.[19] Mitterrand, as the Party's federator, unifier, and indispensable electoral asset, established an unchallenged dominance of attractive power. Thus assembled a heterogeneous collection of social democrats, marxists, technocrats, and *arrivistes* around an inner core of *mitterrandistes de foi*—the traditional 'desert crossers', most of whom had been with Mitterrand since the 1960s and many from the

[18] Georges Lazzarino, 'Les problèmes de l'unité des forces démocratiques dans les Bouches du Rhône', *Cahiers du Communisme*, (43), Feb.-Mar. 1967, pp. 239–44.　　　　[19] J.-F. Bizot *et al.*, op. cit., pp. 37-102.

Fourth Republic: men such as *mendésiste* Radicals like Charles Hernu and Pierre Bérégovoy and others such as Louis Mermaz, André Rousselet, and François de Grossouvre. These men were rewarded with the plum jobs in 1981—Pierre Bérégovoy heading the Elysée secretariat (and thence to the National Solidarity Ministry in 1982), Rousselet and de Grossouvre to Mitterrand's *cabinet*, Hernu to the Defence Ministry, and Mermaz to the chair of the National Assembly. Below these 'Mitterrandists of the first hour' are those who were too young at the time: the Jacobin Marxist, Pierre Joxe, leading the 1986 parliamentary group; Édith Cresson, Minister of Agriculture and then of Trade, and one of the women deliberately raised to prominence by Mitterrand for electoral purposes; Lionel Jospin, a pragmatic, colourless technocrat who was awarded the Party's leadership by Mitterrand in 1981 and whose job was to seek to prevent collision between the radical activists and the moderate ministers; and Laurent Fabius and Paul Quilès, who were given important dirty jobs to do for Mitterrand in his fight with Rocard after 1978.[20] Alongside these comes the entourage of advisers and collaborators, again ranging from conventional technocrats through social democrats to Marxists—men such as the economists Jacques Attali (at the Élysée in 1981), Jacques Delors (Finance Minister), and Christian Goux (Assembly Finance Committee chairman), and the university teachers J.-C. Colliard and Maurice Benassayag (at one time editor of *La Nouvelle Revue socialiste*).

Beyond the closest Mitterrand supporters, the current has come to comprise other small satellite groups. The most important of these is that of the recusant Communist Jean Poperen who, since Valence in 1981, has been the Party's number two. This group originally saw itself as the Left of the new Parti Socialiste and therefore felt upstaged by the more attractive CERES. Poperen's group was not part of the Mitterrand coup in 1971, but was painlessly absorbed into the leadership in 1973, where it had no higher ambition, it would seem, than to serve. However the group has a broadsheet called *Synthèse Flash* which comments on weekly events and serves up yet another variety of the Party's Marxist

[20] See J.-F. Bizot *et al.*, op. cit., on Joxe, Jospin, and Mermaz, pp. 82-9 and 92-7.

analyses, but has neither the originality nor the attractively polemical quality of many CERES writings, even if it is more rigorous. (Poperen himself is the author of many weighty works on the French Left.[21]) Apart from Poperen, who is a deputy in suburban Lyons, the group consists mainly of the ERIS circle and has always been loyal to Left union. The social base of this small current is somewhat more working class than others and numbers CGT members.

Finally the Molletists: although influential because of its position as the balance holder from 1969 to 1971, there is no longer an identifiable Molletist group of any importance. Guy Mollet died in 1975 and those of his erstwhile allies who have not followed him to the graveyard have been blown to the four winds—some, such as the anti-Communist notables Lejeune, Montalat, and Moch, right out of the Party. But equally, a few of the anti-Communist troupers of the Nord–Pas-de-Calais—such as Notebart and Delelis—allied with the Mitterrandists, less because they approved the Union of the Left than because they had particular grievances about the control of their local federations. The renewal of the Party after 1969 changed control inside departments such as Pas-de-Calais and Haute-Vienne where they had been important, and such Molletists as remain are now spread between Mitterrand's group and the Nord current. Thus the Mitterrand current has, like the Party itself, distinctly catch-all qualities —for obvious reasons, being the current of the *patron*. Perhaps the most mysterious aspect of it is the patron himself. This man, as the biographer Giesbert[22] has written, is a mystery: a Socialist Party leader from a Catholic petty-bourgeois background; attracted briefly in the 'thirties by Jacques Doriot; a non-supporter, although a twenty-year-old student, of the Popular Front in 1936; a man who hesitated between Pétain and de Gaulle in 1940 and who was elected *sans doctrine* as a Right-supported Radical in 1946; one of the Fourth Republic's most persistent ministerialists; the opponent of presidential rule in 1958 who was to convert the socialist Left to presidentialism in 1965.

Born in 1916, the son of a modest provincial station master,

---

[21] See J. Poperen, *La Gauche française*, Fayard (Paris), 1974.

[22] F.-O. Giesbert, *François Mitterrand ou la tentation de l'histoire*, Seuil (Paris), 1977.

Mitterrand trained in Paris as a lawyer whilst one brother went into the military via Saint-Cyr and another into industry via the *École polytechnique*. His early political development was obscure, with ambiguity clouding even the Vichy years. He was not obviously in the Resistance until 1943 (by which time he was twenty-seven), though he was to serve as a junior minister in de Gaulle's post-Liberation government. In June 1946 he stood in his first parliamentary contest as a representative of the Radical *Gauche républicaine*, and was elected as such five months later in the rural Nièvre department of Burgundy, which provided him with his electoral base for the rest of his thirty-six-year parliamentary career. Between 1947 and 1957 he served eleven times as a minister, most notably as Minister of the Interior in the Mendès France government of 1954, and as Minister of Justice in the Mollet government of 1956–7. He was pre-eminently a national politician, of mild Centre-Left credentials, and lacked both the party roots and the local organization of Socialists such as Mollet, Defferre, and later, Mauroy. He headed at national level nothing more significant than the tiny UDSR, a small assemblage of deputies deeply committed to the 'third force' politics he was so forcibly to reject in the 1970s, and at local level the minor municipality of Château Chinon. His ministerial career in the Fourth Republic was highly conventional, and on the issue that was finally to destroy that regime he was able to declare in 1954, 'L'Algérie, c'est la France'—a sentiment he would not be allowed to forget, particularly since his tenure at the Justice Ministry was to coincide with the stepping up of brutal anti-terrorist measures against the FLN in Algeria. If it was a capacity to survive that accounted for his time-serving in such governments before 1958, his political acumen served him better when he sided with the very small number of Fourth Republic politicians who rejected de Gaulle and the new Republic in 1958, for it was upon that prudent stance that his subsequent career was to be built.

Mitterrand's book, *Le Coup d'État permanent* set out his criticisms of the Gaullist regime and of the method of its coming to power, but was written more with the 1965 presidential elections in view than as a considered reflection on French politics. It is probable that Mitterrand had no future under the Gaullist regime, for although a Resistance leader in the latter stages of the occupation, he was too much his own man to fit into de Gaulle's authoritarian network and was never one of the *fidels*. De Gaulle would moreover have been unlikely to tolerate a rival of Mitterrand's ability and ambition within a Fifth Republic fashioned for his own purposes, and Mitterrand was not the politician to allow his progress to depend on the whims of others. There was little choice for him but to move into opposition, even though this might be costly in the short and medium term. For Mitterrand, a long period in the wilderness stretched ahead.

Mitterrand faced another problem too: if the Gaullists, who had brought together a solid Centre–Right coalition, were to be beaten, an alliance of the parties of the Left, including the Communists, had to be created. Mitterrand's career in the Fifth Republic was based on this perception: the UDSR was abandoned in favour of a grouping of the non-SFIO Left, the Convention des Institutions Républicaines which could serve as a catalyst for Left unity around the person of its leader. It was a two-pronged movement: on the one hand the strategy of Left union which Mitterrand, before other non-Communist politicians, made his own, and on the other his own presidential candidacy through which he became the main opposition leader with the necessary credentials for a future president unencumbered by a disqualifying legacy from the Fourth Republic. During the years 1958–65 he consolidated his position within the Left, but not without certain difficulties. In October 1959 came the *affaire de l'Observatoire*, when it was claimed that an attempt on Mitterrand's life had been fabricated for publicity purposes. This allegation, though untrue, nevertheless removed Mitterrand from the public arena for some time. With considerable courage he rebuilt his political career (as he was to have to do again after the failure of the FGDS in 1968), relying only on a small group of supporters and his own undoubted talents as a politician.

It was Mitterrand's ability to bring together the small warring groups on the French Left to give them a common purpose and his ability to find talented supporters to work with him in different organizations that were his major resources. When, in 1965, the Communists accepted him as the anti-Gaullist presidential candidate it was because they saw his lack of party backing as posing no threat to their party, but in standing as the Left's candidate against the seemingly invincible de Gaulle and forcing him on to a second ballot, he was established as the main non-Communist politician on the Left. However, Mitterrand's attempt to unite the Left from outside the Socialist Party, and without a large party of his own, proved ultimately too difficult, and when the events of May 1968 broke up the Left alliance it was clear that he would have to work within the Socialist Party or not at all.

For Mitterrand the 1970s, as distinct from the 1960s, was the decade of Left amity contrived from within the Socialist Party rather than from without and sometimes against it. The Socialist Party became Mitterrand's Party in the sense that its rebirth and re-creation were largely his work, but the Party had an existence before him and contains within its ranks other personalities who are capable of leading it; it is not his party in total. He does however, despite a frequently proclaimed dislike of party management, have a distinct talent for party organization, and much of the content of his collected speeches is devoted to parties and to the party system. It is probably best to see Mitterrand, not as a political thinker nor a man who can mobilize enthusiasm around ideas nor as an enthusiast for certain policy issues, but as a consummate manipulator of support. In this way he really is the last of the Fourth Republic politicians: he has that talent which thrived in the old Assemblies for negotiation and coalition building. It is also a talent which a divided Left and a splintered Socialist movement needed when he appeared in the early 1960s as a challenge to de Gaulle.

The word most often used to describe François Mitterrand is 'enigmatic'. Despite a long and distinguished political career it is difficult to discern any guiding principle, even though he was recognized early on as a young and brilliant Fourth Republic Minister who might become an eminent member of France's political élite. It is also noticeable that Mitterrand's writings, although voluminous, are unrevealing: it is true that he attacks political opponents, replies to personal slights, and comments on events, but the bulk of his published musings are reflections on nature, poetry, literature, and art. His collected political speeches do not show a consistent political philosophy. He is evidently more concerned with foreign affairs than with economic policy, but he is a frequent defender of justice and civil liberty. His speeches, often referred to as stylish, are marked to some extent by a quasi-Marxist rhetoric, although the vision of the world they impart is essentially humane and certainly not Marxist.

The political tradition from which Mitterrand and his Fifth Republic Party, the CIR, sprang was that of the republican, as distinct from the socialist, Left—stronger on politics than on economics, and having as its principal aim the defence of republicanism against the Gaullists. When eventually the CIR came to define its economic preferences the outcome was a reformist and essentially (with some exceptions in the case of certain people) non-Marxist *'socialisme du possible'*. Mitterrand himself, with disarming frankness, admitted in 1970 that 'reformism seems to me the only possible way, but it has so bad a reputation that one hesitates to say so.'[23] Some followers (notably Joxe) hold that Mitterrand, although initially a republican and not a marxist (he was not even formally a Socialist until 1971) has subsequently been educated into more advanced views by some of his friends (again, notably Joxe), but there is no evidence to support this view.

Perhaps it should come as no surprise that, with his eclectic past, Mitterrand should have succeeded in managing the Party in so impeccable a fashion. Under his leadership there have been no splits or defections except for a few isolated departures of staunchly anti-Communist deputies. This contrasts with the leadership of both Léon Blum and Guy Mollet which did not prevail without the defection of hostile minorities. In 1933 thirty right-wing Socialist deputies (the *néos*) left the Party and in 1939 the left-wing Pivertists defected. Mollet, whilst usually managing successfully to maintain a majority in the Party, and certainly aided by the ending of the system of proportional representation of tendencies after 1945, had retained control in 1958 at the expense of the secession of the PSA (later PSU) founders (Philip, Tanguy-Prigent, Savary, and Gazier) who had opposed his Algerian policy, his support for de Gaulle and the new

[23] J.-F. Bizot *et al.*, p. 58, quoting from Mitterrand's *Un socialisme du possible*, Seuil (Paris), 1970.

regime, and the autocratic nature of his leadership. This defection occurred shortly after the dissidents had secured no less than 30 per cent of the votes at the party congress. Mitterrand's leadership has not required defections of this order, partly because of the more favourable circumstances in which he has been leader.

Michels's theory of the 'iron law of oligarchy' in socialist parties is not without its critics, but there is no doubt that Mitterrand and his entourage have completely dominated the Party, if not entirely for the reasons advanced by Michels, who placed great stress on the 'perennial incompetence' of the mass (the members) and the infinitely greater skills of the leaders.[24] Michels's low evaluation of party members rested on the assumption that they were working class, ill educated, and unselfconfident; modern-day Socialist Party activists—numbering, in France, so many disputatious teachers and articulate professionals—cannot be so dismissed. But in a number of important respects Michels's case for leadership domination has been strengthened by the electoral demands of the Fifth Republic. The French Socialist Party is operating within—and indeed is to a great extent the product of—an institutional and electoral environment which calls for the maximum degree of leadership control over party activists. The frequency of elections, the need for the widest possible appeal to win in two-cornered second-ballot contests, and the presidential system—calling for the assembling of a vast electoral coalition of 14–15 million votes, requires a leader of presidential stature with wide voter appeal. Michels was right when he observed that 'the independence of leaders increases concurrently with their indispensability',[25] but he could never have imagined quite how electorally indispensable a party Leader in a presidential system would come to be, nor how much the organizational and programmatic aspects of party life in the Fifth Republic would come to be affected by the need to elect an executive President.[26] Mitterrand has exploited this aspect to the hilt.

As one major election after another—coming in quick

[24] R. Michels, *Political Parties*, Collier Books (London), 1962.
[25] Ibid., p. 170.
[26] See Hugues Portelli, 'Le présidentialisation des partis', *Pouvoirs* No. 14, 1980, pp. 97–106.

succession after 1973–appeared to nudge the Socialists progressively closer to power, his indispensability seemed confirmed, and it was only when the Left faltered at the brink (in 1978) at the fifth electoral contest during Mitterrand's leadership that patience and nerves began to crack, obliging Mitterrand to confront his first real crisis as leader. Even then, however, the conflict was not of the kind foreseen by Michels–that between the leadership and the mass–but between two presidential rivals from within the leadership, with victory going ultimately to the incumbent who had colonized the party apparatus with his own men.

Moreover, Mitterrand's 'indispensability' derived from more than just his electoral value. It stemmed also from the Party's very factionalism. Significant animosities exist between certain factions and personalities, sometimes unrelated to policy or doctrine, and not always involving a clash of Left and Right: Defferre enjoyed a poor relationship with his fellow moderate, Rocard, and rivalries exist on the left between CERES leaders and hard-left Mitterrandists, such as Joxe. Mitterrand's skill has been shown in his holding the ring and imposing himself upon the Party as the fount of patronage and advancement. Within the Party, nomination to policy-making committees was carefully scrutinized by the leader to ensure both factional balance and individual reliability.[27] Mitterrand was also able to indulge in a considerable amount of faction-juggling: in 1971 when he took up with CERES leaders to win power in the Party; in 1975 when he dropped them; and in 1979 when he reintegrated them into the majority. Albeit enhanced by his presidential victory, Mitterrand's mastery of the Party was also evidenced in the distribution of government portfolios in 1981. All the prominent ministers were either his friends (Badinter, Dreyfus), or else senior figures with whom he had long enjoyed a good working relationship and whom he trusted (Mauroy, Defferre), or protégés who owed him everything (Cresson, Delors, Fabius, Fillioud). A certain degree of faction-balancing lay behind the appointments (the leader of each current was given a high ministerial ranking in the Government), but the factionalists least trusted or approved

[27] R. Cayrol, 'La direction du PS: organisation et fonctionnement', *RFSP*, Paris 1978, p. 210.

by Mitterrand (notably Chevènement and Rocard) found themselves in relatively peripheral posts. As in the Government so in the Party: the men running it after 1981 were, almost without exception, those whose careers had originated in the post-1971 Party under Mitterrand's auspices—Jospin and Quilès and most of the other members of the Secretariat. Georges Marchais's side-swipe at Mitterrand in February 1975 for being 'plus en plus sûr de lui et dominateur' was not intended as a compliment, but it did fairly describe his position within the Party up to his accession to the Presidency of the Republic in May 1981.

After 1981, government office did to a degree expose strains inside the very broad church that is the Mitterrandist current, for whilst all significant posts in Government, Parliament, and Party are held by the President's men, the switch into a deflationary strategy briefly set Left against Right inside the current. The Parliamentary Leader Joxe and the Finance Committee Chairman Goux both opposed deflation, though the former's loyalty to Mitterrand required him to allow Goux, rather than himself, to make publicly explicit the Left's reservations. The President of the National Assembly, Louis Mermaz, likewise instinctively doubted the virtue of the Delors–Mauroy measures, but cleaved loyally to the President. Meanwhile, right-wing Mitterrandists led by Delors, an architect of the austerity programme, stood four square with the men—Rocard and Mauroy—who were isolated by the Mitterandists in the period before the electoral victory of 1981. Joxe and Jospin, as Mitterrand's placemen in Parliament and Party, were however most successful in their role of maintaining discipline among deputies and activists when the President made unambiguous his preferences, for all then duly followed the *patron*. Only when Mitterrand seemed hesitant or did not express a view were ranks broken, and the conflicts inherent in a situation of courtiers and king made more apparent.

The Centre d'études de recherches et d'éducation socialistes (CERES). (Renamed 'Socialisme et République' in 1986)

The most original, intense, intellectual, and best-defined Socialist Party current is its self-proclaimed left wing, the

CERES.[28] Although CERES was established under the SFIO in 1964 with Guy Mollet's blessing, the group became important only after its association with the coup which brought Mitterrand to the leadership of the Party in 1971. From then until 1978 CERES benefited disproportionately from the influx of new adherents into the Party. In 1971 it had 8.5 per cent of the congress votes, at Grenoble in 1973 21 per cent, at Pau in 1975 24.4 per cent, and at Nantes in 1977 24 per cent again (and 40,000 supporters). This, however, was the peak of its influence, for at Metz in 1979 it was reduced to 15 per cent and in a party somewhat reduced in size. After the electoral landslide of 1981 the group provided about the same proportion of the Party's deputies.

CERES was founded by Jean-Pierre Chevènement, Alain Gomez, and Didier Motchane who were joined later by Georges Sarre of the Paris postal workers' union. What distinguished CERES in the mid-'sixties was less its belief that French Socialism was potentially powerful, than that this power could be realized only through alliance with the Communist Party around a Common Programme. It was this that made possible its crucial collaboration with Mitterrand from Épinay in 1971 to Pau in 1975.[29] For CERES the way to a definable French 'Socialism' which was neither 'social democratic' (a CERES term of abuse) nor 'Stalinist' (not a CERES term) lay through the Left alliance of Socialists and Communists.[30]

CERES saw itself as the active conscience of the Party pushing it towards class struggle, involvement in mass movements, and a transition to Socialism. The CERES proto-Leninist organization, suspicious of electoral activity alone, and described by a former member as frankly autocratic, was to play a role in this movement. The organization comprised local and regional groups, meeting regularly, with a steering committee and a secretariat at national level. Because of its

---

[28] See Michel Charzat *et al.*, *Le CERES, un combat pour le socialisme*, Calmann-Lévy (Paris), 1975, and D. Hanley, *Keeping Left? Ceres and the French Socialist Party* Manchester University Press (Manchester), 1986, and Pierre Guidoni, *Histoire du nouveau Parti Socialiste*, Tema (Paris), 1973.

[29] Pierre Guidoni, op. cit., and J.-F. Bizot, op. cit., pp. 200-3.

[30] Jacques Mandrin, *Socialisme ou social-médiocratie*, Seuil (Paris), 1969. (Although pseudonymous, this is a CERES book.) See also J.-F. Bizot, op. cit., Ch. IX.

organization CERES had often (especially in the early 'seventies) been a major magnet for new members, particularly intellectuals and notably in Paris,[31] providing a sheet-anchor for Left union and the Common Programme and an identifiably 'Socialist' ideology based on self-management. In the early years CERES activists were also more likely than others to come from the former *'terres de mission'*—the largely Catholic areas where the Socialist Party made its striking gains in the 'seventies. In the early years of the PS CERES was the most 'religious' of the Party's currents (17 per cent of its activists being, in 1973, practising Catholics) and it did much to establish a route of access to the Party for Catholics. The two departmental federations where CERES retained control in 1979—Belfort and Haut-Rhin—are both in the Catholic east; most of the deputies identifying with the current represented seats either in the East or Paris.

Having crossed the desert from 1975 to 1979, the CERES group re-entered the Secretariat in 1979 at Metz. This was achieved against objections from some CERES activists and despite CERES's echo of the PCF claim that the Party had veered to the Right. In the past CERES had had its differences with Mitterrand who was accused of being high-handed (Motchane noted 'l'empire du milieu se gouverne par mandat du ciel'), but in the Party's Wars of the Roses they firmly took his side against Rocard. CERES caricatured Rocard as the 'American Left', that is, weakly reformist and not inspired or guided by a genuine Socialist view. After Metz CERES acted as Mitterrand's *chien de garde* against Rocard so enthusiastically that they had to tone down their attacks at one point. Only when Mitterrand appeared to hesitate did Chevènement put himself forward as presidential material—then a wholly ludicrous suggestion, since CERES's sectarianism and anti-capitalist language rendered it a group of somewhat limited appeal outside of the Socialist Party at that time.

CERES retains a Paris office with a four-man staff, and publishes a rather academic-looking journal called *En jeu*. Journals, of which there have been several, have always been

[31] Hughes Portelli and Thierry Dumias, 'Les militants socialistes à Paris', *Projet*, Jan. 1976, No. 101, pp. 35–43. (The Paris federation has since been lost to CERES and now has a 'Mitterrandist' majority.)

an important focus for the group. The main brunt of this publication (which had a claimed circulation of 10,000) was given over to the propagating of CERES's ideas by the group's many prolific writers. In the 1970s the group was one of the most active in publicizing *autogestion*, to the extent that it became almost a CERES property, but with the entry of the Rocardians into the Party the notion was perceptibly dropped, after having been none the less a rallying cry in the early 1970s, giving CERES, and the Party as a whole, a distinctive theme. In addition to its now somewhat muffled devotion to self-management, CERES was rhetorically staunchly anti-capitalist. In CERES's publications attacks on capitalism and the alienating workings of the capitalist system were prominent; it was also committed to planning in association with *autogestion*. But the practical details were never made entirely clear, despite the evident need to reconcile centralized planning with decentralized decision-making, and CERES was always suspicious of small-scale production ('small is beautiful') as an end in itself. However, the CERES view of production for use rather than for profit and the need to replace free-for-all competition with a Socialist plan was influential.

A further distinguishing hallmark of CERES was its nationalism, which was demonstrated in many ways, but was well to the fore in its attitude to the nuclear *force de frappe*.[32] It was not until 1977 that the PCF accepted the French nuclear deterrent; the Socialist Party did not come round to this view until later, but in office it was as 'Gaullist' as other parties. Like many in France, CERES was marked by the collapse of 1940 and drew the conclusion, before other segments of the Left, that a nuclear deterrent was necessary. The group was hostile to the Atlantic Alliance and was frequently anti-American. One of the charges against the United States is its 'neo-colonialism' in the Third World, although CERES was indulgent towards the USSR's behaviour which it had refused to categorize as 'imperialist'.[33] CERES was also hostile to a supra-national vision of Europe, although this was combined with a ready perception of where French interests lay in agriculture (hence hostility to enlargement and tampering

[32] See J.-P. Chevènement, *Le Vieux, la crise, la neuf*, Flammarion (Paris), 1975.
[33] Ibid., p. 253.

with the CAP). Didier Motchane, although a member of the European Parliament, was witheringly contemptuous of that institution, and the group has long since concluded that the 'socialist' potential of European institutions is not high. An appeal was once made by CERES for an 'alternative' Europe (as the British Left would call it) which potentially existed alongside the current institutions and which could be woven together from the unlikely strands of the Portuguese radical Left, the Mediterranean Left, PASOK, etc. to form an anti-capitalist *Europe du sud.*

CERES's experience of participation in the five years of Socialist government was a mixed one. Although it maintained discipline within the party apparatus as well as in government, its two most important ministerial figures left office by March 1983. Nicole Questiaux resigned in June 1982 because she refused to restrict social-security spending and J.-P. Chevènement, Industry Minister, followed early in 1983. However the 1984 Fabius government did retain two CERES members in junior posts, even if the Cabinet showed a marked shift to the Right.

Chevènement's 1983 departure was clearly serious for CERES. Despite the group's rhetoric which flowed from the Industry and Research super-Ministry under Chevènement, the administrative record of this department was not good. Under him the pattern of distribution of aid to industry, and its rationalization, had not changed greatly since Raymond Barre's time. Nor were corporate plans being developed properly for the nationalized sector; government intervention was thus sometimes excessive and usually haphazard. Chevènement probably saw no future in this climate and resigned in February 1983 (a decision not made public until after the local elections in March).

Outside the government, CERES made little progress despite an attempt to foment left-wing opposition to the government's strategy in the run-up to the 1983 party congress. In the event, a synthesis of views was achieved at the congress and in 1984 Chevènement returned to office as Education Minister and at the very time the Communists were leaving government.[34] After the 1986 parliamentary election the

---

[34] On CERES in government see Hanley, *op cit*, pp. 232-253.

group was renamed *Socialisme et République*, and whilst retaining the same personnel and structures, the introduction of the word 'republic' implied a mellowing process. Chevènement indeed acknowledged that the union of the Left—a CERES *cause célèbre* for some twenty years—was dead.

The Rocard current

The group which has self-consciously developed a non-Marxist Socialism, and in the process become the main target for left-wingers, is the Rocard group which emerged after the defeat in the 1978 elections, offering a new policy and a new man. It is usually spoken of as 'social democratic', a label it took no great pains to refute. Although Rocard was a late-comer to the Party (entering just after the 1974 *assises*) he found sympathizers and brought with him many ex-PSU members. He had, in any case, been a member of the SFIO until 1958. Thus, although there was no official Rocard current in 1974, there was a network of contacts and friends which facilitated its later development. They were centred on the personality of Rocard, who had been the PSU's presidential candidate in 1969, but the challenge within the Party came after 1978 on the implied grounds that Mitterrand's Union of the Left was defunct and that Rocard and the Rocardians could bring the Party victory by concentrating on the floating vote with a moderate reformist programme.

There are two sides to the 'Rocard phenomenon'. One side is the *copain-copain* matey style which makes Rocard a Socialist activist *bon enfant*, a characteristic which is endearing, if not exactly unique amongst Socialist grandees. The other side is the sedulously cultivated and planned political campaign. This latter was the making of Rocard as a public-opinion favourite after his entry into the Party in 1974. In a manner of speaking he has been manufactured as a political figure by a close group of friends and merchandized on the political market. Perhaps this is to caricature the Rocard group, but no other French politician of the Left has been so dependent on a team which in media and technocratic manner has projected a potential presidential candidate. Thus Rocard motor-cycling from meeting to meeting as the PSU candidate in the 1969 presidential elections was transformed into the responsible administrator in suit and tie which has been so popular with public opinion since June 1978. It was not a transformation made against Rocard's will, but the two styles do not entirely marry.

Rocard's group includes some of the most adventurous thinkers and lively personalities in the Socialist Party.[34] Although not as disciplined or organized as CERES, they do have a considerable network of contacts, an office in Paris (until 1981), and a review, *Faire* (which in 1982 was dissolved and replaced by *Interventions*), whose audience was heavily concentrated among graduates, higher managerials, and *professeurs*. (Of all the PS currents, the largest proportion of activists from higher-managerial backgrounds were to be found among the Rocardians in 1981;[35] and of the forty-five deputies identified with Rocard in the National Assembly elected in 1981, a higher proportion were drawn from the ranks of *professeurs supérieurs* than of any current in the Party's parliamentary ranks.) In addition to aid from *Faire*, which was theoretical, enormous support came from the distinctly pro-Rocard leanings of the popular Socialist Paris daily newspaper *Le Matin* which gave much backing to Rocard's challenge for the 1981 presidential nomination.

Mitterrand has depended on the support of the Party's right (Mauroy and Rocard) to give the Socialists governmental appeal and to capture floating voters. Rocard's challenge came both as an appeal for the Party's nomination in 1981 and as an ideological 'moderate's' objection to the Socialists' direction through the 1970s. In reality the objections which Rocard was making went back to the practical reformism of the Mendès France government and *la gauche réaliste* by which it was inspired. Rocard was supported by the large non-Communist ex-Catholic CFDT unions and their leader Edmond Maire. Rivalling CERES, he found sympathizers among the many Catholic newcomers to the Party after 1969, and hence was strong in Socialist missionary areas such as Brittany. In 1979 the two federations controlled by Rocard's supporters were both in the west (Finistère and

[34] J.-F. Bizot *et al.*, op. cit., pp. 146–69.
[35] R. Cayrol and C. Ysmal, 'Les militants du PS, originalité et diversités', *Projet*, May 1982, p. 577.

Maine et Loire). After 1981 Rocardian deputies were concentrated in three types of region: the affluent Paris suburbs; the West, and parts of the South-West.[36]

In fact Rocard's group was offering a more pragmatic reformist kind of socialism than Mitterrand's, even though Mitterrand himself was travelling ideologically light. Rejecting the usual anti-capitalist language of the Left, Rocard spoke of the need for a market-oriented system and an obligation towards responsible financial management when in office. This entailed a hostility to excessive nationalization as well as to the place generally given to the Plan in Socialist thought. This last point is ironic, given Rocard's post-1981 internal exile at the Planning Ministry, and it was also gratuitous since the role of the Plan in the French economy has long been marginal.[37] But Rocard also developed the theme of self-management, and in more detail than CERES had done. It was also part of the Rocard group's influence to push the problem of regionalization higher up the agenda of the Party.

The Rocard group also posed problems for the party leadership in the debate about the causes and consequences of the economic crisis. Rocard himself had never been enthusiastic about the Common Programme and much of his discussion of how to deal with inflation was implicitly highly critical of that document. In this the Rocard group concurred with the economic policy of the CFDT and with many Socialist sympathizers who regretted the Left's lack of realism on the issue of inflation,[38] though in essence all Rocard did was to take the standard Keynesian economics of the northern social-democratic parties and adapt them to French purposes.

One issue on which Rocard's predisposition probably ran counter to the sympathies of his supporters was that of the Common Market. When in the PSU, and for some time thereafter, Rocard had not bothered to conceal his contempt for the EEC. It was not so much hostility as a healthy scepticism about the possibilities of supranationalism and the working of the institutions. However, his supporters (many of whom

---

[36] See D. Hanley, 'Les députés socialistes', *Pouvoirs*, No. 20, 1982, pp. 55–66.
[37] See Stephen S. Cohen, *Modern Capitalist Planning: The French Case*, Widenfeld (London), 1969 and Holmes/Estrin *op.cit.*
[38] Florin Aftalion, *Socialisme et économie*, PUF (Paris), 1978, Ch. V.

came from areas benefiting from the EEC) were more enthusiastic and the group therefore took a distinctly pro-
Market line. In general, therefore, Rocard was the very model
of a modern moderate *militant*: 'social democracy' may or
may not be a good description of his approach, but its appeal
to the reformist floating vote on such issues as decentralization, market *laissez-faire* combined with limited government
intervention, and an egalitarian concern for the less well off,
seemed to be shown in the opinion polls.[39]

Mitterrand's candidature and victory in 1981, however,
dealt the Rocardians a blow from which they had little hope
of an early recovery. Many rightly concluded that their
future during the seven long years of the Mitterrand presidency would not be bright and Rocard himself, although
initially a ranking Minister of State, was very pessimistic
about his own prospects. Mitterrand's supporters, anticipating a challenge at the Party's Valence Congress, secured the
main positions against such a possibility. Thus, in the share-
out of party posts in October 1981 Rocard paid for his
insubordination of 1978–80, his current being awarded only
one seat in the Secretariat instead of the three to which its
vote at the Metz Congress entitled it (see Table 10.1). Moreover, by March 1983 the two other members of Rocard's
group who had gained ministerial posts in 1981—Jean-Pierre
Cot and Louis le Pensec—had both left office; the former in
protest at Mitterrand's policy in black Africa, and Le Pensec
over the downgrading of his ministry (Marine Affairs) in the
government reshuffle of March 1983. Rocardians were also
prominent, one of them a close associate of Le Pensec,
among the victims of disciplinary action taken against local
politicians who refused to campaign in alliance with the PCF
in the municipal elections of 1983, and who actually ran
against Communist mayors in defiance of the Party's ruling.
In the third Mauroy government Rocard was moved to the
Ministry of Agriculture. The Planning Ministry had been in-
sufficiently testing for someone of his calibre and had also
left him with too much time on his hands to make embarrassing speeches on the deficiencies of the Government's
economic strategy. Agriculture was a portfolio which seemed

[39] J.-L. Parodi, 'Les leaders socialistes devant l'opinion', *Projet*, April 1979,
p. 491.

Table 10.1

Representation of Currents in Government, Parliament, and Party (1981)

Currents	Government June 1981		Deputies June 1981		Secretariat Oct. 1981		Bureau Exécutif Oct. 1981		Comité Directeur Oct. 1981		Congress delegates Metz 1979
	N	(%)	N	(%)	N	(%)	N	(%)	N	(%)	(%)
Mitterrand*	24	65	134	50	9	60	14	52	67	51	47
Mauroy	6	16	53	20	2	13	5	18	23	17	17
Rocard	3	8	45	17	1	7	4	15	20	15	21
CERES	4	11	36	13	3	20	4	15	21	16	15
Total	37†	100	268**	100	15	100	27	100	131	100	100

* Including Defferre current.   † Excluding seven non-PS ministers.   ** Excluding one unclassifiable deputy.

likely to make or break the politician who remained more popular with public opinion than any other Socialist figure. But Rocard remained, even after his 1985 resignation, the pollsters' favourite and it was on that strength that his hopes were pinned even if the long period until the 1988 presidential elections gave ample time for his rivals to emerge.

Conclusion

If the analysis of the party currents reveals any permanent cleavage, it is the division between CERES and the rest of the Party, but within French Socialism there are as many views across the entire spectrum as in Britain or Germany. Until the failure to win in 1978 the Socialists were united essentially on the desirability of François Mitterrand as Party leader and presidential candidate. Even Rocard's challenge did not seriously call Mitterrand's leadership into question, so the Party has not yet been tested by a root-and-branch internal conflict. It is probable that had Rocard been the 1981 candidate, the Party—even CERES—would have united behind him, but that must remain an open question.

Intra-party rivalry has therefore been contained within limits and the history of the Party from 1969 to 1981 is one of considerable unity and success. The 1978 elections were a setback, but only in the context of continuous advance, and constituted the Party's only experience of failure. With such a short and successful history it is impossible to say whether the Party is institutionally better designed, more stable than, or freer from the debilitating problems faced by the SFIO. Like all Fifth Republic parties it must be able to offer an effective challenge for the Presidency or suffer in consequence, as did the once dominant Gaullists in the mid-1970s and the UDF after Giscard's defeat in 1981. This requirement has clearly had an impact on the Party, where currents whose bases are largely regional (Nord and Bouches-du-Rhône) or ideological (CERES) have inevitably been pushed aside by the more purely presidential groupings of Mitterrand and Rocard.

If Socialist factional rivalries were somewhat attenuated by the victory of 1981, at least two problems remained. In the medium term there was the potential problem of how to reconcile the conflicting demands of activists and voters. The history of other Socialist parties in office suggested that conflict would be inevitable. In fact, however, both the presidentialization of the party's factional life and the demands and experience of office to which all factional leaders were exposed, served to blunt the edge of factional conflict. In the longer run, there was the question of the succession to Mitterrand, whose dominance and stature and whose skill in party manipulation would be very difficult to replace. An effective party in the Fifth Republic requires credible, presidential leadership. The Socialists would thus be required to avoid an indulgence in factional conflict of a sort that would jeopardize the major gains the party had made, as it approached the period of *après Mitterrand.*

CONCLUSION

Léon Blum, Socialist leader of the Popular Front government in 1936, made the celebrated distinction between the exercise and conquest of power. Socialists might hope either to exercise power in coalition with non-socialist parties, and thus merely to introduce some reforms in constricted circumstances, or to conquer power by winning a majority on their own with which to apply their own programme. The scale of the Socialists' arithmetical majority in 1981 appeared on this analysis to meet Blum's condition for the conquest of power: were the party unable to apply its programme after 1981 it was hard to imagine, on the face of it, more favourable conditions. The parliamentary base for the Mitterrand presidency was, unlike that for Blum's government of 1936, virtually indestructible both in terms of its size (the Socialists having on their own, without the Communists, a substantial majority), and its cohesion (disciplined partisan majorities having come, largely through the presidentialization of politics, to characterise French politics). Such factors gave the Socialists absolute security of tenure at least until the parliamentary elections of 1986. Nevertheless, the Party was entering office at a time of economic recession, when alibis for 'restraint' would readily present themselves, and indeed did so when Finance Minister Jacques Delors called, as early as November 1981, for a 'pause' in the reform programme, a word straight out of the vocabulary of Blum's Popular Front government.

The Socialist Party in the 1980s underwent a transformation: by October 1985, when it met in congress at Toulouse, it had developed a taste for power in place of the opposition mentality more evident in the 1970s. To acknowledge this was not to claim that it had undergone a 'Bad Godesberg' process, and been transformed from a socialist into a social democratic party; such a transformation did not occur because in essence it was not required, the Socialists' programme having been drawn in the first place from the mainstream of western European social democracy. The reform programme of 1981-6 was one merely designed to fit French conditions and to bring French institutions into the modern age; thus, for example, the broadcasting High Authority, decentralisation, and women's rights, whilst radical, were not, in a west European sense, daring or novel. This is not to denigrate the reforms nor the difficulties encountered in applying them, but merely to put them in perspective. The French Socialist party, for all its use of a heady vocabulary, should not be seen as a pioneer amongst socialist parties.

Two objections however, can be raised to the presentation of the PS as a mainstream western European social democratic party. The first, and more important, involves reference to the extensive nationalization programme undertaken in 1981. It should, however, be noted that the industries nationalized—almost all of them in notoriously bad shape—did not form part of an overarching 'socialist strategy', notwithstanding the rhetoric of *'autogestion'* developed in the 1970s. Industrial groups were nationalized and then turned over to technocratic managers who sought to do what private managers had been unable to achieve, namely to make them show a profit. There were no end of *post facto* justifications for nationalization after 1981, but the motives were not clear apart from being the presumed price for Communist support in the period before 1981.[1] Moreover, nationalization in the French context was not 'radical' and public opinion, unlike that in Britain, did not see it as such. The second reason for doubting the moderate credentials of the PS concerns the economic policy followed in 1981-2. But again, despite socialist attempts to talk it up, the policy of reflation through increasing demand was recognizable and not unlike that of the British Conservative government's dash for growth in the early 1970s. The policy suffered however, from foreseeable balance of payments problems as France reflated in the teeth of world recession. Had similar measures been adopted in other countries the policy might have worked; it was not outrageously socialist, merely misguidedly unilateral. When in 1983 the Socialist government finally turned its back on the policy, it was not in order to become monetarist, but to

[1] See David Soskice in H. Machin and V. Wright, *op. cit.* pp. 169-72.

restrict internal demand so as to correct the balance of payments deficit. None of these economic policies strayed outside
the main western European social democratic tradition, nor
did they betray an 'alternative logic' as socialists sometimes
argued, nor indeed did they appear bizarre at the time—few,
even on the Right, opposed reflationary growth in 1981.

Presidentialization

Socialist parties in power are conventionally expected to
provoke the disaffection of their rank and file. This did not
happen in the case of the PS after 1981 for one principal
reason, namely the presidentialization of the party. In
common with at least two of the other three major French
parties, the PS has as its central vocation the promotion and
sustaining of presidential candidates. The post-Épinay (1971)
party was indeed built around the person of François Mitterrand with the objective of getting him to the Elysée; all else
was embellishment and detail. To Michels' arguments for the
inevitability of oligarchy in socialist parties have to be added
the electoral imperative of the activists holding ranks behind
their leader in the quest for public office. Moreover, presidentialized systems of power do more than encourage oligarchy; by personalizing executive power they promote a
concentration of power in the hands of party leaders. Notwithstanding the Socialist Party's democratic nature and
factionalised character, a presidential culture came to
permeate the party.[2] Before 1981, formal power structures
were largely by-passed by Mitterrand's own personal network
of advisers. In 1981 Mitterrand campaigned not on the
Party's radical-sounding *Projet socialiste* but on his own far
blander *110 propositions*. Moreover, the very wide vote
aggregation required of presidential contenders in a deliberately bipolarised (second ballot) contest where the victor
needs some 16 million votes—a target well beyond the range
of any single party—serves further to free presidential candidates from party constraint.

It might however be assumed that the taste for ideology

[2] H. Portelli 'Le présidentialisation des partis' *Pouvoirs*, No. 14, 1980 pp. 97-
106, and P. Avril, 'Le Président, le parti et le groupe', *Pouvoirs*, No. 20, 1982,
pp. 115-26.

in a socialist party would preclude or frustrate such a process of presidentialization. Such a 'taste' reflected both a tradition in French Socialism and the requirements of an alliance with the PCF. Thus, the Socialists in their cultivation of the Communists during the 'seventies, had come to be identified with concepts—or rather slogans—such as the 'break with capitalism' (*rupture avec le capitalisme*) and the 'class front' (*front de classe*). For radicals, such *marxisant* phrases comprised the end and the means to which the Party was now committed. In effect, however, the marxist-sounding *front de classe* was a concept foreign to Marx, and in its objective of creating an alliance of all social groups other than large scale employers, sufficiently nebulous to provide ideological cover for what was in essence an electoral strategy. The *front de classe*, far from being the means to a *rupture avec le capitalisme*, was designed to create *un parti attrape-tout*. With such a catch-all electorate acquired and with many Communist voters secured and with the Communist Party itself in decline, the Downsian requirements of bipolarised presidential competition served effectively to relegate ideology and limit the room for activist discontent.[3] The experience of office after 1981 served further to close the gap between a radical rhetoric and an entirely reformist practise, a contrast termed by commentators as the *double langage* of social democracy.[4]

Thus was it without difficulty, after Mitterrand's election and the formation of the Mauroy government, that the potentially troublesome relationship between Government and Party was secured by weekly meetings between President Mitterrand, Prime Minister Mauroy and Party leader Jospin, with the latter's role soon defined as one closer to apologist for the government than spokesman for activist hopes; in his liaising role Jospin in effect held the ring for President and Government.

Not even the highly factionalised character of the party—its major distinguishing hallmark in French politics—insulated it from the presidential infection: in effect, factional life was reduced to a competition of rival *présidentiables* and only

[3] A. Downs, *An Economic Theory of Democracy*, Harper and Row (New York) 1957.
[4] See R. Cayrol, 'Le godillot et le commissaire politique' *Projet*, No. 161, Jan. 1982, pp. 32–41.

currents with a *présidentiable* in the van now counted. Effectively however, ideology was always the servant of ambition, as had been exemplified with Florentine panache by Mitterrand's own dextrous weaving amongst the factions in the ten years before 1981, when he had moved from the *marxisant* emphasis required of a new Socialist leader with palpably shallow socialist roots, through a rejection of the CERES left in the cause of broadening the party's electoral appeal in the 1970s; back to an alliance with the left in 1979 in order to break a dangerous rival, Rocard; and finally to the manifest pragmatism of an electoral campaign in 1981 in which he employed a strategy indistinguishable from that advocated by the isolated and rejected Rocard. Factional conflict focused on presidential ambition clearly may carry a destabilising potential, but less seriously than factional conflict in which ideology counts *per se*.

Despite the formal suspension of factions after 1981, Mitterrand took great care to balance them in the government, even if by 1985 the Rocardians had been reduced to the ranks. Furthermore at the Bourg-en-Bresse (1983) and Toulouse (1985) Congresses, rival motions were submitted and factional strengths accordingly measured. Such strengths continued to be represented proportionately (if with some discrimination against Rocard) in the federations and in the leading bodies of the party, though in an important sense the factions had been decapitated by the disappearance of their leaders into government, with the rank and file correspondingly left leaderless, or at least less rigorously led. Such factional jockeying as there was between 1981 and 1986 was presidentialized, reflecting the rival ambitions of presidential hopefuls such as Chevènement, Rocard and Fabius.

Of the rival *présidentiables*, Chevènement enjoyed three different incarnations during the five years of *la gauche au pouvoir*, first as a technocratic Industry Minister, then as an out of office left-wing critic, and finally as a 'republican' Minister of Education extolling the virtues of the three Rs. Silenced, or at least distracted, by his ministerial responsibilities, Chevènement, as leader of the party's self-styled left-wing, was difficult only during the middle period when out of office for the last year of the Mauroy premiership. During that time he opposed the government's 'Atlanticist' foreign policy, and, more pertinently attacked its economic policy, in place of which he offered what opponents called the 'Albanian solution': instead of Mauroy-Delors-style deflation there should be a defence of purchasing power, higher investment, and—to protect the balance of payments— a withdrawal from the EMS, aid to exports and the introduction of import controls. This critique was also shared by certain left-wing Mitterrandists, such as Pierre Joxe and Professor Christian Goux, but, at the same time CERES' pseudonymous book *Le Socialisme et la France* (by 'Jacques Mandrin') declared rather frankly that for now (1983) 'socialism is not on the agenda'.[5] The firm rejection of growth in 1984 by the new Fabius government coincided with Chevènement's reintegration in government as Education minister, where with great rhetorical verve he defended the *volte face* over the schools question. This was a matter of considerable rank and file destablising potential—the issue having been highlighted by Mitterrand in an attempt to boost activist morale by waving a traditional totem; in fact the surrender to the *école libre* lobby was, significantly, accomplished with activist quiescence.

Ironically it was Chevènement's counter attack around the themes of *'Republican elitism'*, the discussion of standards in schools, and the emphasis of 'traditional' values ('school is for learning') which boosted him with the public as a presidential hopeful. CERES, as a group remained on the Left of the party, if state intervention is taken as the criterion, but it was also as nationalist as ever, a not unhelpful attribute in a new political situation imposing on it, as on the party as a whole, the chase for centrist votes. Whilst Chevènement's 'conversion' into a statesman-like figure was not followed by all of the CERES old-guard, the metamorphosis was reflected in the current's transformation from CERES into *'Socialisme et République'* in April 1986. The current counted some 20 deputies in the parliamentary group elected in March 1986.

Of all the factional chiefs, Rocard had come worst out of the 1981-6 experience, whilst retaining a very high level of popularity with the wider electorate. Though in tune with the Mauroy-Delors deflationary policy after 1982, Rocard's

[5] Jacques Mandrin, *Le Socialisme et la France*, Sycamore (Paris), 1983.

challenge to Mitterrand in the 1978–80 period had destroyed his credibility where it counted most. After two years at the Planning ministry and two more at Agriculture he resigned in 1985—ostensibly over objections to the introduction of proportional representation. In effect his resignation was timely: major EEC-driven cuts were about to damage French farmers, and it also gave him the chance to roam the federations in search of activist support. His supporters—the 'realists'—made their position clear in *Pour réussir à gauche*,[6] and his style of modernization and efficiency with a humanist face was, ironically, to be the corporate image of the new Fabius government in 1984. Rocard's problem was to be right on all the main policies and strategies, but to be weak in public relations and marginalised inside a party whose confidence he would require for his eventual presidential bid. About thirty Rocard supporters remained in the National Assembly after the 1986 election, but weakness in the Party was underscored by under-representation on leading bodies. Thus, after the 1985 Toulouse Congress, before which almost 30 per cent of delegates had backed the Rocardian motion, the current was allocated 25 per cent of the Executive Bureau seats and only three, or 20 per cent, of the places on the 15-strong Secretariat.

Pierre Mauroy, with whom Rocard had been ideologically close, also entertained presidential hopes. No longer as close to Rocard, who had criticised the reflationary excesses of the first year of his premiership, Mauroy's star had waned as his government stumbled into trouble having to defend and justify 'rigour' and was finally blown over with the schools policy débâcle in 1984. As prime minister of the 'Government of the Union of the Left', which ended with the Communist ministers leaving office on his resignation, Mauroy adopted a distinctive and, by 1985 among faction leaders, a lone advocacy of a strategy of *'priorité à gauche'*, believing in the need to recall the Communists from their self-assigned isolation. This now-dated formula, when set against the traditionally moderate orientation of Nord socialism (represented effectively by the mid-1980s by the rising modernist ex-

---

[6] Les Gracques, *Pour réussir à gauche*, Syros (Paris), 1983.

minister and former Mauroy-protégé, Michel Delebarre),
made Mauroy's position appear somewhat eccentric and his
presidential ambitions unrealistic. He lacked in addition the
ability and following to make a serious presidential bid.

The stirrings of rival *présidentiables* had also been reflected
in the dispute in mid-1985 between Fabius (who replaced
Mauroy as Prime Minister in 1984) and party leader Jospin,
over whom should lead the 1986 campaign—a matter resolved
somewhat by Fabius' fall from grace after a weak TV *face à
face* with Chirac in October 1985, his hesitating responses to
the 'Greenpeace affair' and his public dissociation from the
president's invitation to the Polish Head of State General
Jaruzelski in December. The consequence of Fabius' eclipse
was the full presidentialization of the Socialists' campaign
through the unifying intervention of the *patron*, President
Mitterrand, and the Congress at Toulouse in October 1985
demonstrated the existence of a broad consensus in the
party across all factions. The illusion that reflation in one
country was possible had been shattered, and with the PCF
down in the polls at around 10% and unavailable as an ally,
the party had no choice but to bid for the centre ground, to
which end the abandonment of marxist rhetoric and the
embracing of a *rassemblement républicain*. Nor, in the short
run, was Mitterrand's own unifying desire to remain President
to be discounted. During the period of the Mauroy government (1981-4) the Elysée saw to it that Mauroy was unable
to build up a position in the party, whilst Fabius, although
unofficial dauphin, did not have the time. He, however,
started to organize clubs and contact groups, and his vigorous
role in the 1986 election campaign, during which as Prime
Minister he covered the country addressing party rallies,
placed him in a strong position. For Fabius, if not for the
other contenders, the prospect of Mitterrand running again
for the presidency could be regarded with equanimity. The
nomination would be Mitterrand's if he wanted it and this
would effectively end Rocard's challenge. Meanwhile Fabius
had time on his side.

Factionalism was not only subordinated by presidentialization; it was further mitigated by the ideological and sociological heterogeneity of the currents themselves, the factions
lacking clear enough boundaries to pose a threat to the

leadership.[7] Whilst CERES was shown to be the more self-consciously Left-wing of the currents, its activists were not significantly different in the way they ranked issues. At the 1981 congress they were in step with the rest in ranking unemployment, inflation and reduced wage differentials as the most important issues. CERES and Mitterrandist activists showed greater interest in controlling multinational companies, whilst the more social democratic Mauroy and Rocard supporters reflected a greater commitment to 'pragmatism'—cited by two thirds of Rocardians, half of Mauroy's supporters and only one third of the rest. In occupational terms differences were slighter. In an activist base of which 90% was drawn from white collar and professional groups, with the largest component from teaching, there was little to choose between the currents. Only CERES supporters were drawn slightly more heavily from the ranks of routine non-manual and manual workers, and then only one in six. Rocardians were somewhat more likely to be Catholic (40%, as against one third of other currents), and equally less likely to have been raised in a Left-voting family (40%), but this comparatively low figure was also shared by CERES. Equally the 'social democratic' Rocardians and 'marxist' CERES supporters both belonged in similar proportions to CFDT unions, a reflection of their common recruitment in the more Catholic parts of the country. Whilst the variables—occupation, religion, union affiliation—were not entirely randomly distributed across the main currents, neither was there any significant clustering to demarcate one group clearly from another.

Reflecting the presidentialization of the party was the presidentialized election campaign of 1985-6. '*Avec le Président*' declared the Socialist party's posters, and there can be little double that *sans le Président* the party would have stuck some way below its eventual 32% of the vote. The campaign was one of the most presidentialized of any Fifth Republic general election, with Mitterrand addressing two

[7] See R. Cayrol and C. Ysmal, 'Les militants du PS' *Projet*, May 1982, pp. 572-86; R. Cayrol and P. Ignazi 'Cousins ou frères', *Revue française de science politique*, 1983, pp. 629-50; C. Ysmal and R. Cayrol, 'Militants Socialistes', *Projet* No. 191, 1985, pp. 20-32, and H. Rey and F. Subileau 'Le PS: un parti attrape-tout?', *Le Monde* 2 April 1986.

major party rallies and giving numerous press and TV interviews in which he made clear his determination not to be an 'inert' President should he lose his Assembly majority, not to relinquish his role in the reserved domain of foreign and defence policy, and to protect the social policy gains of the Socialist government. Finally in the last week of the campaign it was leaked that Mitterrand would resign if the Right won well on March 16th. Thus yoked to Mitterrand's presidential status—and the unpopular threat to it offered by the rejection of *'cohabitation'* by the Right's leading presidential contender, Raymond Barre—the Socialist vote was increased by some 4% in the February–March period, and by some 10% over the period following Mitterrand's assumption of campaign leadership in October 1985.

The party's campaign, other than baldly enjoining the electors to 'Vote Mitterrand', stressed the themes of modernization through investment and retraining, but jobless totals were high and found by pollsters to be the greatest concern amongst the voters. Other economic indicators were moving well for the government, but time was too short, and although the party rose steadily in the polls it was in the unfortunate position of peaking too late. In effect, the election result was a foregone conclusion, the Left—and thus the Socialists—having had no majority for four years, and with proportional representation introduced for that reason. In the event, the PR was not proportional enough; it was too hard on smaller parties, and thus did not sufficiently balkanise the Assembly in order to permit Mitterrand to make mischief. Proportional representation failed to deny, as had been the Socialist's intention, a majority to the conventional Right (RPR and UDF), by giving seats to the extreme-Right (FN), for with 43% of the vote the conventional Right still emerged with 50% of the seats. With a parliamentary majority for Jacques Chirac, albeit of only three, Mitterrand's ploy had not paid off. Nor with only 32% of the vote had the Socialists themselves polled well enough if they sought to rule the game. Even so the party claimed satisfaction compared with its previous best first ballot election result, Mitterrand's 26% in the presidential election of April 1981, as distinct from the party's coat-tails, and therefore inflated, vote of 37% in the June 1981 general election.

Socialist gains were largely at the expense of the PCF, ecologists, other leftists and previous abstainers, probably in response to a *vote utile* appeal in the new single ballot system. The party was well based in all occupational categories, though significantly stronger in the white collar category (39%) and notably weaker among farmers (11%) and the self-employed (19%). It was strongly based in younger age groups; more (38%) of all voters under 35 voted PS than supported any other party, including the combined RPR-UDF. One third of the higher managerial stratum voted Socialist, as did one third of manual workers. In defeat the party still retained a catch-all profile.[8]

The party's position under power-sharing (*cohabitation*) after March 1986 would not be easy. It would have to exercise restraint in opposing the Chirac government, but as the only credible opposition in the Assembly, and with a broad base in the country, it had a strong base on which to build. Leaving aside the issue of trade union links (weak), the party in policy terms and now experience of office, had come to resemble the social democratic parties of northern Europe and was thus equipped for *l'alternance douce*, about which commentators had been so insistent.[9] But with the Left's aggregate lower (at 44%) in 1986 than at any point in the Fifth Republic, bar 1968-9, the position was difficult, and comparable to Mitterrand's task when he captured the PS in 1971. A new coalition had to be built around the party but with intractable material; votes could now come only from the centre. So much for *la ligne d'Epinay*.

Organization and office

For French Socialists the implicit yardstick of measurement for effective party organization is the Communist Party, but the Socialist Party is a party with solely an electoral vocation and not an agitational or quasi-revolutionary one. Thus, the party should be compared with other social democratic parties, and in this light its low number of activists, its lack

---

[8] Bull–BVA poll: 'La France au fond des urnes', *Libération* 18 March 1986. G. Le Gall, 'Mars 1986: des élections de transition? *Revue politique et parlementaire*, No. 922, March-April, 1986, pp. 6-13.

[9] M. Duverger, *Bréviaire de la cohabitation*, PUF (Paris), 1986.

of a daily paper, and of front and fringe organizations is un-exceptional. It is in effect in membership terms comparable with the Spanish, Portuguese and Italian socialist parties, although not with those which have strong union links such as the British Labour Party. As is to be expected for a Second International party the electoral function is the focus of activity and the French party had certainly become effective in electing local, departmental and regional councillors as well as deputies and in 1981 the President of the Republic.

In 1981 the Socialist party's membership stood at 189,000, in 1982 205,087, and in 1983 213,000, but by the Toulouse Congress in 1985 it was back at 190,000. The party did not benefit from a wave of enthusiasm after the 1981 victory, nor were the recruitment campaigns launched in May 1983 and April 1986 (after the election defeat) a notable success. These recruitment campaigns raised one of the problems of the Socialist Party's search for a role during 1981–6. Whilst France is a society of political street theatre and, although both Left and Right have traditionally been able to stage mass demonstrations from time to time, the idea that the Socialists are a street force is profoundly misleading. During the 1970s, when the party began to grow, the Socialists were a presence in most campaigns over such issues as racism, feminism and human rights, but they never seriously com-peted with the Communists or even the ecologists in this form of politics. Mass demonstrations are not a Socialist forte. Whilst in the 1970s the party had taken up and promoted issues where they excited local or national protest, and become the privileged conduit for 'post-industrial' causes dear to the post-war bulge generation whose presence weighed heavily in the party, in government after 1981, it ceased to act in this way.

Other indicators similarly demonstrated the failure of the Socialist party as a 'transmission belt into the masses'. Launched during the 1981 presidential campaign, the Social-ist daily *Combat* folded soon afterwards with only 16,500 people having subscribed. Other Socialist journals or dailies supporting the Left had their troubles (notably *Le Matin*); the Socialist press in the provinces did not benefit in circu-lation from being associated with the party in power and *L'Unité* (the party weekly) remained more-or-less an internal bulletin. In the unions the most conservative of the major confederations, *Force Ouvrière* grew most rapidly whilst the CGT shrank and CFDT stagnated. During the 1970s the pro-Socialist current in the CFDT grew from 6.8% to 20% but the confederation's leadership was identified with Rocard and a disagreement arose between Maire (who called for restraint) and Mauroy during the first phase of the Socialist government (1981-2). In 1986 the CFDT leadership also found itself out of step with the activists' anti-capitalist rhetoric. In the 1970s the number of Socialist activists in the rival CGT increased but the two Socialist representatives on the CGT board were always isolated, and increasingly so after the PCF's change of line in 1984.

After the Valence Congress of 1981 the party sought the role of guardian of the programme. However this usurped a presidential prerogative; Mitterrand had decided on the 1981 programme and the Prime Minister on the timing of its implementation. For the party as such to insist on a role challenged one of the sedulously maintained fictions of the Fifth Republic, namely that the president and government are above party ties. Here the party leadership were on difficult ground because (despite Jospin's regular working breakfasts at the Élysée) they could not institutionalize their position. Mitterrand maintained the government-party distinction in his presidential message to the Bourg-en-Bresse congress of 1983, and yet his control of the 1986 platform was an essential tool which he would need and could not be pre-emptorily commandeered by the party. Jospin's regular meetings with the president (continuing after the 1986 defeat) were the party leadership's most persistent, if slight, contribution to government.

In the early months of the Mauroy government the party had also tried to be a go-between, a privileged negotiator, between the Assembly group and the government, but the government soon cut the party out by arranging frequent meetings with the Socialist group in the Assembly. At this time the Socialist Assembly group was trying to change government policy on such issues as immigration, advertising on local radio, and the amnesty for Algerian generals, but it relinquished this role or, at least, it expressed it less publicly after a few months. The radical amendments which the Assembly group proposed, and which effectively sank the

Church schools bill in 1984, showed why this process could not be allowed to get out of hand.

With the facade of unity after the election victory of 1981, the party organization suffered in two ways. Firstly, bargaining over positions, and Buggin's turn, led to a degree of administrative stagnation. Secondly, entire branches of the party administration departed for the Ministries and *cabinets* (private offices), ensuring that an organization which had taken twelve years to build up was suddenly denuded of personnel. Rapid promotions took place with the result that a certain degree of administrative incoherence was installed at the rue Solférino. Whilst this inefficiency should not be exaggerated, only on leaving office in 1986 was restructuring of the administration undertaken in earnest with the sacking of some 22 (out of 120) party functionaries. Part of the problem stemmed from the non-complementary nature of the two leaders, Jospin and Poperen. Jospin's base in the party was weak and he consequently possessed none of Mitterrand's authority; people still looked to Mitterrand to decide in the last resort, Jospin being unable to impose solutions and having limited room for manœuvre. A division of responsibility might have been expected with Poperen as the administrative arm of the leadership but his talents lay more in a rhetorical command of marxist cliché, better *chauffer les militants* than to manipulate the apparatus.

Jospin's prestige was somewhat increased by the perceived as respectable 1986 election result, especially because, as head of the Party's Paris list, he had enjoyed personal success. Yet his task as party leader had not been made easier: the election defeat returned all the Socialist Ministers (who had stood) to the Assembly, with the inevitable result that the Socialist parliamentary group increased in authority. Joxe, ex-Interior Minister, not Jospin, was reinstalled as leader of the parliamentary group, which contained all the leaders of all the main factions—the party's *présidentiables*. The role of opposition to the Right moved to the ex-Ministers in the Assembly and to Joxe's highly structured working groups. The tightness of Chirac's parliamentary majority and the nearness of the next major electoral encounter, focused attention on the Parliamentary battle and specifically on the Socialist group's attempts to thwart the Right-wing government's programme. In such circumstances, the position of the extra-parliamentary organs of the Party appeared weak. At the 1987 Lille Congress Jospin attempted to resolve this tension: Mauroy, Fabius, Cresson, Delebarre and other personalities took Secretariat posts to form a more coherent and impressive team and to appeal to the floating voter. Although Poperen was evicted from the leadership and although Chevènement and Rocard did not take posts, there was no significant opposition to the new distribution of power.

The move to the centre

1986 → cohabitatio

The Socialist party of the mid-1980's looked very different from the party constructed in the years after Epinay. The dominant concern after the 1986 election defeat was the desire to return to government and unlike the 1970s the strategy was one of moderation and responsibility. There were many reasons for this, including the exceptional political situation after March 1986—the 'cohabitation' of a Socialist president and a Gaullist prime minister, the 'governmental' image of Socialist leaders and the race for the party's presidential nomination. Yet the main change, and arguably the major domestic political development of the Mitterrand presidency, was the decline of the Communist party.

The major constraint on the Socialist Party after its reorganization in 1969 was the need for an alliance with the Communist Party. With the support of a fifth of the voters, a large organization and control of the major union federation, the Communist party was assumed to be a more or less permanent feature of the French political landscape and Socialist strategy was designed with this constraint in mind. The existence of a large pro-Moscow Communist party loyal to the dogmas of Marxism–Leninism, also served to hinder the Socialist party from developing into a 'catch-all' party able to rally the centre and middle class vote essential to any election victory and successful government.

However, the steady decline of the Communist vote to 15 per cent in 1981, followed by the drop to 11 per cent vote in the European election of 1984 and to under 10 per cent in the 1986 election, eliminated the Communist party as a major force on the Left. In anticipation of this collapse—and in fear of it—the Communists had broken with the Socialists in 1978, after a prolonged polemic which opened in 1974 and continued up to the first ballot of the 1981 presidential election. Neither this radical hostility, which was based on the view that the Socialists were no different from the Right, nor the party's ambiguous and increasingly critical participation in government after 1981, were able to prevent continuing Communist decline. At a time when French public opinion was more pro-American and anti-Russian—in clear distinction to the 1950, 1960s and 1970s—Communist support for the Soviet invasion of Afghanistan and for Moscow's negotiating position in arms control talks were probably vote losers; there was certainly much survey evidence for the declining image of the Communist Party.[10] Moreover if the Communists expected to regain a radical electorate after the end of the government's experiment with reflation in 1983 they were mistaken. Electors may indeed have given the Socialists some credit for trying to prevent industrial decline and even been sympathetic to the need to close-down old industries and to direct investment to those with a clear future. It was also evident that the Communists underestimated the support amongst their own electorate for President Mitterrand and their determination to stop the return of the Right—which meant, effectively, voting Socialist in the 1980s.

These considerations did not stop the Communist party from going into the 1986 election with the campaign theme that the Socialists were selling out the programme and hopes of 1981 and that Socialists were indistinguishable from the Right where it mattered to the 'working-class'. The Right and the Socialists were portrayed in *L'Humanité* as *bonnet blanc, blanc bonnet* and the Socialists accused of preparing to

[10] G. Le Gall, 'Radiographie de l'image du PCF: Double divorce avec la société et les sympathisants' *Revue politique et parlementaire*, Jan.-Feb. 1985, pp. 16-27. J. Ranger, 'Le déclin du parti communiste français', *Revue française de science politique*, Jan. 1986 pp. 46-62; H. Le Bras, 'PC: un déclin inexorable', *Le Point*, 20 June 1986, and M. Kesselman, 'The French Communist Party: Historic Retard, Historic Compromise or New Departure?', in P. Cerny and M. Schain (eds), *Socialism, the State and Public Policy in France*, Methuen (New York), 1985, pp. 42-59.

govern with the Right. Following the election the Communists pressed their theme further by citing the co-existence of Mitterrand and Chirac as evidence of the lack of any difference between them. In the event the Communist across-the-board losses in the 1986 election (reduced to under 10 per cent of the vote in two-thirds of the constituencies) sparked off another wave of dissidence inside the party, and such dissent, because voiced by locally elected councillors who feared for their positions if the decline continued, threatened to de-stabilize the party.

The main electoral beneficiaries of the Communist collapse were the Socialists: as the PS lost votes to the centre it gained some on the Left. However, for strategic purposes, the main outcome was that, by 1986, very few votes remained to be picked up on the Left. Whilst it was possible to envisage that the Communist vote could be squeezed to 5 per cent (in a process similar to that in Spain at the end of the 1970s), not even that would yield the 15 per cent extra share of the vote needed to give the Socialists a majority. Votes now had to be won in the centre. Thus in the 1980s, the strategic game changed from being one of trying to maintain an alliance with the Communists around a radical-sounding programme, to that of wooing voters away from the Right with an appeal to the traditional virtues of patriotism, administrative efficiency and change within continuity, packaged as 'modernistic' socialism. By 1986, therefore, the Socialist Party was calling for an ill-defined modernism and preaching the virtues of their 'balance sheet'. The general move to the centre removed most of the idiosyncratic ideological clashes between currents and threw the 'presidential' nature of the factional war into even sharper relief. (It also virtually eliminated the distinctiveness of Rocard's group which had based its appeal on a view of a 'modernistic' sort). The focus on the individual at the head of the current became, in this way, more intense; Rocard, Chevènement, Mauroy, Fabius, Jospin and others were discussed in terms of their presidential prospects.

Leaders of currents had also emerged from the responsibility of government office with their reputations enhanced and in most cases, except Rocard, with their presidential prospects improved. Party leaders were keen to capitalize on this aspect of their five years in government and this in turn served to tone down and deradicalise the party in the immediate post-election period. Presidential reputations are not built on extremes or on a reputation for maladministration or on the inability to master a brief. Moreover in 1986 the Right's overall parliamentary majority was narrow and the presidential elections were, at most, only two years away. Such factors worked to make the Socialists close ranks and concentrate on their task of opposing the Right. In this they were aided by the powerful presence of over 30 ex-Ministers and their supporters in the Assembly as well as by direct comparisons between them and the new Ministers of the Chirac government. Socialist leadership in opposition in the 1970s had been rhetorical and somewhat unrealistic, but the governmental experience had served to fashion a new style of 'ministerialist' Socialist opposition in the 1980s.

'*Cohabitation*' also worked, in its way, to pull the Party together behind a now beleagured President. The electoral outcome of March 1986 forced onto Mitterrand a Right-wing government with which he had to co-exist for the remainder of his presidential term. Whilst this did not presage the constitutional crisis much predicted at all elections for some 20 years if incumbent presidents were denied a parliamentary majority, it did involve a reversion to prime ministerial government—unknown since the Fourth Republic. The President, *governing* from 1981 until March 1986, was reduced to *presiding* thereafter. Shorn of a majority, Mitterrand had few powers with which to thwart Chirac's conservative government. Powers, such as that to refuse to sign government ordinances designed to by-pass parliamentary scrutiny of controversial legislation, were no more than devices for delaying the inevitability of a government with a parliamentary majority getting its way. This was indeed confirmed in the case of Mitterrand's refusal to sign ordinances relating to the government's denationalization programme in July 1986. Effectively, Mitterrand was left with little more than the very great prestige of his office, a strong popular desire not to see him humbled or embarrassed by Chirac, and his own control during the remaining two years of his mandate, over the timing of the next presidential election. Beyond that, there was the additional hope of division within the Right's numerically tight parliamentary majority. Mitterrand meanwhile, was content to 'preside', basking in the unpopularity of much of the Chirac government's legislative programme, and seeking to imply by his silence as much as by his occasional *'nons'* that it was the Right and not he, which by precipitate action, unreasonable demands and partisan measures, was threatening the harmonious *'cohabitation'* which all opinion polls showed to be the voters' wish.

For the Socialist Party there was thus a perceived need to rally round the president and to produce a presidential platform, based on its government experience, which could win back the floating voter. The continuing exception to this consensus was Michel Rocard who had been banking on the presidential candidacy in a situation of demoralisation and defeat from which point he had hoped to appear as the only candidate capable of leading the Socialists into the next presidential elections. Rocard and supporters aside, the party remained solidly behind Mitterrand who had the option, if he chose, of running for the presidency in or before 1988. Despite the ambitions of the other ex-Ministers none would be seriously embarrassed by the prospect of a further Mitterrand candidacy. Mitterrand was, as he had been for over 20 years, the symbol of unity and the Party's, as much as the Left's, main *'rassembleur'*. The party, despite the challenge from Rocard and the emergence of others with presidential ambitions, recognized this and rallied to Mitterrand's cause once again.

Whilst the Socialist Party had come of age in office and under the pressure of electoral demands, in one sense it remained in the mid-1980s what it had been in the mid-1970s, namely, inspired and dominated by the person of François Mitterrand, whose own political development post-War French Socialism had effectively mirrored. Like Mitterrand, the French democratic Left spent the Fourth Republic in centrist coalitions; like, and eventually with Mitterrand, the Socialist Party spent the 1960s and 1970s in leftist opposition alliances tactically designed to unseat an entrenched conservative government. Finally, with Mitterrand in the 1980s a resurgent Socialist Party during and after five years of office, turned again to a centrist posture required of a party of government and made electorally necessary by the decline of the Communist party.

Neither the experience of the compromises of office, nor the loss of office in 1986, destabilised the party or threatened its newly acquired *vocation majoritaire*. Some factionalists, all uninfluential, continued to baulk at the term 'social democracy', but more representative and more illuminating was the frankness with which the former Prime Minister, Pierre Mauroy, observed in 1986 that the Party had no need to undergo a Bad Godesberg process because the equivalent of such had happened in 1982 'when we embarked on a policy of rigour and pursued it for the remainder of the parliament'.[11] If the compromises of office served as a maturation process for a socialist party which had languished too long in opposition, the loss of office in 1986 was accommodated with ease. Firstly, it had been seen since 1982 as a foregone conclusion: the Left's heady victory of the summer of 1981 (52% in the presidential election and 56% in the parliamentary election) was soon followed by a conservative backlash. A series of electoral outcomes (cantonal elections in 1982 and 1985, municipal elections in 1983 and the European Assembly election of 1984) confirmed the loss of the Left's majority: by 1985 the Left's aggregate was under 40%, and for no other reason than this was proportional representation introduced for the 1986 parliamentary election. Defeat was anticipated: a term had even been coined to describe what would come about when the Socialist President lost his parliamentary majority, *'cohabitation'*. Secondly, the unprecedented political situation after March 1986, and the approach of a presidential election which was expected to unravel the knot of *'cohabitation'*, served both to restrain the President's party and to remind it—if so avowedly electoralist a party needed reminding—of the need to appeal unequivocally to a cautious yet volatile electorate. Thirdly, even though in March 1986 the Left's aggregate was the lowest at any time in a national election for 30 years (bar the very low point of 1968-9), the Socialist Party in defeat retained, with one third of the voters behind it, its status as the largest party of the Left and the largest party in France. This was a distinction held in the 1940s and 1950s, and with such debilitating consequences for the French Left,

---

[11] *Le Monde*, 21 June 1986.

by the Communist Party. Now it was the erosion of that once irreducible Communist rock in the French political landscape that both invited and impelled the Socialist Party to acknowledge its true nature and to do unfettered battle for the centre ground.

Appendices

Chronology 1905–1986

1905 April	Founding of the Socialist Party as the Section Française de l'International Ouvrière (SFIO).
1914 July	Socialist leader Jean Jaurès assassinated.
August	SFIO unanimously votes war credits and two Socialists join the war government ('l'Union sacrée').
1920 December	Socialist–Communist split at the Tours Congress.
1928 April	PCF adopts 'class against class' tactic.
1932 December	'Neo-Socialists' quit SFIO.
1934 February	First joint Socialist–Communist anti-Fascist demonstration.
July	Socialist–Communist pact signed: birth of the Popular Front.
1936 May	Popular Front victory in legislative elections.
June	Formation of Léon Blum's government.
1937 June	Fall of Léon Blum's government.
1938 June	Marceau Pivert's 'Gauche révolutionnaire' quits SFIO.
October	Fall of Daladier government: end of the Popular Front.
1940 June	Fall of France: ninety SFIO deputies vote full powers to Pétain, thirty-six vote against, six abstain.
1941 June	Creation of the Comité d'Action Socialiste in occupied France.
1943 May	SFIO helps to create the Comité National de la Résistance.
1944 April	Tripartism (PCF–SFIO–MRP governments) begins.
1945 August	SFIO refuses PCF offer to merge parties.
October	SFIO and PCF win absolute majority in the Constituent Assembly but the SFIO rejects the Communist offer of a PCF–SFIO government.
1946 September	Guy Mollet elected SFIO General Secretary.
1947 May	SFIO Prime Minister Ramadier expels PCF ministers from Government: end of tripartism.
December	Socialists leave the Communist-dominatd CGT unions to found the Force Ouvrière.
1951 July	SFIO leaves Government.

1954 August	SFIO deputies split over the European Defence Community.
1956 January	Republican Front victory in legislative elections. Formation of the Guy Mollet government.
1957 May	Mollet government falls.
1958 June	SFIO deputies vote forty-two for and forty-nine against de Gaulle's investiture as PM: Mollet, Lejeune, and Thomas (SFIO) join de Gaulle's government.
1958 September	SFIO splits on new constitution: Socialist rebels establish the Parti Socialiste Autonome (later PSU). Mitterrand against new constitution.
November	SFIO backs de Gaulle in legislative elections but is reduced to forty seats (PCF loses 1.5 million votes and holds only ten seats).
1959 January	SFIO ministers quit government.
1960 April	Parti Socialiste Unifié established.
1962 October	Referendum approves the direct election of the President.
November	Mollet opposes support for the Gaullists in second ballot of the legislative elections. SFIO–PCF alliances in some areas.
1963 May	PCF declares single-party socialist regime to be a Stalinist error.
September	Defferre ('Monsieur X') presidential bid launched.
1964 Jan.–Mar.	PCF–SFIO ideological dialogue opens.
February	SFIO accepts Gaston Defferre as presidential candidate.
June	Creation by Mitterrand of the CIR, which backs Defferre.
1965 June	Collapse of Defferre candidature.
September	Mitterrand announces presidential candidature. PCF backs Mitterrand. Signature of FGDS charter (SFIO, Radicals, and CIR).
December	Presidential elections second ballot: Mitterrand 10.5 million votes, de Gaulle 12.6 million.
1966 January	*L'Humanité* attacks Soviet treatment of dissidents Daniel and Siniavski.
May	Mitterrand appoints a *'contre-gouvernement'* (shadow cabinet).
December	FGDS–PCF electoral pact agreed.
1967 March	FGDS–PCF gains in legislative elections (FGDS 19.3 per cent).
1968 January	Mollet calls for a new Socialist Party.
February	PCF–FGDS common platform signed.

May	Student riots and general strike.
June	Gaullist landslide in legislative elections.
August	Russians invade Czechoslovakia.
November	Mitterrand resigns from the FGDS presidency—FGDS dissolved.
December	PCF 'Champigny Manifesto' published. SFIO Congress decides to form a new Socialist Party. Mollett announces retirement.
1969 May	Alfortville Congress of new Socialist Party selects Defferre as presidential candidate.
1969 June	Presidential elections: Defferre 5 per cent, Duclos (PCF) 22 per cent.
1969 July	Issy-les-Moulineaux Congress of the new Parti Socialiste (PS) makes Alain Savary First Secretary.
December	Parti Socialiste leadership agrees to fusion with CIR.
1970 February	Georges Marchais becomes PCF deputy General Secretary. PS dialogue with PCF opens.
March	First PCF–PS meeting.
October	PS meeting (at Bondy) accepts centrist municipal alliances.
December	Publication of PCF–PS *'bilan'* on talks.
1971 March	Mixed results for PS in municipal elections.
June	(11-13) PS Épinay Congress.
	(16) Mitterrand elected First Secretary in place of Savary.
July	PS meeting with PCF followed by proposal to negotiate a common programme.
October	PCF publishes its programme, *Changer de Cap*.
1972 March	(10-11) PS Suresnes Conference adopts a party programme, *Changer la vie*.
	(22) PCF–PS disagreement on how to vote in the 23 April referendum on EEC enlargement.
April	First PCF–PS meeting to negotiate the Common Programme.
June	(27) Successful end to negotiations on the Common Programme.
	(28) Mitterrand's declaration at Vienna meeting of the Socialist International that the PS intends to show that of 5 million PCF voters 3 million can vote Socialist.
July	PS, PCF, and Left Radicals officially sign the *Programme commun de gouvernement*.
1973 March	Left advance in legislative elections (PS + Left Radicals 20.4 per cent; PCF 21.3 per cent).

May	Marchais–Berlinguer talks.
June	PS Grenoble Congress.
July	PS–PCF polemic over defence policy.
September	Socialist advance in cantonal elections. PS Bagnolet Conference on European policy.
1974 April	PS Congress unanimously adopts Mitterrand as presidential candidate. PCF backs Mitterrand.
1974 May	Presidential election second ballot: Mitterrand 12.9 million votes, Giscard d'Estaing 13.4 million votes.
September	PS advances in by-elections and Senate elections.
October	(7) PCF starts polemic with PS.
	(12–13) Assises Nationales pour le Socialisme in Paris. Rocard, Delors, and others join the PS. Left summit meeting cancelled.
1975 January– February	PS Pau Congress: CERES dropped from the Secretariat. Jospin report on PCF–PS relations unanimously approved at a PS National Convention.
June	PS National Convention on *autogestion* adopts the '15 Theses'.
October	Guy Mollet dies.
1976 January	PS favours direct elections to European Parliament.
February	PCF abandons 'dictatorship of the proletariat'.
May	Unanimous agreement at the PS Dijon Conference on municipal election alliances.
June	PCF and PS summit on municipal elections.
November	Socialist advances in by-elections.
1977 March	Left alliance advances in municipal elections: PS gains thirty-nine large towns, PCF sixteen.
May	PS, PCF, MRG start negotiations to update the Common Programme.
June	(17–19) PS Nantes Congress.
July	PS, PCF, MRG committee to update the Common Programme concludes.
September	Left summit broken by MRG walk-out.
	(21–23) Final rupture of Left union negotiations.
November	PS National Convention calls on PCF to restart negotiations.
1978 March	Defeat of the Left in the legislative elections, but PS (24.7 per cent) overtakes the PCF (20.5 per cent) to become the largest party of the Left. Rocard and Mauroy criticize PS strategy.
April	PCF dissenters (Elleinstein and Althusser) make protests about Communist leadership.

1979 April	PS Metz Congress: Rocard and Mauroy leave the Secretariat. CERES return to the Secretariat.
June	European Parliament election confirms PS (23.5 per cent) lead over PCF (20.6 per cent).
December	Soviet invasion of Afghanistan.
1980 January	PS National Convention adopts *Projet Socialiste*.
October	Rocard announces bid for PS presidential nomination.
November	Mitterrand announces bid for PS presidential nomination: Rocard withdraws.
December	PCF runs anti-immigration campaign.
1981 January	PS Créteil convention nominates Mitterrand as Socialist candidate. Jospin becomes PS First Secretary.
April–May	Presidential elections. First ballot: Mitterrand 25.8 per cent, Marchais (PCF) 15.3 per cent. Second ballot: Mitterrand 51.8 per cent (15.7 million votes), Giscard 48.2 per cent (14.6 million votes).
May	Formation of first Mauroy government.
June	(14–21) Socialist landslide in legislative elections: PS 37.6 per cent, PCF 16.2 per cent. PS gains absolute majority of seats (285 including fourteen MRG). PCF reduced to forty-four seats, and loses 1.5 million votes.
	(23) PS–PCF agreement on policy. Second Mauroy government includes four Communist ministers.
October	Private and local radio legalized.
October	PS Valence Congress—unanimous leadership. First devaluation of the franc (4 per cent).
1982 January	PS loses three seats in by-elections.
January	39 hour week instituted.
February	Nationalization Bill passed.
March	Setback for Left in cantonal elections: PS 29.7 per cent, PCF 15.9 per cent.
June	Government imposes wage- and price-freeze and public spending cuts. Second devaluation of the franc (6 per cent.) Resignation of Nicole Questiaux, Minister for National Solidarity.
June	Quilliot rent control law.
July	First Auroux labour laws voted.
August	Corsican Regional Assembly elections. Broadcasting Authority established.
December	PS–PCF agreement on municipal elections.
1983 March	Left vote falls to 44 per cent in municipal elections: PS loses 15 big towns: PCF 16. Third devaluation of the franc (3 per cent). Resignation of J.-P. Chevènement, Minister for Industry and Research. Government reshuffle: the third Mauroy government.

April	Government introduces new austerity package by ordinance.
August	French forces aid Chad government to repel Libyan advance.
September	Austerity budget introduced.
October	PS Bourg-en-Bresse Congress reaffirms unanimous leadership.
December	PS–PCF 'verification' of government agreement. Mitterrand visits Lebanon after attacks on French forces.
1984 February	Lorry drivers' strike.
March	'Restructuring' of coal, steel and shipbuilding industries announced. French troops leave Lebanon.
April	PCF leader Marchais participates in steelworkers' demonstration.
June	Left vote slumps in European Parliament election: PS 21 per cent; PCF 11 per cent. Emergence of large (11 per cent) FN (National Front) vote.
July	Legislation to integrate church schools dropped. Mauroy government resigns; Communist ministers leave government. Laurent Fabius becomes prime minister; return to office of J-P. Chevènement.
November	Pay-TV channel established. Unemployment reaches 2.5 million. Mitterrand–Ghadafi talks in Crete. Elections in New Caledonia followed by separatist demonstrations.
December	Edgard Pisani given special responsibility for New Caledonia.
1985 January	State of emergency declared in New Caledonia.
March	Left parties aggregate under 40% in cantonal elections.
April	Proportional representation system announced for 1986 legislative elections; Rocard resigns from government.
June	Rocard indicates intention to stand for presidency.
July	Fabius and Jospin dispute leadership of Socialists' 1986 election campaign. Greenpeace vessel *Rainbow Warrior* sunk in Auckland, New Zealand.
August	Mitterrand sets up Tricot inquiry into Greenpeace affair; Tricot report absolves French secret service of blame.
September	Defence Minister Hernu resigns over Greenpeace affair; Fabius admits French agents sank vessel.
October	Mitterrand–Gorbachev talks in Paris. PS Toulouse Congress reaffirms unanimous leadership, though one in three delegates back Rocard.

November	Fifth TV channel awarded to Italian Berlusconi.
December	Mitterrand-Jaruzelski talks in Paris; Fabius voices disapproval of Polish leader's visit.
1986 January	Inflation rate falls to 4.7 per cent.
February	Sixth TV channel established. 'Flexible work time' law passed against PCF opposition.
March	Socialists beaten by RPR–UDF alliance in legislative elections (RPR–UDF 43 per cent; PS 32 per cent; PC 10 per cent; FN 10 per cent); Fabius government resigns. Mitterrand appoints RPR leader Chirac prime minister; 'cohabitation' begins.

Socialist Party Participation in Government: 1905–1986

	Leadership	Participation
1914–17		UNION SACRÉE (three SFIO ministers: Guesde, Sembat, and A. Thomas)
1936–8	POPULAR FRONT 1st Blum govt. June 1936–June 1937	Chautemps govt. (Radical) June 1937–Jan. 1938 (nine SFIO ministers)
	2nd Blum govt. Mar.–Apr. 1938	
1940 (May)		UNION NATIONALE Reynaud govt. (six SFIO ministers) Pétain govt. (two SFIO ministers)
1944–51	TRIPARTISM	de Gaulle govt. Sept. 1944–Jan. 1946.
	Gouin govt. Jan.–June 1946	Bidault govt. June–Dec. 1946
	Blum govt. Dec. 1946–Jan. 1947 Ramadier govt. Jan.–May 1947	

Leadership	Participation
THIRD FORCE	
Ramadier govt. May–Nov. 1947	
	Schuman govt. Nov. 1947–July 1948
	Marie govt. July–Sept. 1948
	Schuman govt. Sept. 1948
	Queuille govt. Sept. 1948–Oct. 1949
	Bidault govt. Oct. 1949–July 1950
	Queuille govt. July 1950
	Pleven govt. July 1950–Mar. 1951
	Queuille govt. Mar.–July 1951
1956–9	Mollet govt. Jan. 1956–May 1957
	Bourgès-Maunoury govt. June–Oct. 1957
	Gaillard govt. Nov. 1957–May 1958
	Pflimlin govt. May 1958
	de Gaulle govt. May 1958–Jan. 1959
1981–86	1st Mauroy govt. May–June 1981
	2nd Mauroy govt. June 1981–March 1983
	3rd Mauroy govt. March 1983–July 1984
	Fabius govt. July 1984–March 1986

Election Results

General Elections 1956–1986

(a) Percentage of votes (rounded up or down to nearest 0.5 per cent)

	Communist (%)	Other Left (%)	Socialist (%)	Radical (%)	MRP (%)	Conservative (%)	Gaullist (%)	Other Right (%)
1956	26.0	1.0	15.0	15.5	11.0	15.0	4.0	13.5
1958 (first ballot)	19.0	1.0	15.5	11.5	11.5	23.0	17.5	2.0
1962 "	22.0	2.0	15.0	8.0	9.0	15.0	32.0	–
1967 "	22.5	2.0	FGDS (Soc. and Rad.) 19.0			Centre 13.0	38.0	4.0
1968 "	20.0	4.0	16.5			10.0	46.0	2.0
1973 "	21.0	3.0	UGSD (Soc. and Rad.) 20.5			12.5	35.5	5.0
1978 "	20.5	3.0	24.5			UDF (Giscardians) 21.5	22.5	5.0
1981 "	16.0	2.0	37.5			19.0	21.0	3.0
1986*	10.0	2.5	32.0			} 45.0		National Front 10.0

(b) Seats

	Communist	Other Left	Socialist	Radical	MRP	Conservative	Gaullist	Other Right
1956	150	–	99	94	84	97	22	50
1958	10	–	47	40	64	129	206	
1962	41	2	67	45	38	51	324	4

*One ballot only.

(continued)

	Communist	Other Left	Socialist	Radical	MRP	Conservative	Gaullist	Other Right
1967	73	4	FGDS 116			Centre 44	245	
1968	34		57			33	357	6
1973	73	1	UGDS 102 (Soc. 89; Left Rad. 13)			32	270 (incl. 69 Giscardians)	12
1978	86		114 (Soc. 104; Left Rad. 10)			UDF (Giscardians) 137	RPR 153	1
1981	44		283 (Soc. 269; Left Rad. 14)			RPR/UDF 66	85	National Front 8
1986*	35		216 (Soc. 209; Left Rad. 7)			RPR/UDF 291	35	35

(c) Votes (in millions)

	Communist	Socialist	Centrist	Gaullist	National Front
1978	5.8	7.0	6.1	6.4	—
1981	4.0	9.4	4.8	5.2	—
1986	2.7	8.8	12.3 (Centrist & Gaullist)		2.7

*The number of seats was increased from 491 to 577 in 1986.

Presidential Elections 1965–1981

1. 1965

	5 December (first ballot)	(%)		19 December (second ballot)	(%)
Registered voters	28,333,167			28,223,198	
Voting	24,001,961	85.0		23,862,658	84.5
Abstentions	4,231,206	15.0		4,260,545	15.5
C. de Gaulle	10,386,734	43.7	*de Gaulle*	12,643,527	54.5
F. Mitterrand (Left)	7,658,792	32.2	Mitterrand	10,553,985	45.5
J. Lecanuet (Centre)	3,767,404	15.9			
J.-L. Tixier-Vigancour	1,253,958	5.0			
P. Marcilhacy	413,129	1.7			
M. Barbu	277,652	1.2			

2. 1969

	1 June (first ballot)	(%)		15 June (second ballot)	(%)
Registered voters	28,775,876			28,747,988	
Voting	22,500,644	78.2		19,851,728	69.1
Abstentions	6,275,232	21.8		8,896,260	30.9
G. Pompidou (Gaullist)	9,763,428	43.9	*Pompidou*	10,686,493	57.6
A. Poher (Centre)	5,202,271	23.1	Poher	7,870,601	42.4
J. Duclos (Comm.)	4,781,838	21.5			
G. Defferre (Soc.)	1,128,049	5.1			
M. Rocard (PSU)	814,053	3.7			
L. Ducatel	284,820	1.3			
A. Krivine (Trot.)	236,263	1.1			

3. 1974

	5 May (first ballot)	(%)		19 May (second ballot)	(%)
Registered voters	30,602,953			30,600,775	
Voting	26,012,850	85.0		27,081,383	88.5
Abstentions	4,590,103	15.0		3,519,392	11.5
F. Mitterrand (Left)	11,044,373	43.2	Mitterrand	12,971,604	49.2
V. Giscard d'Estaing	8,326,774	32.6	*Giscard*	13,396,203	50.8
J. Chaban Delmas (Gaullist)	3,857,728	15.1			
J. Royer (Ind. Gaullist)	810,540	3.2			
A. Laguiller (Trot.)	595,247	2.3			
R. Dumont (Ecol.)	337,800	1.3			
J.-M. Le Pen	190,921	0.7			

(continued)

E. Muller	176,279	0.7
A. Krivine	93,990	0.4
B. Renouvin	43,722	0.2
J.-C. Sebag	42,007	0.2
G. Héraud	19,255	0.1

4. 1981	26 April (first ballot)	(%)		10 May (second ballot)	(%)
Registered voters	36,398,859				
Voting	29,516,982	81.1			
Abstentions	6,882,777	18.9			
V. Giscard d'Estaing	8,222,432	28.3	Giscard	14,647,787	48.2
F. Mitterrand (Soc.)	7,505,960	25.8	*Mitterrand*	15,714,598	51.8
J. Chirac (Gaullist)	5,225,848	18.0			
G. Marchais (Comm.)	4,456,922	15.3			
B. Lalonde (Ecol.)	1,126,254	3.9			
A. Laguiller (Trot.)	668,057	2.3			
M. Crépeau (Left Rad.)	642,847	2.2			
M. Debré (Ind. Gaullist)	481,821	1.9			
M.-F. Garaud (Ind.)	386,623	1.3			
H. Bouchardeau (PSU)	321,353	1.1			

Socialist Party Faction Strengths 1971–1987

(percentage of votes cast for rival motions at party congresses)

	Mitterrand, Defferre, and Mauroy		Poperen	Mollet	CERES
Épinay 1971	15	30	12	34	9
Grenoble 1973	65		5	8	21
Pau 1975	68			3	25
Nantes 1977	75				24

	Mitterrand	Defferre	Mauroy	Rocard		
Metz 1979	40	6	17	21		15

| †Valence 1981 | | | | | | |

	Jospin, Defferre, Mauroy, Rocard				
†Bourg-en-Bresse 1983	77		5*		18

	Jospin, Defferre, Mauroy, CERES	Rocard	
†Toulouse 1985	81	29	

| †Lille 1987 | | | | | | |

☐ = component of the Party's ruling majority.

†To demonstrate party unity no rival motions were submitted at the 1981 and 1987 congresses; for similar reasons, the 1983 and 1985 congresses concluded with composite motions.

*Dissident Rocardians.

Attitudes of Party Currents at Metz Congress, 1979

Issue	Mitterrand (Jospin motion)	Mauroy	Rocard	CERES
Left Union	Left union with the PCF sought; rejection of any 'autonomous' strategy.	Left union on its own insufficient: reinforcement of PS through an appeal to the working class.	Close to a rejection of Left union; call for the Party to target its potential voters: the Centre floating vote.	Rejection of 'anti-Communism' and call for a mobilization of the PS through mass appeal.
Economy	'Break with capitalism', nationalization, priority of planning over market, '*auto-gestion*'.	Nationalization, planning, and a social transformation over time.	Sceptical view of nationalization and planning; emphasis on the market.	Nationalization, '*autogestion*', and state investment and growth strategy: a 'break with capitalism' and redistribution.

Europe	A search for consensus with 'progressive forces' in Europe; against nationalism and the 'Atlanticist drift'; favourable to enlargement.	Very pro-European (not supra-national) Favourable to enlargement of EEC. Search for debate with north-European Socialists.	Favourable to EEC, but Rocard personally unenthusiastic.	Against 'Europeanism' and the EEC as the framework for political action.
Party Structure	*Front de classe*, i.e. a wide catch-all Party. Reinforce unity and discipline, more women, increased action in factories, a Party daily, greater help for small federations.	A more collegiate leadership, liberty of expression, increased activity in factories, youth, etc. Unity of Party above all.	Against leadership centralization; call for separation of First Secretary and presidential candidate roles.	Wanted a 'mass party', but a mass party in which activists play a role. Democratic functioning of the Party and hence responsibility of leaders to base.

Attitudes of Party Currents, 1987

	Rocard	Mauroy	Chevènement	Jospin/Fabius (Mitterrand)
Left Union	PS 'vocation' to become *the* party of opposition.	Alliance with PCF still necessary.	Belongs to the past.	PS should only rely on its own forces.
Strategy	Appeal to the 'centre' the 'soft underbelly of the Republic'. Coalitions *could* be possible.	Create a 'wage earners' bloc.	Create a mass popular rally; engage in a rethink through 'clubs'.	Create a mass party for the forthcoming campaigns.
Socialism	Refusal to enter a 'definitional war'.	Appeal to 'Swedish model'.	Socialism still emphasised.	'Social democracy'; language of 'responsibility'.
Other Issues	Priority action against unemployment and Third World debt.	Defence of 'left unity'.	Three points: +national independence +growth – via 'planning' +democracy.	'Modernization' Fabius: concentration on human rights (e.g. South Africa) and unemployment.

Currents in the Socialist Party

The existence of currents in the Socialist Party remained, throughout its period in government, one of its marked features. The currents, structured around an individual, remained much as they had been when expressed at the Congress of Metz in 1979 but the issues at stake changed out of recognition after 1986. The decline of the Communist party almost removed the issue of left unity on which so much of the 1970s debate was focussed but it also precipitated a stampede towards the middle ground with the consequence that the rhetorical centre of gravity moved sharply rightwards. Mitterrand's 'rupture' with capitalism was never a real possibility but that notion, along with the role of the plan, *'autogestion'* (except for Delors who was highly sceptical in 1978), anti-Europeanism, foreign and defence policy and to some extent 'Socialism' itself ceased to be points of discord. Moreover there was, by the mid 'eighties, general agreement about the role of the market, the need to renovate the party and to secure its majoritarian 'vocation', of polling 40%-plus of the vote. The disappearance within a few years of once-salient issues meant that the 'presidential' nature of the currents had become more starkly visible, with the consequence that, on leaving government, the party had too many politicians who considered themselves to be of presidential status.

Thus after March 1986 the inner-party debate ceased to be about how to rally the left but rather about how to win the centre vote essential for a future victory. In this debate CERES, transformed into the moderate sounding 'Socialism and Republic', still saw itself as the party's Left and its emphasis on state intervention, the plan, and Socialism allowed that impression; although Chevènement, like all other serious *'présidentiables'* made a pitch for the centre vote through a *patriotard* style of speech and a moderate image. Rocardians still marked out the right of the party—although they refused such labels—and the emphasis on the market grew more marked just as it did for Fabius whose position depended more on the image of a younger 'Rocard' than on policy differentiation. Mauroy, not a serious outsider, had difficulty in holding a group together and seemed to depend on the (dubious) possibility of a renewed alliance with the Communist Party.

The Second Mauroy Government (June 1981)

*Prime Minister: Pierre Mauroy

Ministers of State
*Interior and Decentralization: Gaston Defferre
Trade: Michel Jobert (Movement of Democrats; ex-Gaullist)
Transport: Charles Fiterman (PCF)
*Planning: Michel Rocard
*Research and Technology: Jean-Pierre Chevènement

Minister
*National Solidarity: Mme Nicole Questiaux

Ministers attached to the Prime Minister
*Women's Rights: Mme Yvette Roudy
*Relations with Parliament: André Labarrère
Civil Service and Administrative Reform: Anicet Le Pors (PCF)

Ministers and Delegate Ministers (with 'host' ministry in brackets)
*Justice: Robert Badinter
*Foreign Affairs: Claude Cheysson
*European Affairs (Foreign Affairs): André Chandernagor
*Co-operation and Development (Foreign Affairs): Jean-Pierre Cot
*Defence: Charles Hernu
*Economics and Finance: Jacques Delors
*Budget (Economics and Finance): Laurent Fabius
*Education: Alain Savary
*Agriculture: Mme Edith Cresson
*Industry: Pierre Dreyfus
*Energy (Industry): Edmond Hervé
*Commerce and Small Business: André Delélis
*Culture: Jack Lang
*Labour: Jean Auroux
  Health: Jack Ralite (PCF)
*Leisure: André Henry
*Youth and Sport (Leisure): Mme Edwige Avice
*Urban Affairs and Housing: Roger Quilliot
  Environment: Michel Crépeau (MRG)
*Marine: Louis Le Pensec
*Communication: Georges Fillioud
*Posts and Telecommunications: Louis Mexandeau
*Ex-Servicemen: Jean Laurain
*Consumer Affairs: Mme Catherine Lalumière
  Professional Training: Marcel Rigout (PCF)

All ministers are Socialist except where indicated.
* See Biographies.

Secretaries of State attached to the Prime Minister
*Public Sector: Jean Le Garrec
*Repatriates: Raymond Courrière

Secretaries of State (with 'host' ministry in brackets)
*Overseas Territories (Interior and Decentralization): Henri Emmanuelli
*Family (National Solidarity): Mme Georgina Dufoix
*Old People (National Solidarity): Joseph Franceschi
*Immigrants (National Solidarity): François Autain
*Defence (Defence): Georges Lemoine
*Agriculture (Agriculture): André Cellard
 Tourism (Leisure): François Abadie (MRG)

The Third Mauroy Government (March 1983)

Prime Minister: Pierre Mauroy

Ministers
Economy, Finance and Budget: Jacques Delors
Social Affairs and National Solidarity: Pierre Bérégovoy
Interior and Decentralization: Gaston Defferre
Transport: Charles Fiterman (PCF)
Justice: Robert Baditner
Foreign Affairs: Claude Cheysson
Defence: Charles Hernu
Agriculture: Michel Rocard
Industry and Research: Laurent Fabius
Education: Alain Savary
Trade and Tourism: Mme Edith Cresson
Urban Affairs and Housing: Roger Quilliot
Commerce and Small Business: Michel Crépeau (MRG)
Professional Training: Marcel Rigout (PCF)

Secretary of State
Government Spokesman: Max Gallo

Delegate Ministers (with 'host' ministry in brackets)
Culture: Jack Lang
Leisure, Youth and Sport: Mme Edwige Avice
Women's Rights:† Mme Yvette Roudy
Relations with Parliament:† André Labarrère
European Affairs (Foreign Affairs): André Chandernagor
Co-operation and Development (Foreign Affairs): Christian Nucci

All ministers are Socialist except where indicated.
* See Biographies.   † Denotes attachment to Prime Minister's office.

Posts and Telecommunications (Industry and Research): Louis Mexandeau

Employment (Social Affairs and National Solidarity): Jack Ralite (PCF)

Secretaries of State
Without Portfolio but with responsibilities for the Plan:† Jean Le Garrec
Civil Service and Administrative Reform:† Anicet Le Pors (PCF)
Communication:† Georges Fillioud
Budget (Economy, Finance and Budget): Henri Emmanuelli
Consumer Affairs (Economy, Finance, and Budget): Mme Catherine Lalumière
Public Security (Interior and Decentralization): Joseph Franceschi
Overseas Territories (Interior and Decentralization): Georges Lemoine
Defence (Defence): François Autain
Ex-Servicemen (Defence): Jean Laurain
Energy (Industry and Research): Jean Auroux
Health (Social Affairs and National Solidarity): Edmond Hervé
Family, Population, and Immigrant Workers (Social Affairs and National Solidarity): Mme Georgina Dufoix
Old People (Social Affairs and National Solidarity): Daniel Benoist
Repatriates (Social Affairs and National Solidarity): Raymond Courrière
Environment and Quality of Life:† Mme Huguette Bouchardeau (PSU)
Education (Education): Roger-Gérard Schwartzenberg (MRG)
Agriculture and Forestry (Agriculture): René Souchon
Tourism (Trade and Tourism): Roland Carraz
Marine (Transport): Guy Lengagne

The Fabius Government (July 1984)

Prime Minister: Laurent Fabius

Minister of State
Planning: Gaston Defferre

Ministers
Economy, Finance and Budget: Pierre Bérégovoy
Justice: Robert Badinter
Foreign Affairs: Claude Cheysson
Defence: Charles Hernu
Interior and Decentralisation: Pierre Joxe
Agriculture: Michel Rocard
Industry and Trade: Mme Edith Cresson
Education: Jean-Pierre Chevènement

All ministers are Socialist except where indicated.
† Denotes attachment to Prime Minister's office.

Social Affairs and National Solidarity: Mme Georgina Dufoix
Urban Affairs, Housing and Transport: Paul Quilès
Commerce, Small Business and Tourism: Michel Crépeau (MRG)
European Affairs (and Government spokesman): Roland Dumas
Labour and Professional Training: Michel Delebarre
Environment: Mme Huguette Bouchardeau (PSU)
Research and Technology: Hubert Curien

Delegate Ministers (with 'host' ministry in brackets)
Culture: Jack Lang
Women's Rights: †Mme Yvette Roudy
Youth and Sports: Alain Calmat
Relations with Parliament: †Andre Labarrère
Co-operation and Development (Foreign Affairs): Christian Nucci
Posts and Telecomunications (Trade and Industry): Louis Mexandeau

Secretaries of State (with 'host' ministry in brackets)
Defence (Defence): Mme Edwige Avice
Civil Service: †Jean Le Garrec
Communications: †Georges Fillioud
Budget (Economy, Finance and Budget): Henri Emmanuelli
Consumer Affairs (Economy, Finance and Budget): Mme Catherine
  Lalumière
Old People and Repatriates (Social Affairs): Joseph Francdeschi
Overseas Territories (Interior and Decentralisation): George Lemoine
Transport (Urban Affairs, Housing and Transport): Jean Auroux
Universities (Education): Roger-Gérard Schwartzemberg (MRG)
Social Economy: †Jean Gatel
Ex-Servicemen (Defence): Jean Laurain
Energy (Industry and Trade): Martin Malvy
Health (Social Affairs): Edmond Hervé
Foreign Affairs (Foreign Affairs): Jean-Michel Baylet (MRG)
Repatriates (Social Affairs): Raymond Courrière
Agriculture and Foresty (Agriculture): René Souchon
Environmental Affairs: †Haroun Tazieff
Technological Education (Education): Roland Carraz
Marine Affairs (Urban Affairs, Housing and Transport): Guy Lengagne
Commerce, Small Business and Tourism (Commerce, Small Business
  and Tourism): Jean-Marie Bockel

All ministers are Socialist except where indicated.
†Denotes attachment to the Prime Minister's Office.

Biographies

Jean Auroux: b. September 1942, Thizy (Rhône); teacher (*professeur*); Minister of Labour 1981-3, Energy 1983-4, Transport 1984-6; mayor of Roanne 1977- ; deputy for Loire 1978- ; PS spokesman on housing and problems of the handicapped 1978-81; member of CGT union; introduced industrial democracy reform 1982.

François Autain: b. June 1935, Deux-Sèvres; doctor; educated at *lycée* in Nantes; Junior Minister of Defence 1983- ; Junior Minister of National Solidarity (responsible for immigrants) 1981-3; ex-UNEF activist; joined PSU 1968; mayor of Bouguenais (Loire-Atlantique) 1971- ; deputy for Loire-Atlantique 3^c (Nantes) 1978-86; ex-member National Assembly Commission on Cultural, Family, and Social Affairs; CERES activist; obliged to impose immigration controls.

Mme Edwige Avice: b. April 1945; Nevers (Nièvre); administrator in office of Director General, Paris hospitals 1973-8 (Crédit Lyonnais International department 1970-3); educated at Faculty of Law, Paris; Junior Minister of Sport 1981-4, Defence 1984-6; member of CFDT and CERES; joined PS 1972; CERES nominee on PS Comité Directeur and Bureau Exécutif 1977; deputy for Paris 1978- ; rising left-wing activist; promoted 1983 and 1984.

Robert Badinter: b. March 1928, Paris; Appeal Court barrister 1951- and Sorbonne law lecturer; son of furrier; educated at *lycées* Janson de Sailly, Ampère, Carnot (Paris), and Faculties of Law and Letters, Paris, Columbia University, NY; Minister of Justice 1981-5; initiated abolition of guillotine, President, Constitutional Council 1985- ; author of *L'Exécution* 1973; Mitterrand confidant; negotiated Mitterrand–Giscard TV 'face to face' 1981; liberal reformer in place of A. Peyrefitte; appointed constitutional watchdog by Mitterrand to oversee *cohabitation* 1986- .

Pierre Bérégovoy: b. December 1925, Seine-Maritime, manager (*chargé de mission* 1978-81) Gaz de France (fitter 1941-2, railwayman 1942-50); educated at primary and secondary schools and Institut du Travail, Faculty of Law, Strasbourg; Minister of Finance 1984-6, Social Affairs 1982-4; Secretary General to the Presidency 1981-2; member of Economic and Social Council 1979-81; member of SFIO 1944-58; founder member of PSA 1958 and of PSU Secretariat 1973-7; joined PS 1969; elected to Comité Directeur 1969, Bureau Exécutif 1969-81, and Secretariat 1973-81 (resposible for relations with PCF 1975-81); unsuccessful parliamentary candidate 1973 and 1978; led negotiation with PCF on updating the *Programme commun* 1977; ex-manual worker; close Mitterrand aide; moved (1982) from head of presidential secretariat to become social policy co-ordinator; promoted to No. 3 in Government 1983; financially orthodox 1984-6; deputy for Nièvre 1986- .

André Cellard: b. March 1921, Rabat (Morocco); barrister (Appeal Court lawyer 1945-); educated *lycée* in Rabat and Faculty of Law, Aix-en-Provence; Junior Minister of Agriculture 1981-3; deputy for Gers 2e (Condom) 1978-86; member of Radical Party -1969 and of PS 1969- ; member of National Secretariat of FGDS 1965; first joint Secretary General FGDS 1968 (FGDS spokesman on employment); member of PS Comité Directeur 1969-73; Mitterrandist; dropped 1983.

André Chandernagor: b. Sept. 1921, Civray (Vienne); civil servant (Conseil d'État); son of merchant; educated Collège de Civray, Lycée Henry IV Paris, École nationale de la France d'outre-mer and ENA; deputy Foreign Minister (responsible for European Affairs) 1981-3; member of the *cabinet* of Guy Mollet (PM) 1956-7, Gérard Jaquet (Minister of Overseas Territories) 1957, and Félix Gaillard (Radical PM) 1957-8; member SFIO/PS 1946- ; mayor of Mortroux 1953-83; deputy for Creuse 2e (Aubusson) 1958-86; president of Creuse General Council 1973- ; president of Limousin Regional Council 1974-81; elected to SFIO Comité Directeur 1963-6, and PS Comité Directeur 1969; elected to PS Bureau Exécutif 1969, PS representative in French delegation to UN General Assembly 1978; ex-member of National Assembly Commissions of Laws and Foreign Affairs; ex-vice-president PS National Assembly Group; senior parliamentarian; ex-SFIO right-wing anti-communist; centrist (suspended from party offices in 1970 for 'centrism'); colonial; pro-EEC; Mauroy supporter.

Jean-Pierre Chevènement: b. March 1939, Belfort; civil servant (ex-Foreign Ministry), son of teacher (*instituteur*); educated at *lycée*, Besançon, Faculty of Law, Paris, and ENA; Minister for Research and Technology 1981-2, and Industry 1982-3; Minister of Educataion 1984-6; joined SFIO 1964; Secretary General of CERES 1965-71; political secretary PS Paris federation 1969-70; member of PS Secretariat 1971-5, out 1975-9, in 1979-81; author of draft PS programme 1972 and 1980; responsible for negotiating the economic section of *Programme commun* 1972; member of Bureau Exécutif 1971-81 and Comité Directeur 1971- ; deputy for Belfort 1973- ; mayor of Belfort 1983- ; PS national secretary for research 1979-81; author of various books including *Socialisme ou social-médiocratie* (1969), *Les Socialistes, les communistes et les autres* (1976); strongly pro-Union of the Left; useful to Mitterrand when negotiating with PCF 1971-2; embarrassment when bidding for centrist vote 1975- ; dogmatic radical pre-1981 (anti-Rocard, anti-EEC); unexpectedly pragmatic Minister 1981-3; backed Finance Minister's call for a 'pause' in reform programme 1981; promoted to super-ministry 1982; then dropped for being too interventionist 1983, conventional/traditional Education Minister; Old Turk.

Claude Cheysson: b. April 1920, Paris; diplomat (served in W. Germany, Vietnam, Indonesia); son of *Inspecteur des finances*; educated at Collège Stanislas, Paris, and at ENA, École normale supérieure, and

École polytechnique; Minister for Foreign Affairs 1981-4; *Chef de Cabinet* to Mendès France 1954; EEC Commissioner (for Developing Countries) 1975-81; Third World (French Africa) specialist; non-parliamentarian; orthodox moderate; blunder-prone.

Jean-Pierre Cot: b. Oct. 1937, Geneva; university teacher (international law and political sociology, Sorbonne, 1969-); son of university teacher (Pierre Cot, Minister for Air in Popular Front Government 1936); educated Faculty of Law, Paris; Junior Minister for Foreign Affairs (responsible for Co-operation and Development) 1981-2; member of PS 1969- ; mayor of Coise-Saint-Jean-Pied-Gauthier 1971- ; deputy for Savoie 3ᵉ 1973-86; PS spokesman on European Affairs 1976- ; PS representative in French delegation to UN General Assembly 1978; orator; anti-nationalist; prominent Rocardian; social democrat; Third World idealist; resigned 1982.

Raymond Courrière: b. August 1932; lawyer (notary); son of notary; Minister for the Repatriated 1981-6; PS Senator, Aude 1974-81; mayor of Cuxac-Cabardès (Aude).

Mme Édith Cresson: b. 1934, Paris; civil servant; daughter of civil servant (*Inspecteur des finances*); graduate in economics; married to a Peugeot director; Minister of Agriculture 1981-3, Trade 1983-4, and Industry and Trade 1984-6; ex-member CIR; PS National Secretary (Students and Youth) 1975-9; member of European Assembly 1979-81; deputy for Vienne 1981- ; mayor of Châtellerault 1983- (won against the trend); farmer's target 1981-3; pro-privatization 1984-6; pragmatic Mitterrand protégé; leading Socialist woman cabinet minister 1981-6.

Gaston Defferre: b. Sept. 1910 (Hérault) died 1986; newspaper proprietor (*Le Provencal* and *Le Méridional*) and barrister 1931-51; son of barrister; educated at *lycée* in Nîmes and Faculty of Law, Aix-en-Provence; Minister of Interior 1981-4, Minister of Planning 1984-6; joined SFIO 1933; mayor of Marseilles 1944-5 and 1953-86; deputy for Bouches-du-Rhône (Marseilles) 1946-58 and 1962-86; senator 1959-62; Junior Minister in Gouin government 1946, and Blum government 1946-7; Minister for the Merchant Navy in Pleven government 1950-1 and Queuille government 1951; Minister for Overseas Territories in Mollet government 1956-7 (initiator of *loi cadre* permitting North African decolonization); president of the National Assembly Socialist Group 1967-81; Socialist candidate for Presidency 1969 (1.1 million votes, 5 per cent); president of Provence-Côte-d'Azur Regional Council 1974-81; municipal patriarch who presided over declining local power base (narrowly survived 1983); long-time opponent of Communist Party; refused PS-PCF alliance at local level until 1983; opponent of Guy Mollet in party 1954-71; loyal to Mitterrand 1971- ; introduced decentralization reforms 1982 to boost PS local power; one of three survivors of Fourth Republic governments in office post-1981; Protestant; rich; yachtsman; died after losing vote in local party meeting 1986.

André Delelis: b. May 1924, Pas-de-Calais; sales representative; son of local government official; educated at Collège d'Auchel; Minister of Commerce and Small Business 1981-3; deputy mayor (1959) then mayor of Lens 1966– ; deputy for Pas-de-Calais 13e (Lens) 1967–86; old-style SFIO anti-Communist; refused to work with PCF at municipal level and was dropped from PS Comité Directeur 1977; dropped from Government for refusing alliance with PCF in 1983 municipal elections.

Jacques Delors: b. July 1925, Paris; university teacher (Paris) and ex-banker (deputy director Banque de France); son of bank clerk; educated at *lycées* Voltaire (Paris) and Blaise Pascal (Clermont Ferrand), and at Faculty of Law, Paris; Minister of Economy and Finance, 1981–4; President European Commission 1984– ; member of *cabinet* of Gaullist PM, Chaban Delmas (social and cultural affairs adviser) 1969–72; joined PS 1974; elected to Comité Directeur 1977; PS spokesman on international economic relations 1976–81; member of European Assembly 1979–81; mayor of Clichy 1983–; non-parliamentarian; Catholic, ex-CFDT union activist; popular moderate; reassuring to employers; pro 'pause' in reform programme 1981; proposer of austerity and 'realism' 1982–4; promoted to No. 2 in Government 1983; resignation-prone; difficult.

Pierre Dreyfus: b. November 1907, Paris; company director; (president and director general, Renault, 1955–75: president of steel company 1955–76); son of banker; educated at *lycée* Janson-de-Sailly and Faculty of Law, Paris; Minister for Industry 1981–2; *Chef de cabinet* to Robert Lacoste (Industry Minister, 1947–9) and to Bourgès-Maunoury (Industry Minister 1954); ex-member SFIO; non-radical, ex-nationalized industry director; non-parliamentarian; retired 1982.

Georgina Dufoix: b. Feb. 1943; economics graduate; Minister of Social Affairs 1984–6 (previously junior minister 1981–4); deputy for Gard 1986– ; member of CIR 1968–9; municipal councillor, Nîmes 1977– ; Mitterrandist; promoted to full cabinet rank 1984.

Roland Dumas: b. August 1922, Limoges; Appeal Court barrister 1950– ; son of *fonctionnaire*; educated at Lycée de Limoges, Faculty of Law, Paris and London University (SOAS); Foreign Minister 1984–6, Minister for European Affairs 1983–4; deputy 1956–8, 1967–8, (Dordogne) 1981– ; Mitterrand confidant.

Henri Emmanuelli: b. May 1943, Pyrénées-Atlantiques; bank manager; son of electrician; educated at *lycée* in Pau and Institute of Political Studies, Paris; Minister for the Budget 1983–6; Minister for Overseas Territories 1981–3; deputy for Landes 1978– ; elected to PS Comité Directeur 1979; ex-member National Assembly Finance Commission; PS specialist on economics and finance; Mitterrandist, formerly close to Defferre.

Laurent Fabius: b. August 1946, Paris; civil servant (Conseil d'État); son of antique dealer; educated at *lycées* in Paris (Janson-de-Sailly and Louis-Le-Grand), École normale supérieure, and ENA; Prime Minister 1984–6, Minister of Industry 1983–4, Budget 1981–3; joined PS 1974; manager of Mitterrand's office 1976–81; deputy for Seine-Maritime 1978– ; deputy mayor of Grand Quevilly 1977– ; PS spokesman on budgetary matters 1978–81; member of PS Bureau Exécutif and Secretariat (Press spokesman) 1979–81; led attack on Rocard at Metz Congress 1979; the youngest PM; technocratic face of modern French Socialism; at odds with Mitterrand over Polish leader's visit 1985, but remained his patron's dauphin; burgeoning orator; smooth; Mitterrand's ambitious, adaptable courtier; Rocard's major obstacle.

Georges Fillioud: b. July 1929, Lyons; journalist; son of estate agent; educated at École nationale professionelle, Lyons, and Faculty of Law, Paris and Lyons; Minister of Communications (Broadcasting) 1981–6; ex-editor-in-chief 'Europe No. 1' Radio Station (barred for political activity in 1966); deputy for Drôme 3e (Romans) 1967–8 and 1973–86; mayor of Romans 1977–83; Assistant Secretary General CIR 1970; member of PS Secretariat 1971–7, Secretary for Propaganda 1971–7; public relations man in Mitterrand's 1974 and 1981 campaigns; close Mitterrand aide; set up broadcasting authority.

Joseph Franceschi: b. Jan. 1924; Tunis; teacher; Junior Minister of Social Affairs (responsible for the Old) 1981–2, 1984–6; Minister for Public Security 1982–4; mayor of Alfortville 1965– ; deputy for Val-de-Marne 1973– ; presidential campaign organizer 1974 and 1981; Mitterrandist; appointed to combat terrorism and crime wave 1982.

Raymond Forni: b. May 1941, Belfort; barrister; son of tinsmith; president of National Assembly Legal Affairs Committee 1981–6; ex-production-line worker, Peugeot 1959–60; joined PS 1966; secretary of Belfort section of CERES 1969–73; deputy for Belfort 2e 1973–86; radical defence lawyer.

Christian Goux: b. Dec. 1929, Aix-en-Provence; university teacher at Sorbonne (Economics) 1969– ; son of civil servant; educated at Collège Chaptal and Faculty of Law, Paris; president of National Assembly Finance and Economics Committee 1981–6; joined PS 1972; adviser to Mitterrand 1974 and 1981; elected to PS Comité Directeur 1977; deputy for Var 1981– ; Marxist Mitterrandist; author of works on economics; critical of Government's economic policy (pro-protection) 1981–6.

André Henry: b. October 1934, Vosges; teacher (*instituteur*), 1955–68; Secretary General of FEN 1974–81 (FEN official 1968–74); son of lock-keeper; educated at École normale d'instituteurs, Mirecourt; Minister for Leisure (*Temps Libre*) 1981–3; permanent Secretary

Syndicat National des Instituteurs 1969–74; joined PS 1974; teachers' union organizer; spokesman for 550,000 teachers; defender of Socialist interest in a union federation with strong PCF element; professional opponent of private schools; not offered Education Ministry in 1981; non-parliamentarian; defeated as PS mayoral candidate at Épinal 1983; unsuccessful minister; dropped 1983.

Charles Hernu: b. July 1923, Finistère; journalist; son of *fonctionnaire*; educated at Collège des Minimes, Lyons; Minister of Defence 1981–5; Radical deputy for Seine 1956–8; PS deputy for Rhône 1978– ; mayor of Villeurbanne 1977– ; ex-president of CIR; ex-*mendésiste* Radical; ex-Secretary General of FGDS; quit over 'Greenpeace affair', protesting innocence 1985; Mitterrand acolyte; Catholic freemason.

Edmond Hervé: b. 1943 Côtes-du-Nord; university teacher (Constitutional Law, Rennes); son of farmer; Minister of Health, May–June 1981 and 1983–6; Junior Minister of Industry (responsible for Energy) 1981–3; mayor of Rennes 1977– ; deputy for Ille et Villaine 1981– ; member of SFIO 1966–9; ex-CERES activist; avoided choosing between CERES and Mitterrand at Nantes Congress 1977; Mauroy supporter 1979.

Lionel Jospin: b. 1938; university teacher, ex-civil servant (Ministry of Foreign Affairs); educated at ENA; First Secretary of PS 1981– (succeeded Mitterrand); joined PS 1971; ex-PSU; member of PS Secretariat 1973– ; National Secretary for activists 1973–5, for the Third World 1975–7, and for International Relations 1977–9; chairman of PS committee on PS–PCF relations 1975–7 (issued reports on the 'state of the Union'); deputy for Paris 1981–6; Haute-Garonne 1986–; Mitterrand protége; led fight back against Rocard-Mauroy criticisms post-1978 election; replaced Mauroy as No. 2 in Party 1979; Mitterrand's guarantor of Party loyalty 1981– ; ex-Maoist; stolid.

Pierre Joxe: b. November 1934, Paris; civil servant (Cour des Comptes); son of Louis Joxe, former diplomat and Gaullist minister; grandson of historian Daniel Halévy; educated at Lycée Henry IV, Faculty of Law, Paris, and ENA; president of PS National Assembly Group 1981–4 and 1986– ; Assistant Secretary General CIR 1970; member of PS Bureau Exécutif 1971–9 and 1981– ; deputy for Saône et Loire 1973– ; PS Treasurer 1979–81; Minister of Interior in Fabius government 1984–6; anti-EEC; left-wing Mitterrandist; member of CGT; opposed opening PS to CFDT activists and Left Christians; *marxisant*; tough parliamentary manager; law and order buff as minister.

André Labarrère: b. January 1928, Pau (Pyrénées Atlantiques); teacher (*professeur*) in *lycées* (1956–8 and 1968–) and university (Quebec 1959–66); son of shopkeeper; educated at École Henry IV and Collège Beau Frêne, Pau, and Faculty of Letters, Paris; Minister for Relations with Parliament 1981–6; mayor of Pau 1971–; deputy for Pyrénées Atlantiques 1967-8 and 1973- ; member of CIR 1967-9; member of PS Comité Directeur 1969- ; member of Bureau Exécutif 1969-71; joined PS before rest of Mitterrand's CIR 1969; former Mauroy ally.

Catherine Lalumière: b. 1935; lawyer (administrative law); wife of Professor of Public Law, Paris (drafter of decentralization laws); Minister for Consumer Affairs 1981-6 (Minister for Civil Service and Administrative Reform, May-June 1981); deputy for Gironde (Bordeaux) 1981- ; elected to PS Comité Directeur 1979; ex-spokesman on decentralization policy; rising PS woman; featured in poster campaign 1981; unsuccessful PS mayoral candidate against Chaban—Delmas in Bordeaux 1983.

Jack Lang: b. September 1939; university teacher (Law) 1976- ; ex-theatre director; son of commercial director; educated at Lycée Henri Poincaré (Nancy) and Faculty of Law, Paris; Minister of Culture 1981-6; Founder and Director of *Festival mondial du théâtre universitaire*, Nancy 1963-72; director of *Théâtre du palais de Chaillôt*, Paris 1972-4; Paris councillor 1977- ; special adviser to François Mitterrand 1978-81; PS campaign organizer in European elections 1979; PS spokesman on the Arts 1979-81; favours resisting *'atlantisme culturel'*; deputy for Loir et Cher 1986- ; vain, modish.

Jean Laurain: b. January 1921, Metz; teacher *(professeur)*; son of ornamental plasterer; educated at *lycée* in Metz and Faculties of Letters in Nancy, Lyons, and Strasbourg; Minister for Ex-Servicemen 1981-6; deputy for Moselle 1978- ; ex-Free French.

Jean Le Garrec: b. 1929, Morbihan; executive IBM; educated at Lycée de Cahors and Faculty of Law, Toulouse; Minister for Civil Service 1984-6, Planning 1983-4, Employment 1982-3, Public Sector 1981-2; deputy for Nord 1981- ; member of CFDT; member of PSU 1967-74; assistant national secretary PSU 1973; joined PS 1974; member of PS Comité Directeur 1975- ; PS spokesman on immigrant workers 1979-81 (member of Mitterrand's personal 'cabinet'); ex-Rocard supporter; after Metz Congress 1979 helped Mauroy to organize his Action Socialiste group. Pierre Mauroy's right arm and spokesman.

Georges Lemoine: b. June 1934, Rouen; university teacher, Sorbonne; son of railwayman; Minister for Overseas Territories 1983-6; Junior Minister of Defence 1981-3 (Junior Minister for Energy, May-June 1981); founder-member of CIR 1965; mayor of Chartres 1977- ; deputy for Eure-et-Loir 1978- ; former member of bureau of PS National Assembly Group; member of National Assembly Foreign Affairs Commission 1978-81; elected to Comité Directeur 1973; Mitterrandist.

Louis Le Pensec: b. January 1937, Finistère; university teacher (Economics), Rennes; son of farm worker, educated at *lycée* in Quimperlé and Faculty of Letters and Economics at Rennes, Faculty of Letters Paris; Minister for Marine Affairs 1981-3. Mayor of Mellac 1971- ; deputy for Finistère 1973- ; PS spokesman on regional affairs 1973- ; ex-personnel office Saviem motor company; ex-member CIR; Breton regionalist, pro-minority languages; Rocardian; opposed demotion of ministry 1983 and was dropped; Rocard man on PS Secretariat post 1985.

Pierre Mauroy: b. July 1928, Nord; technical school teacher; son of teacher (*instituteur*); educated at *lycée* in Cambrai, and École Normale Nationale d'Apprentissage in Cachan; Prime Minister 1981-4; National Secretary Young Socialists 1950-8; Secretary General of Technical Education College Union of FEN 1955-9; secretary of Nord federation of SFIO 1961-9 and of PS 1969- ; member of SFIO Bureau Exécutif 1963-9; Deputy Secretary General 1971-9; mayor of Lille 1973- ; deputy for Nord 1973- ; president of Nord-Pas-de-Calais Regional Council 1974-81; failed to inherit PS leadership 1969; helped to install Mitterrand as leader 1971; No. 2 in PS under Mitterrand 1971-9; backed Rocard's criticisms after 1978 elections and lost place in PS Secretariat 1979; rejoined Mitterrand for 1981 campaign; social democrat but still pro-Left union post–PCF exit 1984; low-flier.

Louis Mermaz: b. August 1931, Paris; university teacher (History), ex-*lycée* teacher; President of the National Assembly July 1981-6; Secretary-General of CIR 1965-9; previously Secretary-General of UDSR (Mitterrand's Fourth Republic party); elected to PS Comité Directeur 1969; Bureau Exécutif 1971-9 and 1981, Secretariat 1973-9 (National Secretary for Federations 1975-9); deputy for Isère 1967-8 and 1973- ; mayor of Vienne 1971- ; president of the Isère General Council 1976- ; Transport Minister May-June 1981; the long-time reliable Mitterrand aide; important parliamentary manager; grey.

Louis Mexandeau: b. July 1931, Pas-de-Calais; teacher (*professeur*); son of farmer; educated at *lycée* in Arras, Faculty of Letters at Lille and Paris, Institute of Political Studies, Paris; Minister for Posts and Tele-communications 1981-6; member of PCF 1952-57; ex-member of CIR; PS secretary Calvados 1971-3; deputy for Calvados 1973- ; PS spokesman on education 1975-81; author of radical Mexandeau report (proposing nationalization of private schools) 1976; not given Education Ministry 1981.

François Mitterrand: b. October 1916, Charente; barrister and journalist; son of vinegar producer (ex-station master); educated at Collège Saint Paul, Angoulême, and Faculties of Law and Letters, Paris; President of the Republic, May 1981- ; deputy for Nièvre 3e 1946-58 and 1962-81; senator for Nièvre 1959-62; National President of UDSR 1946-58; Minister for Ex-Servicemen 1947-8; Junior Minister in PM's Office 1948 (in three govts.); Junior Minister for N. African Affairs 1952; Minister of the Interior 1954-5; Minister of Justice 1956-7; president of Nièvre General Council 1964-81;

mayor of Château-Chinon 1959-77; presidential candidate 1965 (7.7 million votes, 32 per cent, at first ballot, 10.6 million, 44.5 per cent at second ballot); president of FGDS 1965-8; president of CIR 1970-71; joined PS 1971; First Secretary of PS 1971-81; co-signatory of PCF–PS–Rad. Gauche *Programme commun* 1972; presidential candidate 1974 (11.0 million votes, 43.2 per cent, at first ballot; 12.9 million, 49.2 per cent, at second ballot); presidential candidate 1981 (7.5 million votes, 25.8 per cent, at first ballot; 15.7 million, 51.8 per cent at second ballot); POW 1940; briefly a Vichy official, then *résistant*; elected as right-wing Radical against Left opposition 1946; Fourth Republic ministerialist; anti-Fifth Republic in 1958; presidential unifier of PS 1971- ; surprise victor 1981; sphinx; enigma; *force tranquille*; governing pre-1986, presiding post-1986.

Jean Poperen: b. January 1923, Angers; university teacher; son of teacher (*instituteur*); educated at *lycées* in Angers, Rennes, and Paris (Louis-le-Grand), and Faculty of Letters, Paris; No. 2 to Jospin in PS 1981-7; member of PCF 1943-58; National Secretary of Communist Students 1945; member of PSA–PSU 1958-67, 1960-7; member of National Bureau of PSU 1960-7; established UGCS (Union des groupes et clubs socialistes) 1967, joined PS 1969, elected to Comité Directeur of PS 1971; opposed Mitterrand 1971, then backed him 1973- ; member of PS Secretariat 1973- ; National Secretary for Propaganda 1975-9, and for Elections 1979-87; deputy for Rhone 1973- ; mayor of Meyzieux (Rhône) 1977-87; author of books on the French Left; ex-Left unity propagandist; elections specialist; brother was a member of PCF Politburo; anti-CERES; polemicist; dropped from Party leadership 1987.

Mme Nicole Questiaux: b. December 1930, Nantes; civil servant (*Conseil d'État*); daughter of engineer; educated at Institute of Political Science, Paris, and ENA; Minister for National Solidarity (Social Security) 1981-2; joined PS 1971; member of *Comité Directeur* 1971- ; PS spokesman on European Community 1975, but resigned 1976 through hostility to European integration; PS National Secretary for Communication 1979-81; member of CERES 1979- ; specialized in social-policy questions as a civil servant; non-parliamentarian; anti-spending cuts; sacked 1982.

Paul Quilès: b. January 1942, Algeria; engineer; son of army officer; educated at *lycées* in Casablanca and Paris (Louis-le-Grand) and École polytechnique; PS National Secretary for Organization and Federations 1979- ; engineer with Shell Oil 1964-78; PS Energy specialist; member of Economic and Social Council 1974-5 (CFDT representative); deputy for Paris 1978- ; entered PS Secretariat and Bureau Exécutif 1979; CERES ally at PS Metz Congress 1979; used post as National Secretary for Organization to campaign for Mitterrand's nomination; presidential campaign director 1981; loyal Mitterrand proxy in party organization 1978-81; pro 'rolling heads' 1981; defeated as PS mayoral candidate in Paris 1983. Minister for Urban Affairs and Housing 1983-5, Defence 1985-6.

Roger Quilliot: b. June 1925, Pas-de-Calais; university teacher (Clermont Ferrand); son of primary school teacher; educated at *lycée* in Paris (Louis-le-Grand), and Faculty of Letters at Lille and Paris; Minister for Urban Affairs and Housing 1981-3. Member of PS Comité Directeur 1969-71; mayor of Clermont-Ferrand 1973- ; senator for Puy-de-Dôme 1974-86; deputy 1986- ; ex-Mollet protégé; author of *La SFIO et l'exercise du pouvoir*; Mauroy man; social democrat; brought in rent control.

Michel Rocard: b. August 1930, Seine; civil servant (*inspecteur des finances*); son of atomic physicist; educated at *lycée* (Louis-le-Grand), Paris, and Faculty of Letters, Paris, and ENA; Minister of Planning 1981-3, Agriculture 1983-5; National Secretary of Socialist (SFIO) Students 1955-6; National Secretary of PSU 1967-73; PSU presidential candidate 1969 (814,000 votes; 3.7 per cent); PSU deputy for Yvelines 4e 1969-73, and PS deputy for Yvelines 1978- ; resigned from PSU and joined PS 1974; member of PS Bureau Exécutif 1975-81; replaced Chevènement on PS Secretariat 1975-9; National Secretary for the public sector 1975-9; mayor of Conflans-Saint-Honorine 1977- ; challenged Mitterrand after 1978 elections and was dropped from Secretariat 1979; opinion-poll star 1978- ; sought presidential nomination for 1981; CERES and PCF *bête noir*. Protestant; once left wing, now social democrat; pro low growth 1982 and lower living standards 1983; ministerially sidelined 1981; moved to difficult post 1983; quit over PR 1985; weak in party; ambition without means.

Mme Yvette Roudy: b. April 1929, Gironde; journalist; daughter of town-hall clerk; educated at primary and technical schools (Bordeaux), and secondary and higher education by correspondence; Minister for Women's Rights, 1981-6; Secretary 1948-52; translator in American company -1963; Secretary General of Mouvement démocratique féminin; founder and editor of *La Femme du 20e siècle*; joined CIR 1965 (member of CIR Bureau Exécutif); member of PS Comité Directeur; member of PS Secretariat 1979-81; National Secretary for *Action féminine* 1979-81; member of European Assembly 1979-81; translated into French *La Femme mystifiée* by Betty Friedan 1965; *Ma Vie* by Eleanor Roosevelt 1967; *La Place de la femme dans un monde d'hommes* by Elizabeth Jeannewan 1969; author of *La Femme en marge* 1975; deputy for Calvados 1986- ; successful minister.

Alain Savary: b. April 1918, Algiers; former diplomat; son of railway engineer; educated at *lycée* Buffon and Faculty of Law, Paris; Minister of Education 1981- ; Minister for North African Affairs in Mollet government 1956 (resigned); left SFIO in 1958 and joined PSA; deputy General Secretary of PSA (1959); member of Bureau National of PSU 1960; founder of UCRG 1965; First Secretary of PS 1969-71;

deputy for Saint-Pierre-et-Miquelon 1951-9 and Haute Garonne 1re (Toulouse N.) 1973–86; President of Midi-Pyrénées Regional Council 1974–81; lost Party leadership to Mitterrand 1971; reliable moderate in sensitive post but quit when schools policy aborted 1984; grey.

Bibliography

Books on the French Socialist Party

AFTALION, F., *Socialisme et économie*, PUF (Paris), 1978.

ALEXANDRE, P., *Le Roman de la gauche*, Plon (Paris), 1977.

AMBLER, J. (ed.) *The French Socialist Experiment*, ISHI (Philadelphia), 1985.

ATTALI, J., *La Nouvelle économie française*, Flammarion (Paris), 1977.

— and GUILLAUME, M., *L'anti-économie*, PUF (Paris), 1974.

AYACHE, G., and FANTONI, M., *Les barons du PS*, Fayolle (Paris), 1977.

BACOT, P., *Les dirigeants du Parti Socialiste*, Presses Universitaires de Lyon (Lyons), 1979.

BAUCHARD, P., *La Guerre des deux roses*, Grasset (Paris), 1986.

BAYART, J. F., *La Politique africaine de François Mitterrand*, Karthala (Paris), 1984.

BENSAÏD, D., *L'anti-Rocard*, La Brèche (Paris), 1980.

BERSON, M., DELFUSE, G., and ORY, P., *Les Chemins de l'unite*, Tema (Paris), 1974.

BIRNBAUM, P., *Les élites socialistes au pouvoir*, PUF (Paris), 1985.

BIZOT, J.-F., et al., *Au parti des socialistes: plongée libre dans les courants d'un grand parti*, Grasset (Paris), 1975.

BLEITRACH, D., et al., *Classe ouvrière et sociale démocratie: Lille et Marseille*, Éditions Sociales (Paris), 1982.

BORZEIX, J.-M., *Mitterrand lui-même*, Stock (Paris), 1973.

BUNODIÈRE, C., and COHEN-SOLAL, L., *Les nouveaux socialistes*, Tema (Paris), 1977.

BROWN, B., *Socialism of a Different Kind*, Greenwood (Westport), 1982.

CAPDEVIELLE, et al., *France de gauche vote à droite* FNSP (Paris), 1981.

CAYROL, R., *François Mitterrand 1947-1967*, FNSP (Paris), 1967.

CERNY, P. and SCHAIN, M., (eds) *Socialism, the State and Public Policy in France*, Methuen (New York), 1985.

CHARZAT, M., and TOUTAIN, G., *Le C.E.R.E.S., un combat pour le socialisme*, Calmann-Lévy (Paris), 1975.

CHEVÈNEMENT, J.-P., *Le vieux, la crise, le neuf*, Flammarion (Paris), 1975.

303

CLUB, J. M., *Un parti pour la gauche*, Seuil (Paris), 1965.

CODDING, G. and SAFFRAN, W., *Ideology and Politics—the Socialist Party in France*, Westview (Boulder, Colorado), 1979.

COHEN, S., *La Monarchie nucléaire* Hachette (Paris), 1986.

COLOMBANI, J. M., *Portrait du président* Gallimard (Paris), 1985.

COTTERET, J.-M., EMERI, C., GERSTLE, J., and MOREAU, R., *Giscard d'Estaing-Mitterrand: 54,774 mots pour convaincre*, PUF (Paris), 1976.

COTTERET, J. M. and MERMET, G., *La bataille des images*, Larousse (Paris), 1986.

DAGNAUD, M. and MEHL, D., *L'Élite rose*, Ramsay (Paris), 1982.

DEFFERRE, G., *Un nouvel horizon*, Gali (Paris), 1965.

—, *Si demain la gauche . . .*, Robert Laffont (Paris), 1977.

DELFAU, G., PLEZU, G., and PINGAUD, B., *Battre la campagne*, Tema (Paris), 1974.

DELORS, J., *Changer*, Stock (Paris), 1975.

DREYFUS, F.-G., *Histoire des gauches, 1940-1974*, Grasset (Paris), 1975.

DUHAMEL, A., *La république de M. Mitterrand*, Grasset (Paris), 1982.

DUHAMEL, O., *La gauche et la Ve République*, PUF (Paris), 1980.

DUPAY, F. and THOENIG, J. C., *L'administration en miettes* Fayard (Paris), 1985.

DUPOIRIER, E. and GRUNBERG, G.,*Mars 1986: La drôle de défaite de la gauche*, PUF (Paris), 1986.

DU ROY, A., and SCHNEIDER, R., *Le roman de la rose*, Seuil (Paris), 1982.

DUVERGER, M., *Bréviaire de la cohabitation*, PUF (Paris), 1986.

DUVERGER, M., *Lettre ouverte aux Socialistes*, Albin Michel (Paris), 1976.

ESTIER, C., *Journal d'un fédéré, La Fédération de la Gauche au jour le jour—1965-1969*, Fayard (Paris), 1970.

ÉVIN, K., *Michael Rocard ou l'art du possible*, Simoën (Paris), 1979.

FAUCHER, J.-A., *La gauche française sous de Gaulle, 13 Mai 1958-13 Mai 1968*, J. Didier Séuil (Paris), 1968.

FOSSAERT, R., *Le contrat socialiste*, Seuil (Paris), 1969.

GIESBERT, F.-O., *François Mitterrand ou la tentation de l'histoire*, Seuil (Paris), 1977.

GUIDONI, P., *Histoire du nouveau Parti Socialiste*, Tema (Paris), 1973.

HANLEY, D., *Keeping Left? CERES and the French Socialist Party*, Manchester University Press (Manchester), 1986.

HAMON, H. and ROTMAN, P., *La deuxième gauche*, Ramsay (Paris), 1982.

HERNU, C., *Priorité à gauche*, Denoël (Paris), 1969.

HOFFMANN, S., ROSS, G. and MALZACHER, S. (eds.), *The Mitterrand Experiment*, Polity Press (Oxford). 1987.

HURTIG, C., *De la SFIO au Nouveau Parti Socialiste*, Armand Colin (Paris), 1970.

JAFFRÉ, J. *et al.*, *La gauche au pouvoir (Pouvoirs*, No. 20), 1982.

JOHNSON, R. W., *The Long March of the French Left*, Macmillan (London), 1981.

JOXE, P., *Le Parti Socialiste* Épi. (Paris), 1973.

JUDT, T., *Marxism and the French Left*, OUP (Oxford), 1986.

JULY, S., *Les années Mitterrand*, Grasset (Paris), 1986.

KERGOAT, J., *Le Parti Socialiste*, Le Sycomore (Paris), 1983.

LACORNE, D., *Les notables rouges*, FNSP (Paris), 1980.

LACOUTURE, J., *Léon Blum*, Seuil (Paris), 1977.

—, *Mendès France*, Seuil (Paris), 1981.

LANCELOT, A. *et al.*, *1981: Les élections de l'alternance*, FNSP (Paris), 1986.

LAUBER, V., *The Political Economy of France From Pompidou to Mitterrand*, Praeger (New York), 1983.

LEFORT, R. G., *La gestion sociale-démocrate*, Palmer (Paris), 1984.

LIGOU, D., *Histoire du socialisme en France*, PUF (Paris), 1961.

LONCLE, F., *Autopsie d'une rupture*, Simoën (Paris), 1971.

LOSCHAK, D., *La Convention des Institutions Républicains: François Mitterrand et le socialisme*, PUF (Paris), 1971.

MACHIN, H. and WRIGHT, V., (eds) *Economic Policy and Policy-Making under the Mitterrand Presidency: 1981-84*, F. Pinter (London), 1985.

McCARTHY, P., (ed.) *The French socialists in Power, 1981–86*, Greenwood Press (Westport), 1987.

MAIZEY, S. and NEWMAN, M. (eds.), *Mitterrand's France*, Croom Helm (London), 1987.

MANCERON, C., *Cent mille voix par jour: Mitterrand*, Robert Laffont (Paris), 1966.

MANDRIN, J., *Socialisme ou social-médiocratie*, Seuil (Paris), 1969.

—, *Le socialisme et la France*, Éds. Le Sycomore (Paris), 1983.

MARTINET, G., *La conquête des pouvoirs*, Seuil (Paris), 1969.

MATOUK, J., *La gauche peut sauver l'enterprise*, Éd. Ramsay (Paris), 1977.

MAUROY, P., *Héritiers de l'avenir*, Stock (Paris), 1977.

MAUROY, P., *A gauche*, Albin Michel (Paris), 1985.

MENDÈS FRANCE, P., and ARDENT, G., *Science économique et lucidité politique*, Gallimard (Paris), 1973.

MITTERRAND, F., *Le coup d'état permanent*, Plon (Paris), 1964.

—, *Ma part de vérité*, Fayard (Paris), 1969.

—, *Un socialisme du possible*, Seuil (Paris), 1970.

—, *La rose au poing*, Flammarion (Paris), 1973.

—, *La paille et le grain*, Flammarion (Paris), 1975.

—, *Politique*, Fayard (Paris), 1977.

—, *Ici et maintenant*, Fayard (Paris), 1980.

MOLLET, G., *Les chances du socialisme. Réponse à la société industrielle*, Fayard (Paris), 1968.

—, *Quinze ans après*, Albin Michel (Paris), 1973.

MOSSUZ, J., *Les clubs et la politique en France*, A. Colin (Paris), 1970.

MOTCHANE, D., *Clefs pour le socialisme*, Seghers (Paris), 1973.

NUGENT, N., and LOWE, D., *The Left in France*, Macmillan (London), 1982.

PATERSON, W. and THOMAS, A., (eds) *The Future of Social Democracy*, OUP (Oxford), 1986.

PARTI SOCIALISTE, *Pour le socialism: Livre des Assises*, Stock (Paris), 1974.

—, *Projet socialiste*, Club Socialiste du livre (Paris), 1980.

PFISTER, T., *Les socialistes*, Albin Michel (Paris), 1977.

PFISTER, T., *La vie quotidienne à Matignon au temps de l'union de la gauche*, Hachette (Paris), 1985.

PHILIPPE, A., *Les socialistes*, Seuil (Paris), 1967.

PIERRE, C., and PRAIRE, L., *Plan et autogestion*, Flammarion (Paris), 1976.

POPEREN, J., *La gauche française: le nouvel âge 1958–1965*, Fayard (Paris), 1972.

—, *Nous sommes tous les archaïques*, Guy Roblot (Paris), 1978.

—, *Le nouveau contrat socialiste*, Ramsay (Paris), 1985.

PORTELLI, H., *Le socialisme français tel qu'il est*, PUF (Paris), 1980.

PUDLOWSKI, G., *Jean Poperen et l'UGCS*, Saint-Germain-des-Près (Paris), 1975.

QUILLIOT, R., *La SFIO et l'exercise du pouvoir 1944–1958*, Fayard (Paris), 1972.

—, *Une écharpe de maire*, Horvath-Roanne (Paris), 1982.

ROCARD, M., *Parler vrai*, Seuil (Paris), 1978.

— et al., *Qu'est-ce que la social démocratie?*, Seuil (Paris), 1979.

ROCHU, G., *Marseille-Les années Defferre*, Moreau (Paris), 1983.

RONDIN, J., *Le sacré des notables*, Fayard (Paris), 1985.

ROUCAUTE, Y., *Le Parti Socialiste*, Huisman (Paris), 1983.

SAVARY, A., *En toute liberté*, Hachette (Paris), 1985.

SAVARY, A., *Pour le nouveau Parti Socialiste*, Seuil (Paris), 1970.

SOLOMON, A., *Le PS mis au nu*, Laffont (Paris), 1980.

TOUCHARD, J., *La gauche en France depuis 1900*, Seuil (Paris), 1977.

URI, P., *Pour gouverner*, Robert Laffont (Paris), 1967.

—, *Changer l'impôt (pour changer la France)*, Éditions Ramsay (Paris), 1981.

VERDIER, R., *PS-PC: une lutte pour l'entente*, Seghers (Paris), 1976.

WILLARD, C., *Socialisme et Communisme français*, A. Colin (Paris), 1967.

WILLIAMS, S., (ed.) *Socialism in France from Jaurès to Mitterrand*, Pinter (London), 1983.

WRIGHT, V., (ed.) *Continuity and Change in France*, Allen and Unwin (London), 1984.

Articles

BACOT, P., 'Le comportemet électorale des instituteurs: Mitterrandistes et giscardiens', *RFSP*, Dec. 1977, Vol. 27 (4), pp. 884-914.

—, 'Le front de classe', *RFSP*, Apl. 1978, Vol. 28 (2), pp. 271-95.

BOURRICAUD, P., 'Élections, blocage et ouverture', *Projet*, June 1973.

BROYER, P. *et al.*, 'Les candidats communistes aux élections législatives de 1973 et 1978', *RFSP*, April 1979, Vol. 29 (2), pp. 213-29.

CAYROL, R., 'Le Parti Socialiste à l'entreprise', *RFSP*, 1978, Vol. 28 (2), April, pp. 296-312.

—, 'La direction du Parti Socialiste: organisation et fonctionnement', *RFSP*, 1978, VI. 28 (2), April, p. 201-19.

—, 'Les militants du Parti Socialiste', *Projet*, 1974, Sept.-Oct., pp. 929-940.

—, 'Parti Socialiste: enfin les difficultés commencent!', *Projet*, Sept., pp. 917-928.

—, 'Le godillot et le commissaire politique: six contradictions à propos du Parti socialiste', *Projet*, 1982, Jan., pp. 32-41.

— and ÉVIN, K., 'Comment contrôler l'union? Les relations PC-PS depuis 1971', *Projet*, Jan. 1978, pp. 64-74.

— and YSMAL, C., 'Les militants du Parti socialiste—originalité et diversités', *Projet*, May 1982, pp. 572-86.

CAYROL, R., and YSMAL, C., 'Militants socialistes: le pouvoir use', *Projet*, Jan.-Feb., 1985, pp. 20-32.

CAYROL, R., and IGNAZI, P., 'Cousins ou frères? Attitudes politiques et conceptions du parti chez les militants socialistes français et italians' RFSP, 1983 Vol. 33, pp. 629–650.

CHARLOT, J., 'Le double enchainement de la defaite et de la victoire', *Revue politique et parlementaire*, May-June 1981, pp. 15-28.

—, 'La fluidité des choix electoraux', *Projet*, Dec. 1975, pp. 1171-8.

—, 'Intentions de vote des Français', *Projet*, Feb. 1977.

DONEGANI, J. M., 'Itinéraire politique et cheminement religieux: l'example des catholiques militants du Parti Socialiste', *RFSP*, Aug.-Oct. 1979, Vol. 29 (4-5), pp. 693-738.

ÉDOUARD, J., 'Le groupe parlementaire à l'Assemblé nationale: renouvellement et continuité', *Nouvelle Revue Socialiste*, Apr. 1974, Vol. 1, pp. 34-42.

FERRETTI, R., 'Les militants de la fédération du Bas Rhin du PS: éléments pour une sociologie', *Nouvelle Revue Socialiste*, 1975, Vol. 14-15, pp. 8-16.

LE GALL, G., 'A gauche toujours le rééquilbrage', *Revue politique et parlementaire*, 1981.

—, 'Le nouvel ordre électoral', *Revue politique et parlementaire*, July-Aug. 1981, pp. 1-32.

—, 'Du recul de la droite vers l'hégémonie du PS', *Revue politique et parlementaire*, May-June 1981, pp. 29-41.

—, 'Une nouvelle donne avant les présidentielles?', *Revue politique et parlementaire*, June 1979, pp. 33-44.

GARRAUD, P., 'Discours pratiques et idéologie dans l'évolution du Parti Socialiste', *RFSP*, Apr. 1978, Vol. 28 (2), pp. 257-76.

GUÉDÉ, A., and FABRE-ROSANE, G., 'Sociologie des candidats aux élections législatives de mars 1978', *RFSP*, Oct. 1978, Vol. 28 (5), pp. 840-58.

— and ROZENBLUM, S. A., 'Les candidats aux élections législatives de 1978 et 1981', *RFSP*, Vol. 31, 1980 (5.6), Oct.-Dec. 1981, pp. 982-99.

HARDOUIN, P., 'Les charactéristiques sociologiques du Parti Socialiste', *RFSP*, Apr. 1978, Vol. 28 (2), pp. 220-56.

HOLTON, R., 'Industrial Politics in France: Nationalization under Mitterrand', *West European Politics*, Jan. 1986, pp. 67-80.

JAFFRÉ, J., 'L'opinion publique et les élections législatives', *Projet*, June 1978, pp. 737-44.

—, 'La concurrence au sein de la gauche en 1967 et en 1968', *RFSP*, Feb. 1973, Vol. 23 (1), pp. 110-18.

— and OZOUF, J., 'Des municipales aux législatives au fil des sondages', *Projet*, June 1977, No. 116, pp. 728-46.

JOHNSON, D., 'How the French Left learned to love the bomb', *New Left Review*, July 1984, No. 146, pp. 5-36.

JUILLARD, J., 'Mitterrand entre le Socialisme et la République', *Interventions*, Nov.-Dec. 1982, Vol. I, pp. 87-102.

KESSELMAN, M., 'Systèmes de pouvoir et cultures politiques au sein des partis politiques français', *Revue Français de Sociologie*, 1972, Vol. 13 (4), pp. 485- .

LANCELOT, A., 'Le rouge et le vert, les elections municipales des 13 et 20 mars 1977', *Projet*, June 1977, No. 116, pp. 703-28.

—, 'Les premières élections européenes des 7 et 10 juin 1979', *Projet*, Sept.-Oct. 1979, pp. 1003-20.

LAVAU, G., 'The changing relations between trade unions and working class parties in France', *Government and Opposition*, Autumn 1978, pp. 437-57.

LE GALL, G., 'Radiographie de l'image du PCF: double divorce avec la société et les sympathisants', *Revue politique et parlementaire*, Jan.–Feb. 1985, pp. 16-27.

LE GALL, G., 'Mars 1986: des élections de transition?', *Revue politique et parlementaire*, March-April, 1986, pp. 6-18.

LIEBER, N., 'Ideology and tactics of the French Socialist Party', *Government and Opposition*, Autumn 1977, pp. 455-73.

MADELIN, H., 'Les divorcés de la gauche', *Projet*, Nov. 1977, pp. 1026-30.

— *et al.*, 'La France politique après les élections', *Projet*, May 1978, pp. 530-49.

MÉNY, YVES, 'Decentralization in Socialist France: the Politics of Pragmatism', *West European Politics*, January 1984, pp. 65-79.

LE MONDE, 'Dossiers et documents': 'Les Élections législatives du juin 1981'. 'L'Élection présidentielle 26 avril–10 mai 1981'. 'Les Élections législatives de mars 1978'. 'L'Élection présidentielle de mai 1974'. 'Les Élections législatives de mars 1973'.

PARODI, J.-L., 'La France quadripolaire a l'épreuve de la proportionelle', *Revue politique et parlementaire*, June 1979.

— and PERRINEAU, P., 'Les leaders socialistes devant l'opinion', *Projet*, Apr. 1979, pp. 475-92.

PERRINEAU, P., 'Le PS, de l'affirmation à la crise d'identité', *Projet*, July 1984, pp. 796-801.

PORTELLI, H., 'Que se passe-t-il au Parti Socialiste?', *Projet*, Jan. 1978, pp. 55-63.

—, 'Les socialistes et l'exercice du pouvoir', *Projet*, Oct. 1982, pp. 921-32.

— and DUMAS, T., 'Les militants socialistes à Paris', *Projet*, Jan. 1976, pp. 35-43.

PORTELLI, H., 'Le présidentialisation des partis', *Pouvoirs*, No. 14, 198, pp. 97-106.

RÉMOND, R., 'La querelle de l'école', *Projet*, Nov. 1977, pp 1031-42.

—, 'L'anticléricalisme n'est pas mort', *Projet*, Sept. 1977, pp. 905-16.

—, 'Échec de la gauche: est-ce la faute des catholiques?', *Projet*, June 1978, pp. 732-6.

REY, H., and SUBILEAU, F., 'Le PS, un Parti a trappe-tout?', *Le Monde*, 2 April 1986.

ROUSSEAU, A., 'Attitudes politiques des catholiques', *Projet*, Feb. 1978, No. 122, pp. 207-18.

DU ROY, A., 'Qui est socialiste en France?', *L'Express*, 14 Apr. 1979.

SCHONFIELD, W. R., 'La stabilité des dirigeants de partis politiques: le personnel des directions du parti socialiste et du movement gaulliste', *RFSP*, June 1980, Vol. 30 (3), pp. 477-505.

—, 'La stabilité des dirigeants des partis politiques: la théorie de l'oligarchie de Roberto Michels', *RFSP*, Aug. 1980, pp. 846-86.

SUBILEAU, F., 'Le militantisme dans les partis politiques sous la cinquième République: État des travaux de langue française, *RFSP*, Oct.-Dec. 1981, Vol. 31 (5-6), pp. 1038-56.

VIVERET, P., 'La gauche piégée dans l'État', *Projet*, June 1982, pp. 666-74.

Index

318 *Index*